CCAR Journal
The Reform Jewish Quarterly

MW01226089

Contents

At the Gates — בשערים

"Enlarge the size of your tent, extend the size of your dwelling, do not stint! Lengthen the ropes, and drive the pegs firm." Thus does Isaiah (in 54:2) rally his countrymen after the Babylonian conquest. His metaphoric tent and pegs derive from both earthy Israelite experience and Torah descriptions of the Tabernacle. From desert encampments to the Tabernacle to the Temple to synagogues throughout Jewish space and time, and in our time to the diverse places where Jews and those who share their lives come together to "do Jewish"—this is the *shalshelet* of our people's gathering places. From the beginning to now, the central challenge has remained the same: How to encompass and include while maintaining a central core. How to be flexible but firm, both confident and realistic. How to achieve unity of purposeful commitment while also acknowledging one another as distinct individuals.

Back in 1984, studying at HUC-NY, I encountered an unusual sort of article that remained in my consciousness over the years: Lawrence Kushner's "The Tent Peg Business." It turned out that it wasn't only me who vibrated with this piece and kept referring back to it. Over time, it became a classic. And so it's wonderful that this issue of the *Journal* includes an update of "Tent Pegs" as the cooperative venture of two Kushner rabbis, Larry and his daughter Noa.

Several other pieces also consider various roles of the synagogue and/or rabbis: David Whiman's article "Synagogue Work Will Drive You Crazy" and Joel Wolowelsky's "Yom HaAtzma-ut as a Religious Holiday," as well as Elliot Gertel's book review essay "A Congregation, a Rabbi, and a Religious Movement." To these is added an important cluster of articles on "Progressive Judaism Around the World: Paradigms of Peoplehood," guest edited by Larry Englander. Larry believes that our sense of Jewish Peoplehood is the crucial factor in understanding the panorama of Reform Jewry around the world. His knowledge of and devotion to both Israeli and Diaspora Jewish life have enabled him to make major contributions to his congregation, the CCAR, this publication, and the Jewish People.

In balance, as it were, to this interesting range of professionally oriented articles come a number of pieces that focus on biblical texts. Daniel Berry, whom you may remember as the co-author of the Spring 2012 piece "Why Jews Wear Costumes on Purim," tackles the "Two Creation Narratives." *Sefer B'reishit* also draws the attention of Michael Oblath in his "The Garden of Eden: Peeling Back the Layers." Mordecai Roshwald brings us "The Binding of Isaac (A Different Version)." And David Zucker presents "Throwaway Women: Ruth as Response." After you read David's article, be sure to turn to his review of *The JPS Bible Commentary—Ruth.*

To these riches, add the fifth piece to appear under our still-new *Maayanot* (Primary Sources) rubric. In it, our teacher Stephen Passamaneck examines the Laws of *M'sirah* in *Shulchan Aruch, Choshen Mishpat*, Chapter 388. Just a few months ago, Steve fully retired after fifty years of teaching at the College-Institute. We wish him continuing vigor and acuity during this stage of his life.

And finally, this issue features seven fine poems. That the *Journal* has long (perhaps since its beginnings) included poetry gives me a pride and pleasure that is undoubtedly shared by many of you. On that basis, I will take the liberty of ending this column with a lesser-known but, to my mind, very great poem by Robert Frost: "The Silken Tent." Its central image rounds back to the Isaiah verses with which I began while encoding a deep spirituality.

> She is as in a field a silken tent
> At midday when a sunny summer breeze
> Has dried the dew and all its ropes relent,
> So that in guys it gently sways at ease,
> And its supporting central cedar pole,
> That is its pinnacle to heavenward
> And signifies the sureness of the soul,
> Seems to owe naught to any single cord,
> But strictly held by none, is loosely bound
> By countless silken ties of love and thought
> To everything on earth the compass round,
> And only by one's going slightly taut
> In the capriciousness of summer air
> Is of the slightest bondage made aware.

Susan Laemmle, Editor

"Like Oil and Water": Progressive Judaism and the Nations of the World

Lawrence A. Englander

During my first year of rabbinical school at HUC-JIR in Jerusalem, I remember studying the following midrash describing the status of the Jewish people among the nations of the world:

> *Your name is like oil poured forth* (Song of Songs 1:3):
>
> 1. Just as olive oil in its original state [as raw olive] is bitter but afterward becomes sweet, so "Though your beginning was small, yet your end shall greatly increase" (Job 8:7).
> 2. Just as this oil is improved by crushing, so Israel does *t'shuvah* through chastisements.
> 3. Just as this oil does not mix with other liquids, so Israel does not mix with the other nations of the world.
> 4. Just as this oil brings light to the world, so Israel is a light to the world, as Scripture states, "Nations shall walk by your light" (Isa. 40:3; *Shir HaShirim Rabbah*, 1:2).

That was in 1971. With regard to statement 1, my classmates and I thought of how our people had spread from *Eretz Yisrael* to permeate almost every civilization on Earth. We remembered with pride the song from our NFTY days, "Wherever you go, there's always someone Jewish." We smiled confidently as we read statement 2: Our people may have suffered in times past, but we no longer need to find a justification for being "crushed" since we now enjoy a freedom and economic prosperity greater than any other time in Jewish history. As for statement 4, we recalled the teaching of our Reform ancestors that the "Mission of Israel" is to bring justice,

LAWRENCE A. ENGLANDER (C75) is rabbi of Solel Congregation of Mississauga, Ontario, and is a former editor of the *CCAR Journal*.

freedom, and peace to all the peoples of the world—a message that the Reform Movement has carried since its inception.

It was statement 3 that gave us the most trouble. Had we not integrated ourselves so thoroughly into Western culture that we could easily count Jews among political leaders, entrepreneurs, and movie celebrities? The Jewish People and General Culture were no longer like oil and water; on the contrary, we had mixed so well into these societies that we were also helping to shape them. Anti-Semitism was almost nonexistent—and besides, we now had the State of Israel to act in defense of persecuted Jewish communities and bring them to safety.[1] Comfortably swaddled in our blanket of security and confidence, we studied this midrash as a quaint relic of our past existence whose warnings were no longer relevant.

But then, just weeks ago, I began to read the essays that follow in this issue. It seems that the prophecy in statement 1 has been compromised in present times: you can no longer find Jews everywhere you go. There has been an exodus of Jews from Arab lands and from many places in Africa and Asia. In Germany, Austria, and areas of the Former Soviet Union, the Jewish remnant from the Holocaust has found other places to live; most Jews who do live there now have immigrated from other countries. The downturn of the global economy, especially in Europe, has provoked a sober second look at statement 2: it is hard to sustain synagogues, schools, and other Jewish communal institutions when you experience a severe reduction of income.

As in the past, times of austerity are not good for the Jews; consequently, the liquids in statement 3 have separated yet again. Anti-Semitism is on the rise, and even the most tolerant European governments (not to mention many Jews) tend to regard Israeli government policies with suspicion. Ironically, within the Jewish State itself, our Progressive communities face opposition from our own kin: Chareidim and Chardalim[2] refuse to recognize us as viable streams of the Jewish People. As for statement 4, how do we advance the Mission of Israel if our gentile neighbors refuse to accept the message?

The essays in this issue give us insight into a world rather different from the one most of us experience in North America. For one thing, the specter of the Holocaust still looms darkly over the countries where the Nazis had decimated the Jewish population. Perhaps the testimonies of rabbis working in these countries will help to shake us out of our naïveté. This is not to say, however, that everything in these locales is gloom and doom. On the contrary, you will read about the noble history of Jewish communities in many parts of the world and their indelible contributions to their country of birth. Moreover, the multinational experience of our people has given to us all a rich blend of Jewish cultures.

It is our hope that these essays will engender a lively discussion among our readers and the people whom you teach. To begin this process, I offer the following questions for your consideration. They center around the notion of Jewish Peoplehood—a notion that appears to be a stronger component of contemporary Jewish identity than we find in Canada and the United States, where we tend to define ourselves more as a religion. So the first question is this: Does the sense of Jewish Peoplehood form a stronger bond between one Jew and another, wherever we live? Does it impart to us a greater responsibility to care for each other?

Chazal seemed to think so.[3] In comparing two prophets, they depicted Elijah as expressing "love for the parent" (i.e., God) but not "love for the child" (i.e., the Israelite people). Jonah, in contrast, demonstrated the opposite. Despite his religious zeal, Elijah's prophetic gift was taken from him shortly after the contest on Mount Carmel. But Jonah, even though he hoped to protect his own people by disobeying God and leaving the Ninevites unrepentant, was given a second chance. For the Rabbis, love of people trumps even the love of God. The ideal prophet, of course, would possess both—as did Jeremiah in this passage in the *M'chilta*.

This brings us to the second question. In a few of the essays, the authors point out that community programming has shifted more toward Jewish cultural events and Israel-centered discussions rather than on text study, liturgy, and theology. If this be so, what is the status of the "love of parent," expressed through communal prayer in these Progressive congregations? How does this outlook affect Jewish traditional practice of the ritual mitzvot? What is it that gives their constituents a Jewish identity that is distinct from that of their non-Jewish neighbors? If Jeremiah is the ideal, then perhaps the Jewish communities on either side of the globe have much to learn from each other.

Our third question: How does this sense of Peoplehood affect our relationship with those members of the Jewish People who refuse to acknowledge the Progressive communities as equal partners? How successful have these Progressive communities been in attracting members despite being shunned by the Orthodox establishment? Are we repeating history in allowing *sinat chinam* (baseless hatred)[4] to tear our people apart? And what can the worldwide Progressive community do to resolve this impasse?

Fourth: What is the relationship between each Progressive community and the general population? If anti-Semitism and anti-Israel sentiment are prevalent among the populace, what role does the state government play in fostering or mitigating them? Despite these challenges, is there still a sense that Jews have a messianic mission to perform among the nations of the world?

I believe the essays that follow have a great deal to teach us, wherever we may live. I wish to thank the authors for their detailed, candid—and sometimes painful—testimonies of the communities whom they serve. I also thank my editorial team, Rabbis Tony Bayfield and Andrew Goldstein, both of London, for adding their insights into the process of preparing this conversation. My heartfelt gratitude also goes to the editor of this *Journal*, Susan Laemmle, for developing the idea for this cluster and for shepherding it through with patience and skill.

The reader will notice that many countries do not appear in this series. It was not for lack of trying: other potential authors were approached but, for different reasons, declined to participate. If these essays generate sufficient interest, perhaps the editorial board might consider launching a sequel so that Asia and the southern hemisphere, in particular, will be better represented.

These essays prompted me to take a second look at the midrash with which we began. The following analogy may sound trivial at first, but I believe it captures the present relationship between *Am Yisrael v'umot haolam*. If Israel is like oil, the nations of the world can be compared to balsamic vinegar. When these liquids are combined, they produce an attractive pattern and a delicious taste. But each maintains its separate identity. Perhaps our destiny as Jews, wherever we are, is to *blend* within the majority society but not to *dissolve* into it. The degree to which we attain this balance may determine our success in preserving our unique heritage and advancing our prophetic mission.

Notes

1. At that time (1971), we were still demonstrating for the release of Soviet Refuseniks, and the plight of Ethiopian Jews had not yet appeared on our radar screen. Now both communities are able to live securely in Israel and elsewhere.
2. A Hebrew acronym for Chareidi Dati Le'umi (ultra-Orthodox ultra-nationalists).
3. See *M'chilta, Bo, piska* 1.
4. See, e.g., BT *Yoma* 9b.

A Perspective from Europe

Walter Rothschild

Since this is a journal for rabbis and Jewish professionals working hard in the real world, let us be honest; if necessary, brutally
honest. Our work, bridging the gap between the earthly and the
Divine, the short-term and the eternal, the ancient texts and the
modern needs, is never easy. But some things make it even more
difficult. These are some personal perspectives based on a childhood in a refugee community in Britain, activity in European Progressive Jewish youth movements, and then twenty-eight years in
the rabbinate, more than a half of which has been spent in Germany and Austria, with occasional experiences in the Netherlands,
Poland, and the Balkans.

A. Questions

Any rabbi working in mainland Europe (I exclude here the
British Isles) in the post-Shoah period is confronted from the
very outset with a specific set of theological, political, and personal problems. Over the years these problems may ripen and
evolve and develop and overlap and grow, but they do not go
away. They nag at one, in the back of the mind, all the time.
I myself—born postwar but the son of a refugee, grandson of
an innocent man who was incarcerated and injured in Dachau,
former son-in-law of a man who, as sole survivor of his family,
survived Auschwitz—find that not a day goes by that I am not
confronted with a new story from the past, a new challenge for
the present.

Here is a small sample of the questions with which one is confronted, consciously or unconsciously, at every moment:

RABBI WALTER ROTHSCHILD (LBC84) served eleven years in Leeds and has
since then worked mainly in Europe, especially Germany and Austria. He is a
board member of the Union of Progressive Jews in Germany. In his spare time he
writes.

1. Why? Why bother? Why bother creating or reviving or re-creating Jewish communities in cities, in countries where God seemingly allowed all the Jews to be deported or to be wiped out where they were? Is this what God actually wants? Does God actually desire Jews to live here again? (Think of the curse against Jericho in Joshua 6:26.) If so, couldn't God perhaps send a sign and be a little more helpful from time to time?

This is, of course, by no means a new question. Zionism was one response to it and, following the establishment of the State of Israel, there has been no shortage of voices declaring that the surviving Jews should abandon these accursed countries and should move to their ancestral and divinely willed homeland. Of course the debate on the other side is also not new. Does God really want certain countries to become totally *Judenrein*? Is this not in a way giving Hitler yet another posthumous victory? Nevertheless, there are occasions when one puts great effort into organizing a *beit din* in a city such as Bratislava or Skopje whereby, with a lot of travel and trouble, one can perhaps help seven or eight people become accepted as Jews—in a place where, a few decades ago, tens of thousands were deported and wiped out. And so often one asks oneself: Is this what God *really* wants of me?

2. Do we actually want Judaism anymore? I know of no empirical research into the religious beliefs of European Jews postwar, but my own rabbinic experience teaches me that a very high proportion have no belief in God, or at least in an active God, a saving God, a God who can intervene in history. And why should they? But many believe nevertheless in being Jewish and in staying within groups. Many believe in supporting Israel but not living there. It is, ironically, the converts to Judaism who usually display symptoms of belief, idealism, and commitment that jar with the experiences and attitudes of the older Jews.

So we find ourselves here not serving an existing vibrant Jewish community but creating a Jewish community of new Jews, lost Jews, and found-again Jews—Jews without faith or non-Jews with faith.

There is almost no continuity with the past. Even in towns where one has a postwar Jewish community, there is almost no link to the prewar one. Even when an older synagogue was not destroyed and remains today in use, the chances are high that it spent some years deserted or used as a storehouse and was only restored later.

3. What Europe? When we speak of Europe, can we draw at least a distinction between countries that very clearly participated willingly in the destruction of European Jewry and those that can be classed to some extent as victims? Can one distinguish between, say, Germany and Belgium? Germany and the Netherlands? Austria and Macedonia? Historians can show evidence of willing cooperation with the Germans in most countries, but nevertheless some countries did manage to retain a modicum of self-respect in that their governments or governments-in-exile did not openly encourage such collaboration. This does not mean that *all* Danes or Bulgarians, for example, were friendly and philo-Semitic; but at least there is a difference between what they did as a sovereign nation and what some of their individual citizens did when they joined the SS. So can one differentiate?

This is an interesting and unending debate with many twists. For example, the Bulgarians protected Bulgarian Jews but cooperated in the extermination of many Yugoslav Jews. The further one delves into the history, the more one realizes that no one came out of the war with clean hands. Every country closed borders to desperate refugees or made moral compromises with the Axis. The term "neutral" has to be understood carefully when the context is one of not opposing evil.

Great Britain was not invaded and fought valiantly to liberate Europe, but before the war its attitude to refugees was at best ambivalent and after the war its attitude to allowing displaced persons to go to Palestine was hostile and obstructionist.

4. What should our attitude be towards the non-Jewish citizens, whether of the older or the younger generations? Do we really want to open up our synagogues and memorial ceremonies to every local politician or do we wish to be more selective? How should we react to younger people who wish to convert to Judaism? How do we cope with the selective memories, the lengthy silences and gaps in official histories, the poor treatment of certain subjects—important to us—in schoolbooks? How do we build up healthy communities, not only on the ashes of 1945 but on the silences and hypocrisies of the following decades?

5. How should we relate to different elements in today's Europe— to the Catholic Christians, to the Protestant Christians, to the Russian

Orthodox Christians, to the secular atheists and the (former?) Communists, to the increasing number of Muslims? Where can we work together, and with which group against which group? There are many possible coalitions, depending on the issue—whether this be the right to slaughter animals in a certain way or to wear certain religious symbols in public, whether it relates to Middle East politics or to the restitution of properties stolen decades ago by a different regime. After centuries of Christian anti-Semitism, are we *really* in favor of religious education in schools? Will it make life better or worse for the Jews? When churches show remorse for what happened to dead Jews but show no sympathy for living Jews, where do we stand? When secular politicians support Israel but oppose circumcision, can we live with this dichotomy?

Jews have returned from exiles before; they have—or some of them have—survived a *churban* before and then Crusades and pogroms and expulsions and inquisitions. So we are not the first generation ever to be confronted with these fundamental questions. But we are the first and second generations to be confronted with the totality and the brutality of the twentieth century. It takes time to find a foundation and an orientation again.

Something I find fascinating and warming is that there are several non-Jews who share the same burning desire to record and preserve. Not philo-Semites as such, but determined and angry individuals who struggle to break the communal amnesia. I want to help them when they take it upon themselves to restore old abandoned synagogues or research vanished communities or preserve former labor camps or sponsor Stolperstein plaques in the sidewalks. They usually meet with social ostracism but I share their helpless anger and their desire to turn it into something positive.

No one ever said it would be easy to be a rabbi, but I truly believe that European rabbis face totally different historic and current responsibilities than do those in, say, Australia or Canada.

B. History and Context

Where do we start? Let us begin with the situation as it was in 1945. Anti-Semitism did not begin in 1933 and it did not end in 1945. An entire continent was left in rubble and ash; the extent of the destruction as evidenced by photos of the time is truly unbelievable. Although there was utter destruction of two cities in

Japan and conflict in North Africa and the Pacific, although armed forces from many continents fought each other (and massacred civilians) in many other countries and over the world's oceans, the fact is that much of World War II was fought in Europe and the western USSR. The aerial bombing by the Luftwaffe was matched and then exceeded by that of the RAF and USAF. Entire cities went up in flames; the dead could not be counted. The numerous towns and villages that were wiped out by the advancing Wehrmacht or by Einsatzgruppen, the labor camps and concentration camps and extermination camps, the camps into which prisoners of war of different nationalities were herded—all these have left a legacy of mass graves, many marked, many unmarked, many still subject to dispute amongst local historians and local politicians. There is a legacy of shifted and rootless populations and borders drawn on maps by the victors. The Soviet Union showed little compunction in changing sides twice and in sacrificing millions of its own population—after all, this process had begun much earlier. Yet in 1945 at the Potsdam Conference it, too, claimed the moral high ground.

It took over a decade after 1945 for the last prisoners to return—or to be returned to their former home countries against their will; for the refugees to leave the displaced persons camps, some to return to their former homelands, some to strike out in new directions; for the initial rubble to be cleared and some basic infrastructure to be restored: some houses and railway lines and water and power, schools and hospitals. It took time to calculate the dead and work out who would never return home. It took even longer to work out who should bear some blame and who should continue in their profession as though nothing had happened. And yet nothing could remain as it had been. In Soviet-occupied Eastern Europe the ideological dogmatism of the Fascists was replaced by another ideological dogmatism, involving an internal 180-degree switch overnight: yesterday's "partisan terrorists" were today's "heroes of the anti-Fascist resistance"; yesterday's "government" were today's "Fascist imperialist oppressors." The names were changed, but the essential vocabulary and even the infrastructure of secret police, censorship, political oppression, and detention camps were retained. Those who were uncomfortable reminders of different ideas were simply "disappeared." This included Jews, such as the first head of the postwar Berlin Jewish community, Erich Nehlhans, who was "disappeared" by the Soviets. Jews who returned to Poland were made less than welcome, and often murdered. Religion was not desired at all in countries like Yugoslavia. These were dangerous times.

This is our historical and social and religious context. When we speak of Judaism in postwar Europe we have to understand what the foundations were. Where there had once been dozens of village communities in a district, there was now no one at all. Where there had once been communities of several thousand Jews in a city, with several competing synagogues, there was now a handful of Jews, maybe a few dozen, with maybe one centralized meeting point and no rabbi. Where there had been settled, educated, cultured Western European citizens, there were now displaced Eastern European survivors, mostly with no, or only an interrupted, education.

Only now are the last members of that generation leaving the scene. They had survived physically because they were strong and determined, and these qualities kept many of them in communal leadership roles for decades—initially to great effect, but then after a while stultifying any change, any adaptation to newer circumstances. They lived in the past, and the Jewish communities to a large extent still do.

C. Progressive Judaism in Europe Postwar

And into this context we speak of a small revival or a resurgence of Progressive Judaism. A Judaism based on an optimistic, universalistic philosophy, a Judaism based on the advances of the Enlightenment and scientific discovery, a Judaism based on critical thinking and inclusivity and adaptation to modern life.

It is a simple fact that almost all those European Reform and Liberal Jews who had survived had done so in exile. The same applies to the rabbis and teachers. Some had settled in Britain, in North America, in Australia, in Palestine, which became Israel. The early beginnings on the continent in the late 1940s or early 1950s were therefore tentative and modest, and in many places they remain so. Even the changes that came with the end of the Cold War and the opening of borders in the 1990s have led to changes that are dramatic in themselves but, statistically, insignificant. In the whole of Austria there is only one Liberal community: Or Chadasch in Vienna. In the whole of Denmark there is also only one. In all of

Belgium there are two groups in Brussels, with a strong component of expatriates, diplomats, and others. In Switzerland there are Liberal congregations in Geneva, Zürich, and some small *chavurot* in Basel. In the Netherlands a start was made by Rabbi Jakob Soetendorp; the burden was picked up by one of his sons, Awraham, and by a Swede, David Lilienthal; and gradually a nationwide network of communities was built up. One way, however, of defining the successes so far—and it may sound tasteless but it indicates the extent of what was lost—is that almost the entire Jewish populations of several European countries could still have fitted into just one more deportation train. (Most such trains had a capacity of about a thousand.)

In many cases the Progressive Jewish communities formed initially with a small kernel of expatriates—usually British or American—who took the initiative and then found a local scattering of lost Jews and an isolated Israeli or two. The bulk of the community now comprises people who have deliberately chosen to become Jewish—in some cases out of theological commitment, in some cases because they have traced Jewish ancestry. It is up to a *beit din* to check whether there may be other, less healthy reasons for their desire.

In several countries the Progressive communities are still wholly excluded from whatever postwar organizations have been established; in others they have won a (usually grudging) acceptance. Enormous amounts of time and effort are wasted on conflicts with those who maintain that they are the only true followers of the prewar communities: those who have obtained state recognition; who control synagogues, cemeteries, and schools; and who monopolize commissions and committees.

The majority of Jews in Europe are essentially secular, but whenever they are driven by a sense of nostalgia or fear to seek a religious organization they will go to something that presents itself as traditional—which means a male rabbi in a dark suit and with a dark beard and dark thoughts, which means a service that is incomprehensible but sounds right. Chabad are, of course, the world leaders in this branch of pseudo-religious marketing, and they are enormously successful in Europe, mainly because they step into what is essentially, still, decades after the Shoah, a vacuum. There are usually no other rabbis or synagogues to compete with their *sh'lichim*, who establish a foothold in a city and build up from there, showing—and this may be one reason for their success—no public awareness of the questions I listed at the outset. They approach politicians openly (though not churches or mosques), and they act as though they are utterly convinced that this is what *HaShem* demands of them. The past exists mainly as a means of leverage over the guilt feelings of those in the present. I find something callous, something disturbing in the way they memorialize the victims of the Shoah—but they are there, on the spot, financed initially from external sources, and successful in raising funds internally as well.

D. Challenges in Europe Today

Let us look at some of the alternative groups, religious or political, with whom we have to deal:

1. The Europeans, those who believe in a unified Europe, achieved much but have suffered many setbacks and suffer also from a poor press. Many of those who benefit from today's open borders or shared currencies or transnational agreements do not realize just how fortunate they are. It is easy to focus on swollen bureaucracies or excessive costs, on erosion of national powers, on currency crises—and one should not forget that Europe has found it hard to work together in terms of foreign policy—and yet, for decades now the armed forces have been essentially unemployed, the watchtowers and borders are not patrolled, and fewer and fewer young men are called up for military training. One should do more to point out that the glass is half-full, not half-empty.

2. The Left have lost their main sponsor, the USSR, which imploded and fragmented, and they are increasingly exposed as ever more information comes to light of the oppressive state systems that had been employed to assert what was referred to as "the will of the people." Although they bleat about social justice, many realize that this was never their real aim. Totalitarianism in this form is out of fashion. Too many idealistic Communists were betrayed by the systems they naively and uncritically believed in. There are always a few unreconstructed remnants here and there, of course, but the times have changed.

3. The Christians. Christian Mission still exists but has ceased to be a really big problem. The Christians of a Europe that spent centuries in bloody inter-Christian conflict have also not yet fully come to terms with the total failure of their respective churches during the grim years of Nazis; not just in terms of the Jews, but how the Protestants formed their own German National Church or allowed baptized Jews to be deported with their unbaptized fellows; how bishops with so few exceptions failed to protest against euthanasia programs or the maltreatment of fellow Christians hauled across Europe and worked to death as slave laborers; how the Vatican remained silent when it could have spoken out. Essentially, although not every bright evangelical spark may have noticed it, Christianity lost all its remaining moral authority in the latter part of the twentieth century. A God of Love was noticeably absent as millions of Christians, too, were crucified in different ways. It is sad and ironic that there are, however, growing groups of Messianic Jews (so-called—many of their members lack any Jewish background) who are prepared to hand out leaflets and sing songs on the pavements—people so ignorant and foolish that they are prepared to combine syncretistically the worst features of both beliefs.

The swastika symbol is called in German the *Hakenkreuz* (a cross with hooks). In the end the hooks were more important than the cross itself. Where Christianity flourishes now in Poland and Russia it is, I believe, as much as a political as it is a theological movement.

But at least the Christians find Judaism interesting and many are now prepared to be philo-Semitic, to join Jews in acts of remembrance, to invite Jews to speak. This is, in a way, progress, but whether in the longer term it is really going to be effective, only time can tell. Did God really want me to work here, mainly talking to non-Jews?

4. The Muslims are growing rapidly, and the majority are still uneducated or undereducated and underachieving in the labor market. Many still live in villages that have been established inside cities, as self-contained communities linked electronically to the homeland in ways that were never experienced by previous migrant groups, who had a greater incentive to assimilate into their host communities. The intelligent among them seek for common ground with Christians and Jews in order to strengthen their social status here, though they do not realize that telling us that "they also accept Abraham and Moses and Jesus" does not necessarily warm every heart; the more isolated and frustrated amongst them turn to authoritarian fundamentalism and even to violence, and the European countries are slowly, perhaps too slowly, becoming aware of the extent of this long-term threat to what is left of their (multi-)cultures. No one, apart from right-wing extremists and racists, has any answers.

5. The Far Right. The only triumphalism one experiences is that of the growing extreme nationalist groups, composed mostly of people who were never taught by their parents' generation the facts of what really occurred in the 1930s and later, who can therefore be only partially blamed for their stupidity. Basing themselves on a fictitious and nebulous mythic past and wrapping themselves in a present dominated by fear of the Other, they work for a future that they themselves do not fully understand. Different groups linked only by their hatred find common cause. We have the irony of nationalist organizations who hate foreigners working internationally with foreign groups who also hate foreigners. Some speak of neo-Nazis, but Slovak or Hungarian or Flemish or Polish nationalists have their own myths and do not necessarily want to refound a National Socialist German Workers' Party. But they hate Roma and they hate Jews and they hate refugees and asylum-seekers from Africa and they hate the European ideal.

So, what should be the response of Reform, Liberal, Progressive Judaism in such a mixed-up continent? What can it be? Statistically we are an infinitesimally small proportion of the population; we often feel threatened, whether the threats be real or merely a product of our paranoia. It is a fact that Jewish buildings and Jewish cemeteries are still often the target of acts of hatred; Israel is constantly portrayed in the media as an aggressor and occupier, and the acid drips through the communal consciousness. It takes us all our strength to keep our communities together—we have little energy for exposure in the media or to exercise political influence.

Another issue we must face is, of course, that one speaks of Europe as an entity, but there are several dominant and many more minor languages, educational systems, government attitudes to religion and other divisions. It is true that one can get by in

English in many senior positions—such as international rabbinic meetings—but it is usually hard to find competent people willing to spend their ministry serving Jews who speak and pray in Croatian or Hungarian or Portuguese or Danish or Italian or Spanish or Danish or others. Within Germany now, thanks to the immigration from the Former Soviet Union, one needs Russian skills more than German. But the Soviet emigrants who were committed to Judaism or Zionism went to Israel; those who were young and skilled and sought social advancement went to America; and the rest, the pensioners, came here, because here, at least, the heating works. They come with very different attitudes to how communities should be organized; they need and respect a strong leader and they bow down to hierarchies. This is how they lived in the USSR; those of us who represent a Progressive Jewish outlook, based on the Enlightenment and the importance of the individual and on freedom of choice, often find ourselves speaking a wholly different social and theological language.

E. And *Davka* . . .

To add to the diversity and the fragmentation: Our different national Progressive movements also have different approaches to certain issues such as patrilineality and conversion. We may share common outlines of liturgy but there are many different details—some of them significant. And then there are issues of distance, the duration and expense of travel, the differences in culture. All of these make it hard to meet as European Progressive Jews or as European rabbis, although, when a few of us *do* manage it, it is always worthwhile.

In view of all the above, the mere existence of *any* Progressive Jewish communities in many of these countries is a remarkable achievement. Few are more than twenty years old. In the last months of 2012, I celebrated the tenth anniversary of the small congregations in Pinneberg and Bad Segeberg, north of Hamburg, the tenth anniversary of the state federation (Landesverband) to which they belong, and dedicated a new synagogue in Elmshorn. None of these communities is over two hundred strong, each depends enormously on the enthusiasm and strength of less than a handful of individuals, and the demographics are of an aging (and often immigrant) population. The Union of Progressive Judaism in

Germany now has twenty-four constituent communities, but some of these are truly tiny. The European Union for Progressive Judaism is adding constantly to its constituent base new small communities, often little more than *chavurot*, in Norway or Hungary or Poland. We form a minority within a minority, and yet we remain active; we build tiny huts rather than large palaces, but nevertheless we build.

It sometimes feels that I spend about a half of my rabbinic endeavor in remembering the dead Jews—unveiling plaques, dedicating stumbling stones, saying *Kaddish* at sites of former horror—and the other half interviewing and teaching non-Jews who wish to convert. It's a truly schizoid experience, very different than my rabbinate in Britain where, although there were continental refugees in the congregations, my main work was based in a comfortable middle class suburb where no one had been murdered.

From a truly tiny, microscopic base, one can build and build and expand and expand until, at the end, one has perhaps a small community. With the enthusiasm and dedication of a few individuals one can perhaps inspire a few more to join them before the first group of activists wears out with exhaustion. It's a constant challenge. The future remains unclear. What is God's real plan? What role are we playing in fulfilling it—if we are actually doing so?

Let's hope. And, now and again, let's pray.

Goulash Judaism:
The Case of Hungary

Ferenc Raj

For a person like myself who spent most of his childhood and youth under Communism in Hungary, the collapse of Communism was a huge, and I must admit, a pleasant surprise. When this major event of the late twentieth century occurred, I was already living in America. It gave me, a former pariah of that oppressive regime, a great satisfaction to watch on the television the removal of the Communist symbols that represented spiritual suffering for so many of us who, while living in a Communist country, could not freely practice our respective religions. However, during the last twenty years we quickly learned that, for all religions in general and for Judaism in particular, freedom does not offer an instant and successful spiritual revival.

In Communist Hungary, the government, though its officials never admitted it, closely controlled all the religious denominations through an institute called Állami Egyházügyi Hivatal (loosely translated as Office of Church and Government Relations). Through this office, the ruling Communist Party was able to appoint, or at least approve or disapprove of, the leaders of church and synagogue organizations. This not so subtle pressure brought about some positive side effects; for example, a spontaneous cooperation among Orthodox, Neolog, and secular Jews who were not willing to allow the government to impose restrictions upon them that would prohibit the teaching of the Hebrew language and contemporary Jewish culture. Let me give one personal example: when I was a young rabbinic student attending the Neolog rabbinical seminary, I was invited by Jenő Schück, the Orthodox chief rabbi of Miskolc, to run a

FERENC RAJ (Budapest67; Ph.D., Brandeis University) is rabbi emeritus of Congregation Beth El in Berkeley, California, and founding rabbi of Bet Orim Reform Jewish Congregation in Budapest, Hungary.

program for about fifty Jewish youths from ages five to sixteen for two consecutive summers.

Today, close to a quarter of a century after the collapse of Communism, interdenominational relations among Hungarian Jews hardly exist. Jewish denominations as well as Jewish cultural organizations are acting as independent agents, each declaring itself as being authentic, while the others are not. Hungary's Jewish population is still the largest of all the former Soviet satellite countries; depending on the surveys and the definition of "who is a Jew?" the actual number ranges between 60,000 and 200,000. Nevertheless, those who participate in any Jewish activity are probably less than 20,000.

It is curious that such a small community draws so much attention in the Hungarian media and daily culture. Hungarians enjoy klezmer music, theater performances with Jewish themes, and especially Jewish food. In almost every better restaurant in Budapest, one will be able to order matzah ball soup and cholent. Unfortunately, in spite of this interest in things Jewish, anti-Semitism is still a major concern, as the ultra right is gaining ground in Hungary.

Anti-Semitism in Hungary, like in many of the other East and Central European countries, is deep rooted. It should be noted that Hungary never acknowledged its participation in the political process that led to the Holocaust. Rather, it put all the blame on Nazi Germany. Hungary has never apologized for being part and parcel to the chain of actions that caused the almost total annihilation of the Jews living in the provinces, nearly half a million people.

In 2010, Jobbik, Hungary's neo-Nazi party, received 844,169 votes, representing 16.7 percent of all the votes. The party currently occupies forty-five seats in the Hungarian parliament.

Fidesz-Christian Democratic People's Party (KDNP), a center-right-wing coalition, won a two-thirds majority of seats in the parliament by gaining 52 percent of the votes. Though the current government condemns anti-Semitism, its actions lack a clear separation from Hungary's Nazi past. For example, viciously anti-Semitic writers, such as József Nyírő, Dezső Szabó, and Albert Wass, have been included in the new school curriculum set to be implemented in September 2013.

Representatives of the Jobbik in the parliament are delivering wildly anti-Semitic speeches. One such speech referred to the infamous Tiszaeszlár Blood Libel as true, and just a few months ago, Márton Gyöngyösi, deputy floor leader of the Jobbik's faction, suggested that Jews in the parliament and in the government should be registered, since they are a security concern to the homeland.

In addition to these anti-Semitic threats, Hungary's current government that has been in power since 2010 introduced a new Church Law. On December 30, 2011, the Hungarian parliament enacted Act number CCVI of 2011 on the Right to Freedom of Conscience and Religion and the Legal Status of Churches, Denominations and Religious Communities (Religious Freedom Law). It entered into force on January 1, 2012.

As a consequence, Hungary's erstwhile overall Jewish organization, the MAZSIHISZ (Alliance of Jewish Communities of Hungary) was broken up into two denominations, Neolog and Orthodox, and Chabad/Lubavitch was given a chance, with the full support and approval of Prime Minister Orbán's government, to declare themselves the heirs of the nonexistent Status Quo Ante Movement of pre–World War II Hungary, whose members were not as extreme as the Orthodox, but more observant than the Neolog. These were the three Jewish movements that received the coveted Church status.

Apart from the recognized churches listed in the appendix of the Religious Freedom Law, all other religious communities, previously registered as churches, lost their status as churches and could only continue their activities as associations. If intending to continue as churches, religious communities are required to apply to the parliament for individual recognition as such.

Historically, Reform Judaism was the first Jewish denomination in Hungary that was given an official Church status by the revolutionary government during the 1848–1849 anti-Habsburg uprising, led by the world-renowned freedom fighter Louis Kossuth.

Reform Judaism in Hungary was abolished by the oppressive Austrian regime in 1852. The rabbi of the community, David Einhorn, left for America where he became one of the most respected leaders of the Reform Movement.

After the collapse of Communism, Reform Judaism emerged once again in Hungary. As of today, there are two Reform congregations in Budapest, Hungary: Sim Shalom, the first to form, led by the British trained Rabbi Katalin Kelemen; and more recently,

Bet Orim, whose founding rabbi is the author of this article, Ferenc Raj, a member of the CCAR.

Neither Bet Orim Reform Jewish Congregation nor Sim Shalom Progressive Jewish Congregation, both members of the European Union for Progressive Judaism (EUPJ), was listed in the appendix of the Religious Freedom Law. They applied for individual recognition but did not obtain reregistration from the Hungarian parliament and consequently lost their status as churches, together with the state subsidies that had been due to them as such. They now continue their activities as associations.

Nevertheless, Sim Shalom and Bet Orim have tremendous possibilities in a difficult environment that is full of suspicions towards anything new. There is a subtle, but occasionally open hostility towards Reform coming from the spiritual and the lay leaders of the Orthodox, Neolog, and Chabad/Lubavitch groups. They say that since Reform Judaism does not accept the *Shulchan Aruch* as the most important and valid Code of Law, Reform Judaism is not authentic.

As rabbi of Bet Orim, I am happy to report that slowly but surely we are reaching more and more people who were pushed to the periphery of the Hungarian Jewish world due to their lack of knowledge or their halachically questionable Jewish lineage. Another group that gravitates towards us consists of Liberal Jews who firmly believe in pluralism.

In a scholarly article, Professor Géza Komoróczy, a non-Jewish expert of Jewish life and then director of the Center of Jewish Studies of the Hungarian Academy of Sciences at the Eötvös Lóránd University in Budapest keenly observed:

> Jewish proselytizing is taking place in Hungary. While Judaism has traditionally rejected proselytizing, in late antiquity, in the Mediterranean region, the Jewish religion attracted gentiles in great numbers. The new proselytizing has as its pool those former, now secularized, Jews, emotional or cultural Jews, and half- and quarter-Jews who now may come nearer to Judaism and the Jewish community. However, this will occur only if community life is attractive to them and provides them with a degree of social and emotional comfort they are seeking. In contradistinction to the nineteenth century, attraction cannot be created by adopting motifs of Christian ritual or way of life. For today it is the *difference* and richness of a separate tradition that makes Judaism attractive.[1]

I strongly believe that Reform Judaism is best fitted for this task of which Professor Komoróczy speaks. It is even more than a labor of love; it is a mitzvah. Is there anything more beautiful than helping a lost person to come home, where after a long and arduous journey she or he may find love, happiness, and spiritual and intellectual nurturing among brothers and sisters?

Note

1. Géza Komoróczy, "Jewish Hungary Today: The Jewish Cultural Heritage in the Contemporary Culture of Hungary," in *Jewish Centers and Peripheries: Europe between America and Israel Fifty Years After World War II*, ed. S. Ilan Troen (New Brunswick, NJ, and London: Transaction Publishers, 1999), 137.

Beit Warszawa, Jewish Music, and *Shabbes*

Haim Beliak

Beginning in 1995, Beit Warszawa's founder Severyn Ashkenazy applied his professional sensibilities and experience to creating a *Shabbes*. Ashkenazy is a successful hotelier and he brought a profound Jewish love for creating *Shabbes* hospitality. A nourishing Shabbat dinner with a Jewish cultural program for those Jews who self-identified and would show up for Friday evening became a regular part of Warsaw's scene. *Shabbes* at Beit Warszawa became justly famous for an atmosphere suffused with warm candle light, flowers, music, and excellent food. All of this became synonymous with *Shabbes* in Progressive Judaism's Poland. Jewish visitors from outside of Poland and people exploring the meaning of Judaism from inside Poland are enchanted by our *Shabbes*. For many years government ministers and university professors, musicians and artists, intellectuals and seekers found their way to *Shabbes* at Warszawa.

Initially, repeat attendees admitted to only a passing curiosity about Judaism and perhaps a desire for a hot meal. In time, however, many admitted that they were not merely curiosity seekers, or what I like to call cultural anthropologists of the Jewish tribe, but that they yearned to return to their Jewish faith. Eventually, out of the *Shabbes* dinners and programs, Beit Warszawa emerged as a bona fide World Union for Progressive Judaism (WUPJ) congregation. The Shabbat congregation's ritual practice employs communal singing, which is greatly prized in Poland. The *Shabbes* Evening Service is conducted 95 percent in Hebrew. The siddur, based on the American *Mishkan T'filah* and the Israeli Progressive

RABBI HAIM BELIAK (C76) is the executive director of Beit Polska, the umbrella organization of Progressive Jews in Poland including Beit Warszawa, Beit Lublin, Beit Lodz, Beit Poznan, Beit Bialystok, Beit Konstancin, and Beit Trojmiasto. Beliak with Jane Hunter developed several social justice projects using the Internet and social media: www.JewsOnFirst.org, www.HaMifgash.org, www.StopMoskowitz.org, and www.InclusivePrayerDay.org.

siddur, has a new Polish translation, Hebrew, and transliteration of Hebrew; it has been in use as an experimental edition for nine months and is soon to be published in a more permanent form.[1]

Currently, the congregation is led by Israeli-born Rabbi Gil Nativ, who came to Warsaw with his wife, Ziva, in August 2012 to serve as the rabbi of Beit Warszawa.[2] Nativ was ordained by the HUC in Jerusalem, but he has served in Masorti congregations in Israel and North America. Rabbi Burt Schuman was the pioneering permanent rabbi for five years until his unfortunate illness. Schuman's efforts and successes are the basis of today's on-going synagogue life. Schuman is much beloved for his gentleness and human sweetness.

Today Beit Warszawa sponsors Sabbath services, Hebrew classes, a children's Sabbath school, a summer day camp, holiday and Jewish learning and cultural events, and offers conversion classes. Beit Warszawa, Beit Polska, and the friends of Jewish Renewal have trained eight Sabbath lay cantors and five teachers of the Introduction to Judaism course. Three of the lay cantors have completed their training to lead the much more complex and demanding High Holy Day services. Lay cantors are taught by a master teacher, Cantor Mimi Scheffer of Berlin and Israel.[3] The fostering of a Polish-speaking cadre of learned and committed Progressive Jews continues with two candidates in rabbinical school and two more preparing for either cantoral or rabbinic preparation. The challenge of building a sufficient infrastructure for these future Polish leaders to serve in is a test of resourcefulness and optimism. Beit Polska, as the embodiment of a future Polish Progressive Judaism will for the foreseeable future need the help and wise counsel of Progressive Jews everywhere.

In 2008, Beit Polska was founded as an umbrella organization to minister to the Jewish population of Warsaw as well as to encourage the formation and support of other Jewish congregations elsewhere in the country.[4] The chair of Beit Polska[5] is Piotr Stasiak, a physicist turned businessman turned Jewish community leader. One of the challenges of Jewish life in Poland is working with congregants toward developing a sense of civic responsibility for Jewish life. Poland's immediate Communist past did not encourage communal leadership efforts and the model of Catholic life did not invite lay leadership. Notions of local communal responsibility are not well developed in Poland. The fabulous wealth acquired by individuals in the Former Soviet Union communities did not materialize in Poland.

At a much deeper level, the challenges of acquiring an individual Jewish identity outweigh in many ways the imagination of what a community might be like. Several generations are "missing" from the enterprise of building a Jewish community. In Beit Warszawa, there are very few families with an orderly succession of generations—grandparents, parents, and grandchildren. Many of our members are individuals who have chosen to embrace Jewish while their partners are often supportive and involved but unlikely to embrace Jewish life.

Despite numerous impediments, Beit Polska over the last two years has grown in the number of Progressive congregations/ *chavurot*. The leap from one to seven is difficult and tentative but gradually more and more real. In addition to Beit Warszawa,[6] there are now groups called Beit Lublin,[7] Beit Lodz,[8] Beit Poznan,[9] Beit Gdansk,[10] Beit Plock,[11] and our newest addition, Beit Bialystok,[12] founded in August 2012. A WUPJ congregation that is outside of the Beit Polska structure exists in Krakow under the leadership of Rabbi Tanya Segal.

My own involvement in Poland began in 2008 when I spent several months in Warsaw as a sabbatical replacement for Rabbi Burt Schuman. I found the experience of supporting a Jewish religious and communal revival in Poland truly gratifying and was determined to stay involved. I returned to Poland in 2011 and 2012, spending about ten months there during that time frame. My work was partially supported by a onetime grant from the WUPJ and the European Union for Progressive Judaism (EUPJ). Today, I serve as executive director of Beit Polska and spend six months a year in Poland. My mandate is to continue to nurture existing congregations and to look for opportunities to create new ones.

Beit Warszawa and Beit Polska Struggle for Freedom; Polish Courts Must Adjudicate a Legal Dispute Brought by Orthodox Leaders That Threatens to Take Away the Right of Progressive Jews to Organize and Pray

There are threats to religious pluralism and freedom in Europe. But sadly the threats to Progressive Polish Jews come not from right wing fascists or neo-Nazis but originate in the monopolist efforts of self-styled Orthodox Jewish leaders. In Poland, it is the government that is seeking to support and defend Jewish religious pluralism while the Union of Jewish Religious Communities (UJRC), a pseudo-Orthodox gang of five, threatens to institute monopolistic religious arrangements for their benefit. In every country in Eastern and Central Europe similar struggles are being waged in which Orthodox organizations, working often through unsuspecting government officials, establish official offices often at taxpayer expense. The governments are hesitant to pursue conflicts with the Jewish community for fear of being labeled anti-Semitic. At the same time, many of these governments are familiar with the hierarchy of the Catholic Church and assume that Judaism has similar arrangements. These countries include the members of the Former Soviet bloc countries (Russia, Ukraine, and Lithuania) and Hungary, Austria, and the Czech and Slovak republics.

In Poland the Orthodox effort attempts to block Progressive life by both overt and devious means. By suggesting that the Orthodox rabbinates receive their authority from the Orthodox establishment in Israel, they further insinuate themselves in Polish life. Self-declared chief rabbis in Central and Eastern Europe anoint themselves as the equivalents of cardinals and bishops. At issue in Poland is a claim by the UJRC of a monopolistic lock on Jewish life. Numerous attempts by the WUPJ and the EUPJ to mediate an accommodation have failed. In March 2012, I was party to an attempt to reach an accommodation but again Mr. Kadlcik, the titular head of the group known in Poland as Twarda and the chief rabbi of Poland, Rabbi Schudrich, sought a humiliating surrender not a compromise. The newest player in this tragic waste of resources is a young Reform rabbi hired by the UJRC to form an independent Reform group. In a cynical move the UJRC took advantage of typical congregational intragroup rivalries in Beit Warszawa to set up an independent Reform congregation under the auspices of the Orthodox Rabbi Schudrich. Jews are used to breakaway religious groups dissenting and starting new groups. But this new independent "Reform group" seeks to have the old group declared illegal. The Polish Ministry of the Interior is being sued in an administrative court to revoke its recognition of Beit Polska. The UJRC (Twarda) authorities have eighteen rabbinical positions allocated for Jewish life in Poland. Most of the positions are vacant year after year and the ones that are filled employ only

Orthodox rabbis! Twarda seeks to negate Poland's and the European Union's commitment to pluralism and religious freedom. No one denies the necessity and the value of Orthodox commitment but anyone who is familiar with the challenges of Polish Jewish renewal cannot seriously imagine a community in the sole control of the Orthodox.

The UJRC claims that the 1993 arrangement with the Polish government reached at the end of the Communist era permitted the Union the rights to settle all property claims on communal Jewish properties that had been confiscated during the Nazi era and the subsequent Soviet invasion and domination. The estimated $300 million worth of Jewish communal property has been gradually sold off for undisclosed amounts. No audits have been performed nor are any elected boards empowered to oversee disbursements. The Union retains an enormous war chest with no plans to provide services such as clinics, or to educate Jewish teachers or rabbis for the future. No forward planning is happening for future training of rabbis or developing communal organizations. The estimated five hundred individuals who are recognized as members of the Union may collectively be the richest per capita Jewish community in the world.

In addition, more contributions from well-meaning but unsuspecting (Reform and Conservative) donors and the considerable know-how and funds from the Joint Distribution Committee (JDC) flow to Twarda.[13] The WUPJ and Beit Polska are demanding a clear and separate institutional space be instituted between the Union and the JDC. A concerted misinformation campaign by the UJRC seeks to undermine Beit Warszawa and Beit Polska groups and the morale of individuals seeking a Progressive Jewish milieu. One of the classic claims made by Twarda is that there was only Orthodox Judaism prior to World War II.

Members of Beit Polska have been subject to threats delivered to their employers suggesting that employees are members of a "strange cult." Men and women studying at Progressive congregations have been confronted with threats that if they attended Progressive synagogues they would not be allowed to marry and their status as Jews be questioned both in Poland and in Israel. In a community seeking to find its own direction, the activity of the Twarda group does not benefit the future of Poland's Jews.

At the present time, Beit Polska is working with officials from the Joint Distribution Committee to demand equal access to social services funded by JDC. There is a concerted effort to include Progressive Jews and Progressive rabbis in JDC-funded and -staffed summer camps, family camps, social service agencies, and leadership trips to North America and Israel. The WUPJ and the EUPJ have stood by Beit Polska and Beit Warszawa. When visiting delegations from the March of the Living, the Forum for Dialogue among the Nations, the JDC, and many other organizations have entertained visitors while ignoring Beit Warszawa and new Beit Polska congregations. This is indicative of a culture of disdain for pluralism and Jewish diversity. Many visitors have little understanding that the money contributed largely by Reform and Conservative North American Jews is used to systematically undermine Jewish diversity in Poland.[14]

The newest participant in the attempt to enforce a religious straitjacket on the tiny Polish Jewish community comes from the president of the Abraham Geiger School, Walter Homolka. In an alliance with the UJRC, Homolka introduced the notion that a nineteenth-century German imperial governmental arrangement called an *Einheitsgemeinde* (unified community) would preserve the community. Homolka also offered to reconfirm conversions that had been authorized by the WUPJ and the EUPJ! Besides a lack of courtesy and *menschlichkeit*, Homolka managed to alienate large swaths of the Polish Jewish community who could not understand why Homolka, a German, was offering to meddle in internal Polish matters.

In Poland, World War II Ended in 1989: The New Context of Communal Renewal

There are factors that are unique to Poland and the surprising emergence of a Jewish community. With the withdrawal of Soviet troops and the gradual transformation to what is called the Third Republic in 1991, a new context for Polish Jewish life and indeed for Poland emerged. Today, ethnic Poles make up 98 percent of a largely homogeneous country. This is in contrast to the ethnic makeup of Poland's Second Republic (1918–1939) with its "nervous" demographics in which ethnic Poles were 60 percent of the population. Jews made up 10 percent of the Second Republic's population. That Jewish community despite being superficially protected with the Minorities Treaty was increasingly isolated and disdained until Poland repudiated the treat all together in 1935.

The post–World War I restored Poland contained other ethnic groups including Germans (Volksdeutch), Ukrainians, Latvians, and Lithuanians.[15] A growing anti-Jewish movement shaped the Polish nation-building efforts encompassing conservative, traditionalist, and Roman Catholic expressions. Anti-Semitic stereotypes became the major ideological vehicles in the struggle to define a nation that disappeared between 1784 and 1919. The recurring anti-Jewish expressions were to reappear throughout Poland's failed attempts at national reassertion. Beginning in the aftermath of the failed 1864 revolt and up until the Communist era (1948–1989) and its aftermath, all failed national efforts were the fault of the Jews.[16]

The ethnic homogeneity of today's Poland is credited with opening in many circles a search for a Polish civic society and open stance, even nostalgia for Jewish culture.[17] The demons of the Polish past that sought to portray Jews as the threatening Other are not completely exorcised but they are no longer respectable.[18] Today there is a considerable part of Polish society that is dedicated to understanding and addressing the Polish past:

> In Polish history attitudes toward Jews and other minorities have continued a litmus test of democracy, which embodied in the concept of modern civic nationalism . . . champions of civic and pluralistic Poland in the post-Communist era have "rediscovered" the cultural traditions of Jagiellonian Poland and view them as a historical heritage.[19]

The possibility of a renewed Jewish life in Poland is rooted in the context of a

> liberal position of recognition of the rights of a minority to the maintenance of its ethno-cultural make-up and of recognition of such a minority as an integral part of a national community defined in the civic and pluralist sense.[20]

Today's emerging Polish Jewish community is only tangentially related to previous expressions of Jewish life in Poland. So much was carried away and forgotten. Even before World War II, during the mass murders of World War II, and in the aftermath of World War II during the civil war (1944–1948) and then the assertion of the Communist system in Poland, two contradictory phenomena worked in tandem: excluding Jews who were rebranded as Zionists and claiming that the Jews were in control of the Communist regime.[21] The fact that it was easier to impugn people by simply inventing or suggesting a Jewish background did not cause too much concern even in the post-Communist era. Communists with a Jewish background did not claim that what they were doing was for the benefit of Jews. But this logic did not impress too many Poles. It was easier to blame the Jews.

There are internal dynamics that are uniquely Polish and uniquely Jewish in the current renewal of Jewish life in Poland; there are no remnant expressions of pre–World War II Jewish life that have secretly remained dormant, only to come to life in the post-Communist era. Poland's renewal of Jewish life is a product of imagination, creativity, and invention. It is also subject to all the ghosts of the past.

The current situation is difficult to assess. One important "internal" perspective is provided in the concluding report written for the Institute for Jewish Policy Research. Konstanty Gebert and Helena Datner conclude:

> Twenty years after the fall of communism, the Polish Jewish community finds itself in a rather paradoxical situation. Even though the community is very small in number and insignificant at the national level, Jews still attract a great deal of political attention, and due to internal diversity, it is not possible to draw a single coherent picture of its current situation. Its very revival is something of a miracle, it finds itself today internally torn between the attractiveness of Orthodoxy, which was strongly supported in the past by both the community's own spiritual leadership and external funding, but nevertheless represents a minority within the community, and needs of the majority of Poland's Jews. Their Jewish identities still ill-defined, they tend to look towards Reform and secular models of Jewishness, yet struggle to find enough of real substance there.[22]

This sobering conclusion by one of the most committed and longtime leaders of the revival of Polish Jewry must give one pause.[23] The author's attempt at sober realism is not historical nor is it current. No elements of the rich Polish Jewish past are employed to imagine or even allow an internal Jewish pluralism that once included Progressive Judaism.

American Jewish apprehensions over Poland's commitment to develop a civic society in the new era after Soviet domination contributed greatly to skepticism over the necessity for internal Jewish pluralism in Poland. The admittedly shaky nostalgia for Polish Catholic and Polish Jewish amity in North America contributed to perception on the part of philanthropists that one form of Judaism would be sufficient to address all of Jewish life in Poland. There has not been the kind of comprehensive communal planning that could imagine a Polish Jewish future.

The bulk of the resources invested in building Polish Jewish life in the early 1990s did support projects like the Orthodox led Lauder-Morasha school, which continues to this day long after the Ronald S. Lauder Foundation has withdrawn its major support. It is an excellent institution but it has not produced an Orthodox community or much of a non-Orthodox community. The school did not offer a realistic forum for Jewish life beyond its tiny Orthodox group. From a Progressive Jewish perspective, the failure of the Lauder school to produce a pluralistic Jewish community is not a surprise. A great opportunity is being missed.

Elements of a Polish Jewish Future Community

A brilliant and courageous tiny part of the Polish Jewish community is committed to Orthodoxy having moved from their days of the Flying Jewish University in which they recovered their Jewish identity to a stoic skepticism about a Jewish future in Poland. Faced with the realization that the majority of Polish Jews who identify as such are not Orthodox and yet, not fully secular, this influential group has often despaired about the direction of the community. It is this niche that Beit Warszawa has tried to address as its constituency. Understanding our constituencies in Poland is a challenge. There are groups of Israelis who seek their future in business and education in Poland. (There are eight medical schools in Poland teaching in English, which is an attractive option for Israelis and for former Jewish Poles whose families migrated to Europe.) Estimates vary but Polish officials have suggested that there may be as many as 200,000 Israelis with Polish passports and subsequent access to the European Union. Besides "reinforcements" from outside of Poland, we know very little substantively about the needs and desires of the 5,000 or maybe as high as 20,000 or even 100,000 who have a claim on Jewishness.

Making the Historical Contribution of Poland's Progressive Judaism Visible

The thirteen Progressive (Modern or Reform) synagogues in pre–World War II Poland located in major urban areas proceeded along the lines of moderate religious views and leadership by their rabbis in the development and strengthening of a sense of Peoplehood not only in their synagogues but also in Zionist affairs and Polish national leadership. The key contributions to the Progressive Jewish communities are often elided; the significance of these Progressive Jewish efforts is completely obscured from consciousness in present-day Poland.

An appreciation of the historical contribution of Progressive Judaism in Poland is neither part of trips to Poland nor part of the official history taught in the curriculum of the new Museum of Polish Jewish History. Instead, visiting groups focus almost exclusively on the Nazi murders in visits to Auschwitz, while Polish schools teach about shtetl life to the exclusion of other Polish Jewish expressions. Across the board—visitors to Poland and home born—are left with the erroneous impression that all Progressive Judaism was a German Jewish development of the nineteenth century.

These communities were termed by their Orthodox detractors as the *Yekish* (German) synagogues, but they were rooted in the complex intersection of a Polish Jewish reality that comprehended the modern world's conflicting demands. These Progressive (Postepowe) communities collectively numbered in the neighborhood of one hundred thousand members. While certainly influenced by German Reform they hewed to their own Polish direction. The community in Lviv (Lemberg, Lwow) is the oldest and most illustrious, dating back to the nineteenth century.[24]

The modern synagogues of interwar Poland were very promising. The Great Synagogue on Tlomackie Street in Warsaw was led by rabbinic leaders of great stature, Abraham Poznanski[25] and Mojzesz Schorr.[26] These synagogues were home to acculturated Jewish Poles and Zionists alike. In Chestochowa, a smaller edifice modeled on the Great Synagogue in Warsaw, was a site led by Rabbi Nahum Asz, who served as a bridge figure to the Catholic hierarchy during his life. Asz was known as a defender of the practice of *sh'chita*. Bishop Teodor Kubina from Chestochowa, a friend of Asz's, was the only member of the Catholic hierarchy who forthrightly condemned the July 4, 1946, Kielce pogrom.[27]

The premier Progressive rabbinical model was Rabbi Ozjasz Thon, the leader of the Tempel Synagogue in Krakow, from 1897 to 1936. Thon was trained in traditional studies and received ordination from Orthodox scholar Uri Wolf Salant. He attained subsequent degrees in philosophy and sociology at Fredrich Wilhelm University in Berlin and rabbinical training at the Institute for Jewish Studies (Lehranstalt fur die Wissenschaft des Judenstum) in Berlin.[28] Rabbi Thon wrote a "weekly column in the Zionist daily *Nowy Dziennik*" and held a seat in the Sejm, the Polish Parliament between 1919 and 1935. The Jewish group in Sejm was led by Rabbi Thon for five years.[29] From 1918 to 1926 Thon was president of the Tarbut (Zionist) school system, which eventually was responsible for about a fourth of the Jewish students not enrolled in Polish government schools.

After World War II, Poland's western boundary moved 150 miles to incorporate areas that in the nineteenth century had been Germanized but retained a connection to their Jewish Polish roots. Cities like Wroclaw (Breslau), Poznan (Posen), Gdansk (Danzig), Slupsk (Stolpe), and Bytom (Beuthen) are now part of the Polish reality. For Reform and Conservative Judaisms these communities were the cradle of religious reform. The luminaries of our religious movements—Abraham Geiger, Heinrich Graetz, Leo Baeck, Yoachim Prinz, Max Joseph, and many others—were born or served congregations and communities in these areas. Each of them had an influence on modern Jewish life that is lost to us. The Reform and Conservative movements have not fully explained the many important roots that their movement has to the Polish lands. The inspiring examples of the fruits of their work are not available. I conclude with one example. A hardly noticed hero of Progressive Judaism is Rabbi Max Joseph who wrote one of the first tracts defending the Zionist Movement and later with the rise of the Nazis was one of the first advocates for people leaving for Palestine and settling in Haifa, where he died in 1950.

Israel Is Perceived Positively

When people from Poland seek to visit Israel or to live there after completing the conversion process in Poland they often encounter official suspicion by representatives of the Israeli Ministry of the Interior and Jewish agency representatives. Even though the formal agreement between the Israeli Ministry of the Interior and the various religious movements provides for a direct process of the movements attesting to the integrity of the conversions, something else happens.

The questions asked of the perspective immigrant assume that they are living an Orthodox lifestyle. The request that often hostile Orthodox rabbis ratify the conversions of people who chose a Reform conversion leads to delays.[30] The professionalism and leadership of the Israeli Religious Acton Center's attorneys and staff is absolutely critical to a successful conclusion of the citizenship process. In practice each candidate is examined by the Israeli Ministry of the Interior as if the old Orthodox monopoly applied.

Except for the period from 1949 to 1956, people who sought to leave Poland could do so with relative ease compared to the situation in the Soviet Union. During certain periods of official anti-Semitism/anti-Zionism, *aliyah* was actively encouraged by the Polish authorities. While this "permissiveness" was part of anti-Semitic/anti-Zionist campaigns, the notion of moving west and then deciding to leave for Israel allowed some Soviet Jews to find their way to Israel after 1956 through the 1960s and 1970s. Poland often served as the first destination during the late 1980s for Soviet Jews seeking to immigrate to Israel after the fall of the Soviet system. The motivations for Polish government assistance in the period after 1989 were often attributed to a newfound interest in reconnecting with Western powers. Nevertheless, this help was forthcoming.[31]

It is noteworthy that at least 25 percent of Beit Warszawa and Beit Polska attendees who complete the Step-by-Step classes attempt *aliyah*. The network of young people who remain friends and advisors to each other is impressive because they are active members of Reform and Masorti congregations in Israel and Poland. There is a normal constant stream of people moving back and forth between Israel and Poland. The once distant and detached communities of Poland and Israel actually have a good deal of interchange. It is not unusual for families to spend considerable time in each country. It is hoped that in the future Beit Warszawa will form a kindergarten program that will help to solidify the sense of community.

Memorial Projects and Cultural Festivals

Progressive Judaism in Poland is committed to memorial projects but is resolute in its focus on building congregational life. Considerable philanthropy was directed toward other kinds of efforts: memorial projects and cultural festivals.

The memorial projects seek to preserve remnants of the physical presence of synagogues, schools, and other buildings. These projects transform these buildings to community centers, libraries, and other laudable uses. Those community centers serve the local educational needs of towns seeking to have a "placeholder" for their past. These efforts build friendship and goodwill but often they are a distraction from Jewish congregational life. The mayors and city councils mean well but often these projects come with the hope that the city will realize a tourism boon. In as much as foundations from abroad support these efforts the day-to-day needs of building up Jewish life are ignored.

The cultural festivals such as the successful Krakow or Warsaw festivals have provided a venue for spreading goodwill and Jewish literacy. There, too, remains a certain ambivalence by those committed to building Jewish communal life since an unintended consequence of the reenactment culture reinforces stereotypical representations of Jews.[32] From the perspective of Progressive Jewish ideas of openness, the festivals do attract a certain number of spiritual seekers. If they are fortunate enough to connect to Progressive congregations, an often long-term process begins that sometimes culminates in people formalizing their relationship to Judaism. As Progressive Jews we are open to this process without crossing the line into proselytizing. We make a clear distinction between welcoming people and teaching about Judaism and missionary work, which is universally frowned upon.

A good deal of tourist detritus comes with the cultural festival. Often one sees grotesque presentations of dolls and representations of Jewish ritual objects. The appearance of anti-Semitic tropes is part of the tourist presentation.[33]

It is important to note that the Jewish world in Poland is often dismissive of the people's non-Orthodox spiritual searches. Often people who five and ten years earlier were themselves welcomed into Beit Warszawa become the least tolerant of gentiles. The availability of DNA testing is another strange phenomenon that has somehow served to motivate interest in Judaism. The suggestion that Jewish "blood" can be verified through a DNA test holds a certain fascination for people. These stories of people who discover their connection to Jews are often very dramatic, but we are reminded of the need to foster proper reasons for connecting to Judaism.

Poland Is More a Religious Community Than Not

The formulation of the Polish national narrative—both Catholic and increasingly secular—is complex. Any analysis of the renewal of Polish Jewish life must take into account the importance of Polish Catholic piety as the milieu in which a considerable portion of modern Poland lives. Unlike Christianity in other Communist-dominated countries, the Catholic Church did not die out under oppression. The Church during the eighteenth and nineteenth centuries and most of the twentieth century became the fervent keeper of Polish national identity.[34] The religious nature of part of Poland's society—while diminished from the days of Communism—provides a context sometimes constricting for Jewish piety. It suggests that a careful part of the pedagogy for people seeking to develop a Jewish commitment is the necessity to have a clear pattern of expectations and mitzvot. The community has developed a statement of thirty-five principles that help define our path and direction in Judaism. In the light of an organized campaign of disinformation and even a court case the community has sought to explain how Progressive relates to classical Judaism and how it is unique.[35]

The growth potential for these small communities is difficult to know. Many individuals have worked assiduously to cover any connections to the family's Jewish past. Some have accomplished this hiding coupled with a fear of discovery. The decision by a relative to visit from Israel or the decision of a nephew to embrace Judaism may spell disaster for some who are hiding.

Most moving for me were my two encounters with two separate men just three or four years older than my age (I was born in 1948 in Germany) whose elderly "relative" in their nineties informed each of them that the family had brought him into the family and raised him as Catholic but he was not a blood relative. He would not inherit the family farm!

The impact on an individual in their sixties grappling with their identity was quite stunning. One individual described a combination of shock, curiosity, and even elements of revulsion. This was accompanied with some rejection or distrust when an attempt was made to connect with the Jewish community. The collective effort of Beit Polska has been to be as welcoming as possible. Some individuals express a desire to learn about Judaism but remain faithful Catholics. For others there grows a desire to go one step further by formally connecting with the Jewish community. In March of 2013 five men who had been studying with Rabbi Gil Nativ participated in the first step of conversion, circumcision. This was an unprecedented event but very moving for all concerned. The presence of a group of seekers in a Jewish community represents a host of challenges.

Response to Jewish Renewal in Poland and in North America and Israel

The response of many members of the organized Jewish community outside of Poland to the phenomenon of individuals reclaiming their Jewish identity has often been confused, dismissive, and skeptical. When I talk in North American congregations about the work of building a Progressive Jewish community in Poland, I often encounter a range of responses. Some negative responses are born of mourning and unresolved grief. Others are skeptical and full of questions. (Why didn't "they" move to Israel? What is their motive for connecting to Judaism? Why did their grandparents convert to another religion? Why did their grandparents support Communism? "They" are simply seeking some advantage!) Often, anger and ignorance combine to create a wall of disassociation and rejection toward the very people we should be embracing! The happy news of reuniting with lost brothers and sisters is sometimes met with hostility and suspicion. I think that fostering Jewish life in Poland is a duty and an opportunity directed to Progressive Jews. Helping those who seek to learn about Judaism is our mitzvah. Some will discover that they want to regularize their status and become Jews. Thank goodness there are those who recognize the miracle of return and want to help these congregations flourish.

In Poland, some organizations have tried to capitalize on this phenomenon by seeking to regain public Jewish property for what appears private gain. The fate of the monies from the sale of public Jewish properties remains a mystery. Others saw an opportunity to connect with the burgeoning Jewish community and to foster an old-world, nineteenth century form of Judaism. The once idealized "Klezmer Judaism" often serves the romantic (exoticize) impulses that lead people to seek a deeper Jewish connection, but these do not appear to be representative of what Jews in Poland are looking for today. Nevertheless, the Polish Jewish spectrum seems less about ritual practice and more about strategies of cultural transmission.

The Polish Polish Jewish Context

It is in this larger context of the subsequent period of Poland's Third Republic that a new phenomenon began to appear—Polish Polish Jews.[36] Stanislaw Krajewski writes:

> *Polish* Polish Jews [are] Polish Jews who live in Poland, and . . . treat Poland as their homeland rather than just a place of origin . . . We do not ignore the reality of antisemitism in Poland, we feel it. We know that in the eyes of many Poles, Jews still provide much of the mystical explanation of Poland's misfortunes . . . On the other hand, however, we do feel the existence of pro-Jewish attitudes, popular interest in "things Jewish," and respect for Judaism. Above all, we feel the bond of common experience between contemporary Polish Jews and their non-Jewish peers.

Jews in Poland are numerically inconsequential today, but have an enormous role to play in the future of Jewish memory for all Jews, and also this small community will form a living witness for non-Jewish Poles.

The Museum of Polish Jewish History on the Seventieth Anniversary of Warsaw Ghetto Uprising, April 2013

The future meaning of the Museum of Polish Jewish History will continue to be debated. Certainly the new museum will grow, develop, and change. Its exhibits will respond to the educational needs of visitors.[37] In the future, Jewish youth will encounter in an organized and well-conceived fashion more of Polish Jewish culture than is encapsulated by the remains of Auschwitz and Maijdanek. Polish school children will come to the museum to see part of their past. Jewish youth from around the world will gain a glimpse of aspects of Jewish culture. Whether there will be sufficient input from Polish-speaking Jews living as Jews in Poland is a challenging matter for the community to face. No doubt the Jewish Socialist movements, the Bundists, and the Progressive movements (Postepowe) will receive short shrift in the new museum. For ideological reasons these movements will take a back seat to the caricature of shtetl culture.

The museum will serve as a venue for reconciliation. Beit Polska has had a role in introducing educators from North America and Israel to their counterparts in Poland. The museum will represent an important stage in the process of telling the thousand-year-old narrative of Jewish life in Poland.

Visiting Scholars, Rabbis, and Artists

A dedicated core of teachers from the Reform and Conservative movements are teaching at Polish universities under Beit Polska's auspices. At a very modest cost the Polish institutions of higher learning are welcoming academics from a host of academic fields. These Jewishly informed individuals have provided an opportunity for high schools and university students to learn about the culture of Judaism for the first time. Often where a young Pole meets a Jew is in these forums. The presence of teachers living in the community for a few weeks or a couple of months has provided Jewish role models and teachers for individuals seeking to reconnect to Judaism. In turn, Beit Polska's leaders are visiting congregations in North America, Israel, and Europe to learn about Jewish communal life. The network of twinning congregations has provided an opportunity for shared discussion. Book discussions via Skype have allowed a sense of the larger Jewish world to be as close as one's computer.

There has been considerable discussion of encouraging young Polish Jews to join a special elite school of Ambassadors of Judaism. By offering a sophisticated course to young people that would prepare them to speak and represent Judaism before high schools, student clubs, Rotary clubs, and other emerging civic institutions we would create a boon to Jewish young people's Jewish formation and inform Polish young people about Jews. There is nothing comparable to the experience of representing a group to inspire young leaders and educate Poles more broadly about Judaism.

Notes

1. Wikipedia article: Beit Warszawa, http://en.wikipedia.org/wiki/Beit_Warszawa_Synagogue.
2. Beit Warszawa website, http://www.beit.org.pl/.
3. http://www.mimisheffer.com/index-en.htm.
4. Friends of Jewish Renewal in Poland, http://www.jewishrenewalinpoland.org/.
5. Beit Polska, https://www.facebook.com/beit.polska.
6. Beit Warszawa, http://www.beit.org.pl/.
7. Beit Lublin, https://www.facebook.com/pages/Beit-Lublin/178811312131129?fref=ts.
8. Beit Lodz, https://www.facebook.com/beit.lodz.5?fref=ts.
9. Beit Poznan, https://www.facebook.com/beit.poznan.
10. Beit Gdansk, https://www.facebook.com/BeitGdansk.
11. Beit Plock, https://www.facebook.com/pages/Beit-Plock-%D7%A4%D7%9C%D7%95%D7%A6%D7%A7/262225673911579?fref=ts.
12. Beit Bialystok, https://www.facebook.com/BeitBialystok.
13. "Toward" is the name of the street on which the Union of Jewish Religious Communities has its offices.
14. Cnaan Lifshiz, JTA, http://www.timesofisrael.com/in-poland-orthodox-and-reform-clash-over-control/ and a more in depth article by Nissan Tsur, http://www.jpost.com/Magazine/Judaism/Article.aspx?id=302318&prmusr=GeLTKjYhLJjzsL7EuPo9EDrF5l4SFYnN%2fTWeUG2a6tMYJUaOzPz0ADlBovGoywO8.
15. Joanna Beata Michlic, *Poland's Threatening Other: The Image of the Jew from 1880 to the Present* (Lincoln: University of Nebraska, 2006), 108–30, especially 131ff.
16. Michlic, *Poland's*, 1–2.
17. Ruth Ellen Gruber, *Virtually Jewish: Reinventing Jewish Culture in Europe* (Berkeley: University of California, 2002), 6.
18. Michlic, *Poland's*, 133–39.
19. Michlic, *Poland's*, 3–4.
20. Michlic, *Poland's*, 15.
21. Josef Banas, *The Scapegoats: The Exodus of the Remnants of Polish Jewry* (New York: Homes & Meier Publishers, Inc., 1979).

22. Konstanty Gebert and Helena Datner, "Jewish Life in Poland: Achievements, Challenges and Priorities. Since the Collapse of Communism," *Institute for Jewish Policy Research* (September 2011): 32, http://westburyeurope.org/sites/default/files/attachments/JPR%20Poland%20report%20for%20website.pdf

23. Steve Lipman, "The Revival of Jewish Life in Poland," *Jewish Action* (Fall 2010): 16–18, http://www.ou.org/pdf/ja/5771/fall71/14-18.pdf.

24. Antony Polonsky, *The Jews in Poland and Russia* (Portland, OR: The Littman Library of Jewish Civilization, 2012), vol. 2, 315, and http://www.sztetl.org.pl/en/article/lwow/5,history/?action=view&page=3.

25. http://en.wikipedia.org/wiki/Samuel_Poznanski#Writings.

26. http://en.wikipedia.org/wiki/Moses_Schorr.

27. Polonsky, *Jews in Poland and Russia*, vol. 3, 193.

28. http://en.wikipedia.org/wiki/Hochschule_f%C3%BCr_die_Wissenschaft_des_Judentums.

29. Polonsky, *Jews in Poland and Russia*, vol. 2, 194–95.

30. Gil Kariv, Israel Religious Action Center talk, San Francisco, March 2010.

31. Gebert and Datner, "Jewish Life in Poland," 28.

32. Gebert and Datner, "Jewish Life in Poland," 19.

33. Gruber, *Virtually Jewish*, 49.

34. Adam Zamoyski, *Poland: A History* (London: Harper Press, 2009), 275.

35. Statement of Principles of Progressive Judaism in Poland, http://beit.org.pl/images/PDFs/mission_statement_A4_ENG.pdf.

36. Stanislaw Krajewski, *Poland and the Jews: Reflections of a Polish Polish Jew* (Karkow, Poland: Wydawnictwo Austeria, 2005), 17–19.

37. http://www.jewishmuseum.org.pl/en/cms/home-page/.

Czecho-Slovak Jewry

Andrew Goldstein

I recently met a woman in the Jewish old-age home in Bratislava who had lived all her life in the city. When she was born it had been called Pozsony, then Pressburg, and now Bratislava. The official languages she had to learn in her lifetime had been Hungarian, German, Czech, Russian, and now Slovak (she also spoke Yiddish and English). Such is the fate of a Jew in the most central of Central European cities, and an understanding of the twentieth-century history of Czechoslovakia is vital before trying to consider the present and possible future of its Jewish community.

The nation of Czechoslovakia had only three brief periods of existence. It was established in 1918 by the first Czechoslovakian president, T. G. Masaryk, following the carve-up of Europe at the end of World War I; but it was always, in reality, two different nations, speaking closely related languages and close cultural affinities, yet never completely comfortable together, and whose Jewish communities were and are markedly different. The Czechs look to the west and Germany; the Slovaks to the east, to Hungary and the Ukraine. Bohemia and Moravia (the Czech lands) are predominantly Protestant, and Slovakia fiercely Roman Catholic. Czech Jews since the late 1920s have been mostly secular, very few Orthodox. Slovakia, on the other hand, became a center of ultra-Orthodox Judaism; the Chatam Sofer, Bratislava's most famous Jew, was one of the most virulent opponents of early Reform Judaism, and his yeshivah preached rigid Orthodoxy across Central Europe and beyond.

Czechoslovakia was broken into two by the Nazis in 1939. The country had already lost a large area of borderland (Sudetenland) to Germany following the infamous Munich Treaty in September

RABBI DR. ANDREW GOLDSTEIN has been visiting the Czech and Slovak Republics for over thirty years. He is the rabbinic advisor to the European Union for Progressive Judaism (WUPJ) and coeditor of the current *machzor* and Haggadah of the British Liberal Movement.

1938; and six months later, in March 1939, the Czech lands of Bohemia and Moravia became a German Protectorate. The Slovaks, who always saw themselves as different from the Czechs, declared an independent republic headed by a Catholic priest, Jozef Tiso. In effect it was a Nazi puppet state and, although the treatment of its Jewish citizens followed a slightly different path than in its former partner in Czechoslovakia, the result was the same: the almost total annihilation of its Jewish community. Of 136,000 Jews living in Slovakia in 1938 (including those in the territory annexed by Hungary), 105,000 were murdered in the Holocaust; of 118,000 Jews in Bohemia and Moravia (present Czech Republic) some 80,000 were killed. The vast majority of communities, many of them with long histories, were annihilated, leaving only deserted cemeteries and synagogues to mark their passing.

Czechoslovakia was briefly reunited in 1945 as a democratic nation, but the influence of the Communist party increased (the Red Army had liberated most of the country), and in 1948 Czechoslovakia became a Communist state. For a brief period before the Soviet takeover, Czechoslovakia supported the fledgling State of Israel, but this soon changed and a process of Stalinization followed and extreme anti-Semitic measures were taken. In 1952, Rudolf Slansky, who had been second only to Prime Minister Gottwald in the short-lived postwar democratic republic was, after a show trial, executed along with eleven other prominent Jews. In 1967, the representative of the American Joint Distribution Committee, Charles Jordan, was murdered in Prague and decades of fear enveloped the Jewish community. People attended synagogue (or church) at the risk of imprisonment, losing their job, or ruining the chances of their children getting into university. Religious teaching was forbidden, and many synagogues and cemeteries that had survived World War II intact were bulldozed to make way for housing estates or factories. The historic Jewish quarter of Bratislava and the former Neolog synagogue were destroyed in the late 1960s to make way for a new road. No wonder that a large proportion of the Jewish community, mostly survivors of the Shoah, emigrated at any opportunity, such as the brief Prague Spring in 1968 and its following Soviet invasion. Most of the refugees were of the younger generation and the Czechoslovak Jewish community was near to extinction. In Prague, only two synagogues were open, visited only by a few elderly Jews, and were operated, not by prewar Praguers, but by refugees from Eastern Europe who were more traditional in approach to Judaism than the prewar, largely non-Orthodox/secular Jewish community.

Come the Velvet Revolution and the end of the Communist state in 1989, there looked to be little future for the country's Jewish community. Three years later, the third attempt at a combined nation ended with the Velvet Divorce, and the present-day independent Czech and Slovak Republics were formed. A leader of the Slovak Jewish community told me, "The Nazis killed our body; the Communists destroyed our soul." There was little left of Jewish learning or identity, or numbers. The Nazi period left deep mental scars and a challenge: Do the efforts and finances of the newly emancipated communities go into memorializing the Shoah, restoring historic synagogues (usually without any hope of a future congregation), and supporting the dwindling group of Holocaust survivors, or in encouraging the younger generation back to Judaism and rebuilding the community structures? The Communist period left another challenge, for in those days there was no concept of volunteering, charitable giving, or democratic leadership. And yet, despite the many challenges, an amazing renaissance has taken place, especially in Prague and to a lesser extent in Bratislava in Slovakia.

In reality, after the Velvet Revolution there were, and are, only nine viable communities listed as members of the Federation of Jewish Communities in the Czech Republic outside of Prague. Plzen has a magnificently restored synagogue, the third largest in the world, but currently only has one Shabbat service a month. Decin, Liberec, and Olomouc have active groups that look after their elderly, but only the last two have regular services. Brno, the second largest city in the Czech Republic, is probably the only community with a sustainable program. Its community survived the Communist onslaught better than others because Rabbi Dr. Richard Feder, the chief rabbi of Bohemia and Moravia and the only rabbi in the country, resided there and continued to teach and lead the community even in Communist times, until his death in 1970.

The story is different in Prague; it feels like a Jewish city. Several historic synagogues form the Jewish Museum: the Meisel and Klaus, with brilliant exhibitions of Judaica and Jewish life and history; the Pinkus, with the 80,000 names of those murdered in the Holocaust painted on the walls; the Spanish, often a venue for concerts of Jewish music, and, of course, the Alt-Neu Synagogue, the oldest synagogue (c. 1270) in Europe with continuously held services. There are also several more synagogue buildings and cemeteries and Jewish monuments to discover around the city. And then there are the tourist trinkets in many shops based on the legend of the Golem or T-shirts of Kafka or models of the grave of the Maharal in the mysterious old Jewish Cemetery in the heart of the former ghetto.

But what of the current Jewish community? Throughout the Communist period, regular Orthodox services were held in the Alt-Neu Synagogue led by laypeople from Eastern Europe. The Jubilee Synagogue on Jerusalem Street (its name escaping the Communist anti-Zionist purges) had been a "Reform" synagogue before World War II, as were most of the Prague congregations; in reality they were Neolog, akin to Conservative or Masorti communities today. There was a mixed choir and organ (played at least for the *Kabbalat Shabbat* psalms) and a shortened service. When I visited it in Communist times, the services were conducted by an elderly cantor, Dr. Bloom, with his devoted congregation of well-dressed ladies and a minyan of men. It was a faint reminder of the prewar liturgy and ambience of most of the Prague synagogues.

Today the Prague community is well organized and thriving. There are Orthodox services held in the Alt-Neu and Jubilee synagogues, sometimes also in the High Synagogue. There is a Chabad center, though it does not enjoy the success it has in other parts of the world. There are several Orthodox rabbis in town, and the new chief rabbi is a young Czech Jew trained in Israel. There is a Jewish school, an old-age home, kosher restaurant, and many Jewish educational and cultural activities, as well as organizations concerned with aspects of Holocaust commemoration and research.

The Federation claims it has 3,000 Jewish registered members in the country with 1,400 in Prague, but reckons that there are 10,000–15,000 more Jews who have not registered. Many will not register, remembering the fate of those so listed in Nazi and then Communist times. Most are just not interested in Jewish life—no different from the situation in other countries around the world. Although it must be remembered that there was a hiatus of forty years in which Jewish life was largely forbidden, and so there was no exposure to Judaism even in the home. A good proportion of the present potential community are in, or are the children of, intermarriages, often with only a Jewish father, although the Federation allows membership for patrilineal Jews (but this does not apply in the Prague Orthodox community). And there are a large number of Israelis living in the country, some of them for many years and well involved with the economic life, though rarely the life of the official Jewish community.

What of Progressive Judaism in the Czech Lands? The minutes of the World Union for Progressive Judaism (WUPJ) conference in 1946 indicate that a Progressive Movement was about to be set up: "The Association of Progressive Jews in Czecho-Slovakia have asked for affiliation and Chief Rabbi Frieder, when he visited us earlier in the year, gave it as the view of his young people that Progressive Judaism would be the Judaism of the future. We regret to say that Rabbi Frieder passed away a few weeks ago." The minute continues with a request "for assistance from the World Union in equipping the only Progressive Synagogue which out of a large number partially escaped destruction…the roof is missing." And later there is a reference to raising money in America "for the Progressive Synagogue in Pressberg." The identity of these synagogues needs further research, also the background of the named delegates from Prague and Bratislava. What is certain is that the death of Rabbi Frieder and the onset of the Communist regime must have spelled the end of the attempt to form a Progressive presence in the years after World War II.

Towards the end of the Communist era, an increasing number of younger intellectuals began showing an interest in Judaism; some were halachically Jewish, others sought Orthodox conversion. In 1989, they took over from the elders who had just about kept the community ticking over in the previous four decades. Government recognition was given to the revived Federation of Jewish Communities in the Czech Republic, which was constituted as an official Orthodox body. It had sudden access to government financial support as well as restituted properties, including the many buildings and the vast collections of the Jewish Museum. As in other continental European countries, especially those that were formally Communist, this concentration of power and finance has made the growth of Progressive Judaism difficult. The well-resourced "Orthodox" establishment is unwilling to share its financial wealth with Progressive congregations and is often antagonistic to their activities.

In early 1989, a newly ordained American rabbi, Joan Friedman, was given permission by the Communists to study in Prague. She befriended Sylvie Wittman, a young Jewish worker in the State Jewish Museum, and this led to the founding of the first Progressive *chavurah*, Bejt Simcha, as soon as the Communist era ended. It met in a basement in Sylvie's apartment block and, having moved at least three times, still meets in a basement although now right in the center of Jewish Prague. In the early, heady days of the new democracy, the rediscovery of Jewish roots, of religious identity, was common and Bejt Simcha (as well as the Orthodox community) had great success, especially amongst young, enthusiastic searchers for meaning in the new world. Prague became a magnet for many foreigners, especially Americans, and in their number were many Reform or Conservative Jews. Initially, Bejt Simcha was the meeting place for these ex-pat non-Orthodox Jews, but soon cultural differences led to a split and Bejt Praha was formed. It still meets every Shabbat in the impressive Spanish Synagogue and though it was briefly a member of Masorti Olami, it is now an independent liberal Conservative congregation. Its onetime rabbi broke away and now runs his own official Masorti community. Bejt Simcha had another falling-out, which for a time was most unpleasant with lawsuits and unfortunate national media coverage. The root cause of the disagreement was a dispute that colored many aspects of life in the newly independent country: one group was composed of former dissidents and the other included those who may have colluded with the former regime. The breakaway Zidovske Liberal Union (ZLU) holds Shabbat and holiday services and is associated with the Maccabi sports organization and, amongst other activities, sponsors an annual cycle ride from Prague to the former concentration camp Terezin. Bejt Simcha and ZLU are both members of the WUPJ and both are thriving. There are four non-Orthodox congregations, two Progressive and two Conservative, when a united congregation would have real presence and power: how Jewish!

The Federation has a rule that there can only be one official Jewish community in a town. The tiny communities in Decin and Liberec have declared themselves Progressive and the latter has the services of the Liberal Rabbi Tom Kucera of Munich (who is Czech) on an occasional basis. Kucera has also run several successful weekend retreats sponsored by the WUPJ (with the aid of the Breslauer Foundation), which has brought the concept of Progressive Judaism to a wide audience. He was also involved with the publication of a truly Progressive prayer book, *Hegyon Lev*, with parallel columns of Hebrew, Czech, and transliteration (with occasional additions of English and Slovak). As well as services, Bejt Simcha runs well-organized and publicized conversion courses, its candidates being converted by the European *beit din* that serves European countries in which there is no national Progressive *beit din* (as in Holland or France). However, Prague claims it is historically Orthodox (which, of course, prewar it was not) and so the two Progressive communities can only be associate members or cultural societies of the Federation; but this is, hopefully, about to change. Bejt Simcha has been offered a synagogue building on the outskirts of Prague, but its location and the fact that it is in a decrepit state make it a difficult offer to accept. A centrally located dedicated synagogue building would certainly give a boost to the further growth and influence of Progressive Judaism in the Czech Republic, though an even greater boost would come from a full-time Czech-speaking rabbi. This cannot be stressed enough: in a community that is mostly secular with a high proportion of intellectuals, mostly in intermarriages, there is great potential for Progressive Judaism in Prague and the small provincial communities—if only the lay and rabbinic leadership could be found.

The position in Slovakia is somewhat different. Having more affinity to Hungary than Germany, prewar towns often had both an Orthodox and a Neolog synagogue and community. In general the Jewish community was very traditional and more religious than in the Czech lands, mirroring the power and influence of the Catholic church in Slovakia. Although the Federation of Jewish Communities in Slovakia claims it has fourteen communities (with maybe three thousand Jews in the country), in truth only that in Bratislava has a long-term future. Even here the leadership and most members, though claiming to be "traditional," are in reality secular and lack any real knowledge of Judaism. There is one synagogue open, but with a Chabad rabbi who tries hard but cannot answer the needs of a largely professional, intermarried congregation, it often finds difficulty finding a minyan. After several years visiting to give lectures on Jewish subjects, I offered to come more regularly if I could lead Progressive services, teach from a Progressive point of view, and convert those who wished to regularize their status. I can claim a modest success and there is clearly a need for a non-Orthodox rabbi in Bratislava who could also serve the other smaller communities. As I have said regarding Prague, a competent Slovak-speaking Reform rabbi could play a major role in defining the future of Slovak Jewry despite its Orthodox history.

Meanwhile, a new leadership in Bratislava has recently brought new energy to Jewish life. The community center has been refurbished, a kindergarten started, educational events planned, and successful children's and family residential camps are developing deeper community and Jewish identity; there is a new confidence in the air.

The Jews of both the Czech and Slovak Republics are very pro-Israel and many members have relatives in Israel, and, from the end of Communism, there have been regular visits both ways. The Czech government and media have been pro-Israel at a time when this was not so in most other European countries. Anti-Semitism appears not to be a big problem, although there are more concerns in Slovakia, with a new nationalist movement trying to restore the reputation of the wartime Fascist leader Tiso as well as racists stirring up trouble for the Roma. In the Czech Republic, many deserted synagogues have been restored, often by local non-Jewish enthusiasts, and there is growing interest in keeping alive the memory of former communities. This trend is less active in Slovakia; however, an energetic young leader, Maros Borsky, who spent some time studying at Leo Baeck College in London, has recently developed and opened a new Jewish community museum in the women's gallery of the Bratislava synagogue (www.synagogue.sk) as well as creating an exciting Slovak Jewish Heritage Route, taking in many historic synagogues across the country.

By and large it is good to be a Jew in both the Czech and Slovak Republics; their communities will never experience the glory of their prewar days, but at least in their capital cities they have a future. Both cities and both countries warrant visits for they offer many Jewish sites of interest and fabulous sights in many towns and beautiful and varied rural scenery.

Growth of Dutch Progressive Judaism: A Chutzpah

Menno ten Brink

In September 2010 a demographic survey was published by the Jewish Welfare Organization (Joods Maatschappelijk Werk, JMW) that is indicative for the situation of the Jews in the Netherlands in 2009.[1] The conclusions of the survey are as follows:

- The number of Jews in our country is difficult to calculate directly. Due to fear of registration, we don't like a census. Through indirect figures and counting, it is estimated that in 2010 some 52,000 people with a Jewish background lived in the Netherlands. This figure is slowly on the rise, mostly because the Israeli population in the Netherlands is estimated between 9,000 and 10,000 people.
- Relatively there are more older people (the baby boomers, born after the Shoah between 1945 and 1959).
- The percentage of people born of two Jewish parents is 45 percent; 25 percent have only a Jewish mother and 30 percent only a Jewish father.
- Less than 40 percent have a Jewish partner and this percentage is decreasing: 52 percent of the parents of the respondents have a Jewish partner; 44 percent of the respondents have a Jewish partner, their children 26 percent, and their grandchildren 14 percent.
- People start late with relations (after their study, starting careers), they have children at a relatively high age, and there is a high rate of divorce.

MENNO TEN BRINK (LBC93) is the senior rabbi of the Progressive Jewish community of Amsterdam, coordinator of the *beit din tzedek*, and member of the executive board of the Anne Frank Foundation. He holds an MA in Law at the University of Amsterdam (LL.M) and an MA in Jewish Education. He is married to Riette and has three children (Daniel, 23; Sharon, 20; and Yael, 18). For more information, see www.ljgamsterdam.nl and www.verbond.eu.

- Almost half of the Jewish population lives in the Amsterdam region.
- Most Jews are highly educated and have professions in the higher range.
- Jews tend to judge postmodern values as important in their lives (e.g., self development, democratization, and protection of nature).
- Elderly Jews are reasonably alone, especially the child survivors born between 1925 and 1945 (the first prewar/war generation of elderly people), especially when their spouse passed away.
- Most of the respondents in this survey use the Internet and social media, but they do not take the place of the direct, face-to-face, social life in communities and Jewish organizations (the social media are most important however for the younger generations).

A few results from this survey are important for this article on Progressive Judaism in the Netherlands. In general we can see a tendency of a decline in organized Orthodox Jewish live due to internal controversies and, most of all, the way the Orthodox rabbis act as the leaders of their Jewish organizations. The mainstream members of Orthodox Judaism in the Netherlands are traditional but not orthopraxy; they find that the Orthodox rabbis are out of touch with the way they choose to exercise their Judaism. For example, the chief rabbi of the Amsterdam community made public remarks that homosexuality is an illness and homosexuals should rather be cured than their attitude being sanctioned. He was criticized by his board; but the point was made, and it set a tone. Some years ago, the group "Amos" started in Amsterdam. It is an offshoot of the established Orthodox community, NIHS (Nederlands Israëlitische Hoofdsynagoge). The main reason for starting on their own, under the guidance of a popular Orthodox rabbi who is not Chareidi or Lubavitch, is that their members don't want to be told what to think and what (not) to do. The group is very popular amongst young families, and the mainstream are members of the NIHS. They gather in a rented location and they are not directly affiliated with the established community. However, most of the members of this offshoot are still members of the main Orthodox synagogue movement, otherwise they might lose their burial rights.

Of course there is also a strict Orthodox group. They are a minority in Amsterdam but are nevertheless a coherent group. Most of them are related to the Chabad, as most of the appointed Dutch rabbis are who are the leading rabbis of the Dutch Orthodox community. A strict Orthodox school, the Cheder, exists in Amsterdam, supported also by subsidies from the more Orthodox Christian community in our country. Girls and boys are separated during the school time. Classes start early and end late, due to the long hours of Jewish education. The school is very small. If parents look for mainstream Jewish education, they can find this in Amsterdam: a preschool (Ganon), primary school (Rosh Pina), and a secondary school (Maimonides). These schools are small as well (Maimonides has some 150 pupils); costs are high, also because of the separate Jewish topics and the security that is necessary to protect the schools against terror attacks. Not a lot of the children from the Liberal Jewish Movement visit those schools. One of the major problems is the acceptance of children. Children must be acceptable to the Orthodox rabbinate, meaning that a child should be born from a Jewish mother, or the mother should have been converted before an Orthodox *beit din*. This means that a lot of the children in our Progressive Jewish community are not allowed to be students at those schools, because our converts are not accepted and children from only Jewish fathers are also not accepted. According to the Dutch law, it is legal to open these schools only to students they choose, as it is considered to be a private school. The students at these schools are for a large part children from Israeli parents or Israeli mothers and non-Jewish fathers. The schools could be much larger if they would open their doors for all our members, including children with only a Jewish father. Due to subsidies from the Orthodox Movement and the prohibition by their rabbis to accept these children, it is impossible for them to do this. Judaism is only taught by Orthodox rabbis, with denial of the existence of the Progressive synagogues.

Some twenty years ago the Liberal Movement started a Liberal Jewish day school in Amstelveen (Leo Baeck School), but due to internal problems, and the fact that parents didn't want to bring the children from outside Amsterdam on a daily basis, the school was closed after several years. It is very hard for these institutions to keep their doors open. A lack of students and finances threatens the existence of these Jewish educational institutions. A principal discussion towards acceptance of all children with Jewish backgrounds, including children with only Jewish fathers and converts of our movement, would be necessary to guarantee the existence of these Jewish days schools into the future.

The same tendency of decline of Jewish institutions because of declining numbers and costs is seen in the Jewish care institutions. There are two Jewish old people's homes (one in The Hague and the other one in Amsterdam, respectively Mr Visserhuis and Beth Shalom). Beth Shalom in Amsterdam has two locations (one in Amsterdam the other one in Amstelveen), but financially it is almost impossible to survive on their own, without a larger general umbrella organization. This is also the case for the Jewish psychiatric hospital and clinic, the Sinai Centre, formally in Amersfoort in the middle of the country, but now already for some years in a new building in Amstelveen, within the heart of the Jewish community in the Netherlands. The institute is unique in Europe, but has many difficulties in surviving. The building is expensive and there are not enough Jewish patients, so it is difficult again to subsist on its own. There are other Jewish psychiatric clinics in the rest of the country, but they are too small, mainly staffed with non-Jewish personnel and with non-Jewish patients. At the moment, talks about merging with a large non-Jewish psychiatric organization are in process. Some of the difficult aspects in this merger are to keep Jewish identity, the possibility to keep kashrut (expensive and only for a few people), and the expertise to work with patients with a first- or second-generation Shoah trauma. The Jewish department of the General Hospital, also based in Amstelveen, next door to the Sinai Centre, is basically the same: a lack of Jewish patients, but a well-established Jewish care group for its patients, and a synagogue on the premises, which is very popular, mainly for people that live close to the hospital. On the other hand, we are very proud here in the Netherlands to still have special Jewish institutions for care for the elderly, the sick, and the mentally disabled. We should make sure to fight for their Jewish identity, especially when they are economically forced to be part of a larger and nondenominational organization.

The Jewish Welfare Organization itself (Joods Maatschappelijk werk) is looking for its continued existence. The reason for starting this organization was the Shoah. Now, seventy-three years after the beginning of World War II, the first generations of war survivors are dying out, the second generation is getting older, and the families are less traumatized than in earlier years. The Dutch state is not convinced that this small denominational organization should be subsidized anymore. It seems that the reason for its existence in former years is not there anymore. Moreover, the Dutch state does not want to continue subsidizing these specific Jewish organizations, as others will also claim subsidy from the state, like the growing Muslim population in our country. They look for budget cuts and no increase in this subsidy system. Therefore there is a constant search for a valid reason to exist and the government looks for reasons to stop the subsidy in these economically bad times.

At the same time, we see an increase in reclaiming Jewish identity in Holland. Years after the Shoah people with a Jewish father tend to reclaim their Jewish background and are searching for their Jewish roots. When parents who survived the Shoah and never wanted to have anything to do with their Judaism anymore (it only brought death and despair) are not alive anymore, their children and grandchildren find the freedom to look actively for their own form of Judaism, which ends up in many cases in reclaiming their Jewish identity.

We see an increase in membership in the Amsterdam Liberal Jewish Community. When people want a Jewish life, it is more and more in Amsterdam and Amstelveen, as the Mediene communities (i.e., the Jews in the rest of the country) are decreasing. There are hardly any kosher shops outside Amsterdam. There are only much smaller communities, with the largest in Rotterdam and The Hague, but these cities have hardly a Jewish infrastructure left. As said before, there seems to be an increase in attachment towards Judaism, but a Judaism that is more modern, warm, and welcoming to people that just start their development as "new" Jews. Either they discovered their Jewishness and want to proceed to do more with their identity, or people that have a Jewish father want to be confirmed in their Jewish status after a course in Judaism before our Liberal *beit din tzedek*.[2] What is most attractive to young families (Israeli and Dutch) are the classes at Sunday school (*talmud Torah*). We opened our doors for children with a Jewish father, who should be a member of our synagogues, and after the *talmud Torah*, and months before the bar/bat mitzvah date, the child can choose to be confirmed in the Jewish status (*beit din*, *b'rit milah*, and *mikveh*). In Amsterdam we have some thirty *b'nei mitzvah* a year, which is extraordinary. Most people stay on as members of the synagogue.

In Amsterdam we built a new Jewish Community Centre for Progressive Judaism, close to our former synagogue. The building is the largest ever built Progressive Jewish building on the main land of Europe. We are the most active and largest Jewish community in Amsterdam and its region. In the structure, the Shoah is less prominent than it was in the old building. The new building is open, with a lot of light from inside-out and from outside-in. This is symbolic of the attitude of Reform/Progressive Judaism in the Netherlands: We want to be actively part of the general society while also keeping our own identity. We have something to give to the outside; for example, the dialogue with other religions (we are the first synagogue in Amsterdam with a dialogue committee). About one thousand students from the neighboring technical and professional training institute, mainly students with Muslim background, have an introduction to Judaism in our building, with young members of the synagogue teaching them what Judaism is about, who their neighbors really are.

During the week, hundreds of people visit our building for synagogue services on Shabbat and holidays, for concerts, theater, culture, Jewish adult and child education, lectures on Jewish topics, activities for youngsters and for the elderly, like Café Europe, for Jews from sixty years upward. The Amsterdam Progressive Jewish community is the center of the main Jewish activities in the country, and we are proud of this. Liberal Judaism is not a "dirty" word anymore (except that there is still a *p'sak* against being in our building for Orthodox Jews, but most of the mainstream Orthodox do come, also during services, for a chuppah or bar/bat mitzvah). Our membership in Amsterdam is on the increase and we are heading now for the 1,000th member unit, which makes the membership some 2,200 people. We are almost as large as the Orthodox Movement. We started as one of the first member communities of the WUPJ in the 1930s. Mainly because of German Jews, who fled Nazism, the congregations in The Hague and Amsterdam were established. After the war, almost no survivors were left, but a small group of five people decided to start all over again in Amsterdam, and they succeeded. During the mid-1950s they appointed Rabbi Jacob Soetendorp, who was one of the driving forces for the further development of mainly the Amsterdam congregation. In 1966 a new building opened its doors. The building was big; some said that those people had chutzpah to build such a large building after the war. But in forty years time we had to build another building, with more classrooms for our children, with more space for social and cultural activities, with a *mikveh* and a small prayer room.

There are some larger and smaller Progressive Jewish congregations outside Amsterdam in The Hague, Rotterdam, and Utrecht, nine in total. We have a Levisson Institute, where we train rabbis, *chazanim*, teachers, *gabbaim*, and *baalei korei*, for the professional leadership of our congregations. At the moment, we have ten rabbis serving our congregations, all of them part time. In The Hague and Amsterdam, Rabbis David Lilienthal and Awraham Soetendorp worked very hard for many years towards the further development of Progressive Judaism. I too have worked from 1993 in Amsterdam together with David Lilienthal, and took over in Rotterdam from Awraham Soetendorp. By the end of 2003, Lilienthal had an early retirement, and I took over as senior and full-time rabbi, on my own until September 2012, when Rabbi Ira Goldberg, the sixth graduate of the Levisson Institute, started as part-time junior rabbi with me in Amsterdam. We have a rabbi serving the Dutch army and the prisons in the Netherlands. I am also working as rabbi at the Sinai Centre. We take our active responsibility in the general society in our country and in the main Jewish community. We take our stand and are partners in the negotiations with the other Jewish communities, and the local and national government, when it comes to difficult issues like *b'rit milah, sh'chita,* and anti-Semitism.

There is reason to believe that Progressive Judaism is still on its rise in the small country of the Netherlands. We are working very hard here to further establish a strong and meaningful Progressive Judaism, as part of the WUPJ, within a traditional and modern framework.

Notes

1. Hanna van Solinge and Carlo van Praag, *De Joden in Nederland anno 2009: Continuiteit en Verandering* (Diemen: AMB, 2010).
2. In our Liberal community, people with only a Jewish father need to be confirmed in their Jewish status before the Liberal *beit din tzedek*, after a course and integration in the Jewish community. *B'rit milah* and *t'vilah* are also part of this procedure.

Reform Judaism in Switzerland

Reuven Bar-Ephraim

Everything that happens in Europe happens in Switzerland, too, just some decades later. This popular Swiss saying depicts the situation of Judaism in Switzerland in general and that of Liberal Judaism[1] in particular. Although in most West European countries the Jews received civil rights decades before, in Switzerland this was only the case in 1862. Jews had lived in the area that today is called Switzerland since the middle ages. In 1349 (this time at the same moment as in many other European cities) the Jews were expelled due to the Black Death. Individual Jewish families settled again after some years on Swiss territory, but no communities were established. During most of the eighteenth and nineteenth centuries, the only two villages where Jews were allowed to settle were Lengnau and Endingen in the kanton[2] of Argau, which were also known as the *Judendörfer* (Jews') villages. After the kanton of Zurich in 1862 allowed the Jews to settle within its borders, a stream of Jews from the two Jewish villages began to flow toward the kanton's capital, the city of Zurich. They organized themselves and, in light of the recently received equal rights, they orientated themselves towards a community that would fit the standards of modern life. Striving to create a modern community, they took as their model the German Liberal congregations. In the same year, 1862, the Israelitische Cultusgemeinde Zürich (ICZ) was founded. In 1884 a synagogue was inaugurated, which is in use until this day. The synagogue had the German way of seating (like a theater) with the bimah up front, facing the congregation. The inauguration was accompanied by a mixed choir and a harmonium, both unheard of back in the *Judendörfer*. The Liberal direction in which the ICZ developed didn't fail to meet

REUVEN BAR-EPHRAIM (J93) is the rabbi of Or Chadasch congregation in Zurich, Switzerland, member of the executive board of the EUPJ, and co-chair of the European *beit din*.

resistance. The result was the splitting off of an Orthodox group that established the Israelitische Religions Gesellschaft—Adat Jeschurun (IRG), in 1895. In the course of the twentieth century, also due to the employing of rabbis with more and more traditional tendencies, the ICZ became more traditional in its ritual. The harmonium was voted down in 1937 and the bimah was turned around to face the *Aron HaKodesh*. After World War II, the ICZ identified itself as an *Einheitsgemeinde*, a home for every Jew observant and less observant, with traditional (i.e., Orthodox) ritual.

Because of the Orthodox direction in which the ICZ developed, a change occurred also in the discourse within the ICZ, which left little room for Liberal Jewish thought. Outside of the largest of Jewish congregations in Switzerland, the Liberal ideology was expressed particularly by Rabbi Lothar Rothschild,[3] rabbi of the *Einheitsgemeinde* of St. Gallen. Together with two others,[4] he established in 1957 the Vereinigung für Religiös-Liberales Judentum in der Schweiz (VRLJ).[5] This Union published a periodical, *Tradition und Erneuerung*,[6] and organized Liberal services within the building of the ICZ. In 1978 a group of ICZ members, who were active also within the VRLJ, established a new congregation, another split-off from the ICZ. This congregation, Or Chadasch, was the second Liberal congregation in Switzerland after that in Genève. A similar development occurred, from a group (Groupe Israelite Liberal [GIL])[7] within the Orthodox lead congregation, into a vibrant independent congregation.

Today Liberal Judaism in Switzerland has its own umbrella organization, the Platform for Liberal Jews in Switzerland (PLJS). The largest congregation is the GIL in Geneve with over a thousand members. Since its foundation, the GIL was lead by Rabbi François Garai. He was born in 1945 in Paris and was ordained in Paris in 1968. He became the first Liberal rabbi in Switzerland in the English-speaking Jewish community of Geneva. In 1970 he founded GIL and is to this day the rabbi. He participated in the creation of several Liberal communities in France (Marseille, Lyon, Grenoble, and Strasbourg) and the Federation of Judaism. He has published *The World of Mitzvot* (Jewish liberal practices) and *The World Ethics* and was editor of books and daily prayers of the High Holy Days. Garai is a past president of the EUPJ. He edited a siddur for the GIL.[8] The GIL has its own beautiful community center, which was inaugurated in 2010. The curved triangle shape of the plot that the community received was a great challenge for the architect to use in the most efficient way. He chose to design the building in the shape of a shofar. This choice has an amazing result. It gives the building a dynamic of its own, which suits Liberal Judaism on one hand and the temperament of Rabbi Garai on the other. GIL publishes the highly valued French-language magazine *Hayom*, circulated among both Jews and non-Jews. Or Chadasch in Zurich (where German is spoken) is the second-largest congregation with about six hundred souls. In Basel the eighty-member Liberal congregation Migwan is consolidating and growing.

Since I serve Or Chadasch, which is part of the largest Jewish community in Switzerland in Zurich, I will concentrate the rest of this article on Zurich. Besides Or Chadasch there are three other (all Orthodox) congregations in this city. The already mentioned ICZ which has around 2,500 members, is the largest of Zurich. The other two are the IRG, that developed itself into a west Ashkenazi Chareidi community, and the Agudas Achim, the Polish-oriented Chareidi community. Besides the four official synagogues, there are around twenty-five places of worship, including the synagogues of the two Jewish old age homes and two that are run by Chabad.

Or Chadasch and the ICZ are the only recognized Jewish congregations in the kanton. The two others cannot attain this status, since they are non-egalitarian in their organizational structure, meaning that women do not vote and cannot be voted for office. This recognition for Jewish congregations is relatively new (2009) and gives Or Chadasch in the public realm a far bigger status and weight than it would have if only for its membership. In every interreligious forum, in every discussion with the city or kanton councils, we are being consulted on an equal basis with the ICZ. The part of the "church tax" that our members pay (every inhabitant of Switzerland pays this tax) now flows back into the congregation because of this recognition.

Since its founding, Or Chadasch has been an egalitarian Congregation, not only between women and men, but also towards non-Jews. Half of the married couples are intermarried. Although only Jews can become members, non-Jewish spouses are as integrated as they want to be. Non-Jewish spouses are interred in the same grave as the Jewish spouse in our cemetery, albeit with a neutral ceremony that bears no symbolism from other religions.

As said before, Or Chadasch is member of the PLJS. The found-ing of this Liberal umbrella organization in 2010 was the answer to the turning down of a request by Or Chadasch to become a mem-ber in the large Swiss community umbrella the Schweizer Israel-itsche Gemeindebund (SIG)[9] in 2003. In spite of the fact that we are a much smaller organization, here, too, on the national level, we have the same status as the SIG. Many people inside the SIG do not agree with the Orthodox-vetoed acceptance of the PLJS and try now to get around that and arrange a way to corporate with us.

Between the ICZ and Or Chadasch there are several areas where the two communities work together. On the level of the two boards and on representative levels vis-à-vis the local and national au-thorities, much is done together, as is in the cultural area of orga-nizing Israeli film evenings by a joint committee named Seret. On the rabbinic level, there is no contact. When we asked if we could use their facilities for *taharah* it was declined by the rabbi, as was the request to use their *mikveh*. The present president of the ICZ dreams of a real *Einheitsgemeinde* where, within one organization, a large variation of religious services would be offered, Orthodox and Liberal rabbis would be employed equally, and services could be conducted in various ways. Knowing the Swiss Jewish mental-ity, I presume that messianic times can be welcomed prior to the realization of this vision.

Or Chadasch is a growing community. Each year between 7 percent and 15 percent new members are welcomed. Partly these are people who come from the ICZ, partly they are "our" children coming of age, partly people that come from other communities, partly children or grandchildren of Shoah survivors who only now dare to connect with a Jewish community. Another part of the new members are converts. Our strength and attractiveness lies in the fact that we are open to every Jew, regardless of their lifestyle. We are easily accessible, without demanding a certain way of Jewish life at home, but assisting in developing just that. Although patri-lineal descent is not recognized in our community, we do accept children of Jewish fathers into our Hebrew school, who appear be-fore the *beit din* for conversion prior to bar/bat mitzvah.

Within Liberal Judaism, Or Chadasch leans more towards a traditional way in liturgy and services. The prayer book *Ha'avoda Shebalew*, which was published by the IMPJ in 1982, has been in use since 1992, after a German translation was added. Services are conducted mostly in Hebrew. The harmonium (the banner of Liberal Judaism in this town) is used for accompanying the *sh'liach tzibur* and the congregants in the singing of music by amongst others, Louis Lewandowsky, Debbie Friedman, Jeff Klepper, and Shlomo Carlebach.

Our latest project is called Shabbat Jachad. Central to this idea is that celebrating Shabbat together shouldn't stop with the singing of *Adon Olam* at the end of a service. Beside that, it is known that services are an essential element of Shabbat experience for only a small part of the membership. Shabbat Jachad opens the doors of the community center the whole day, where different activities are going on at the same time. Adjacent to the service, the cafeteria is opened for a drink, a schmooze, reading, or a game of cards. In another room a story can be told to young children. There is also a meal that everyone can attend. Even for those who come just for that, there can be a *shiur* on the *sidrah*, a lecture on literature, and a film for the youth group. The sky is the limit; the goal is to make Shabbat special also for those members who don't come to services.

Besides the different congregations as mentioned before, different organizations exist here, too, with the usual suspects of any Jewish community: Keren Hayesod, New Israel Fund, international (Hashomer Hatsair, Bne Akiwa) and local youth organizations, sport clubs, B'nai B'rith, Hadassah, etc. What strikes me is the lack of an active Zionist federation. Israel-connected activities are organized by any of the above-mentioned bodies or by one of the many "Friends of . . ." foundations (Hebrew/Tel Aviv/Ben Gurion University, Leo Baeck School, Alyn Hospital, etc.). Besides an occasional report in *Tachles* (the Jewish weekly), these events generally take place before convinced audiences. No open discussions about hot items. The two congregational umbrella organizations SIG and PLJS utter their protests with the authorities when they say or do something that might turn out negatively for Israel. In general these organizations try to appear as Swiss as possible and only remotely related to the State of Israel. Clear critical sounds for better and worse can be heard from the mixed Jewish/non-Jewish Swiss-Israel Society and the Jewish Voice for Peace.

Now picture this: The Swiss Friends of Givat Haviva invited some years ago a Palestinian professor to Zurich to read from her new book and to speak about the situation between Israel and the Palestinians. For this event they rented the premises of our congregation. The chairperson of the day was a member of the board of the congregation. She was asked by the board to facilitate the evening. The audience were mostly nonmembers and/or not Jewish. A couple of days after the event, the board of the congregation received a letter signed by a dozen members, in which the undersigned demanded the stepping down of the specific board member. The fight was fought too in the Jewish weekly with many letters to the editor in *Tacheles*[10] pro and contra. Some said that it was a disgrace for the congregation to have an event that hosted this professor and, on top of that, chaired by a member of the board. Others argued that it didn't have anything to do with the congregation. What weren't discussed were the topics of the event (i.e., the situation between Israel and the Palestinians). It appeared impossible to have a conversation without external guests about the conflict. We could discuss liturgical challenges and changes, we could talk about the interior of the synagogue, we could talk about the budget, but talking about the conflict was out of the question. As soon as we tried to talk about the situation, emotions jumped high. Everyone thought that the person with the other opinion represented the end for the state. The ones who think that a solution is only within reach through compromises, removing Israeli rule from certain territories, recognizing the refugee problem and Israel's responsibility in finding a solution, and developing a two-state situation for the better of all the inhabitants of the area, were seen as the ones that are preparing the destruction of the state. The ones who don't want a two-state solution, but rather one state with different status for different populations, were seen by the former as heading towards the end of the Israeli enterprise. If the stakes are that high, discussion becomes impossible.

To help ourselves we organized Taboo Evenings, where difficult issues were discussed. Besides patrilineal descent and the issue of circumcision, one of these evenings was dedicated to the problem of not being able to discuss the Middle East conflict. By talking about not being able to discuss, by presenting the discussion as a taboo within the congregation, we did talk about it without splitting the congregation, without having people ending their membership.

All in all, the fairly young congregations GIL and Or Chadasch are the contemporary phenomenon of a 150-year-old reality within the Jewish community of Switzerland that is here to stay.

Notes

1. "Liberal" is the adjective that is used in Switzerland, for what is known in the United States as "Reform."
2. A Swiss kanton can be compared to a U.S. state.
3. Rabbi Lothar Rothschild (1909 Karslruhe–1974 St. Gallen) was ordained by the Bresslau rabbinic seminary.
4. Rabbi Dr. Eugen Messinger and Victor Loeb.
5. The Union for Liberal Religious Judaism in Switzerland.
6. Tradition and Innovation.
7. In 1970 the La Caummunauté Israélite Libéral (CIL) was founded.
8. The Liberal communities of Europe, with all their different languages, wrestle all the time with written liturgy. Creating a liberal siddur that is translated into the local language is mostly the extra work of congregational rabbis. I would like to mention that most of the time the single rabbi of the congregation is also the siddur committee; so to be able to edit a siddur, next to building a new community center and the other regular rabbinic work, the way Garai did that, is a remarkable achievement.
9. Swiss Israelite Congregational Union.
10. In the beginning of February 2013, after it was thought that this issue was buried, a former member of Or Chadasch, who lives in Israel now, published a full-page ad in a local newspaper, where this event was mentioned and the specific board member again was publicly slandered.

A Sephardi in Sepharad

Rifat Sonsino

Rabbinic Work in Spain

I am a Sephardic Jew, originally from Turkey, who has had the opportunity—I could also say the *z'chut* (the merit)—to return to Sepharad (Spain) to teach Judaism at Bet Shalom of Barcelona, a relatively new Progressive congregation. I retired from the congregational rabbinate in 2003 and now am in the academic world, teaching on a part-time basis at Boston College's Theology Department. Working with Bet Shalom has been a rewarding experience for me and, they tell me, even for the members of the congregation.

Every time I go back to Spain I am filled with mixed emotions. On the one hand, I feel energized by the recollection that I am walking on the same grounds of the old Rabbinic Sages and Jewish grandees, but, on the other hand, I am repelled by the remembrance of those who perished at the hands of the evil Inquisitors and murderous fanatics of the past. Nevertheless, I continue to go back, year after year, because I feel an obligation to teach Judaism, using the language and academic skills that I possess.

This is my story.

Jews of Spain: A Very Brief History

The history of the Jews in Spain is said to go back to the Roman period when a number of Jews, either by choice or by force, moved to different parts of the Iberian Peninsula in the eighth century C.E. In 711, when the Berber leader, Tarik Ibn Ziyad, crossed Gibraltar in order to conquer Spain, a number of Jews followed his lead and joined a small Jewish community already living under the Visigoths. The number of Jews increased in time. They soon reached a high cultural and economic level unheard of before. In

RIFAT SONSINO, Ph.D. (C66) is rabbi emeritus of Temple Beth Shalom, Needham, Massachusetts, and is now on the faculty of Boston College's Theology Department. He is a past editor of the *CCAR Journal*.

the tenth century, Hasdai Ibn Shaprut (925–975) became the court physician of Abd-ar-Rahman III (889–961), the Caliph of Cordoba, and Samuel Ibn Nagdela (993–1056) functioned as the vizier of Granada. The years 1000–1148 are considered to be The Golden Age of Hebrew Literature in Spain, with great luminaries such as Ibn Gabirol, Judah Halevi, Ibn Ezra, Maimonides, Nachmanides, and others leading the illustrious list.

Things started to deteriorate for the Jewish community when the Reconquista began in earnest in the eleventh century, and Christian armies started to push the Muslims back into Africa. By 1212, only the kingdom of Granada remained in the hands of the Moors, and more Jews ended up living among Christians. The rigid rule of the Catholic rulers made things worse for them. In 1265, King Alfonso X (1252–1284) of Castile issued Las Siete Partidas (The Seven-Part Code), which gave Jews some liberties but severely restricted their activities vis-à-vis Christians. There were infamous religious disputations sponsored by the crown in Aragon (1263) and in Tortosa (1413) between rabbis and leading gentile clerics, most of them new Christians. In 1391, violent riots erupted in Seville, Toledo, and Lerida, which resulted in the death of many Jews.

During the medieval times, some Jews converted to Christianity out of conviction and others did it for the purpose of advancing in their professions. These Conversos were, at best, tolerated by the old Christians who often called them Marranos (Pigs). By the fourteenth century, many new Christians were accused of leading a double life, Jews at home and Christians in the streets. In 1480, the Inquisition was finally established in Castile to make sure new Christians were faithful to the Catholic Church.

On March 2, 1492, Granada surrendered to the armies of King Ferdinand and Queen Isabella. At the end of the month, claiming that Jews were corrupting the new Christians, the King and Queen, under the influence of Tomas de Torquemada, the confessor of the queen, issued a decree of expulsion at the Alhambra in Granada, ordering all Jews to leave Castile and Aragon in three months (the date was then postponed). A Jewish delegation, led by Abraham Senior and Isaac Abrabanel, came to see the monarchs, but failed in its mission. So, Jews were compelled to leave Spain en masse. The date was August 1, 1492 (c. Tishah B'Av, 5252).

It is not known how many Jews actually left the country. A good estimate would be about one hundred thousand. Those who went to Portugal were forcibly converted to Christianity in March 1497. The rest spread out to southern France, North Africa, the Balkans, and as far as the Ottoman empire, whose Sultan Beyazid II ordered all governors of the provinces "not to refuse the Jews entry or cause them difficulties, but to receive them cordially," because of their skills and international connections. Besides, the Ottoman Empire was then a mosaic of nationalities, including Greeks, Serbs, Arabs, and others. So, the presence of another group of Jews joining those who already lived in it did not make much of a difference to the leaders of the Empire.

Very few Jews reentered Spain for the next hundreds of years, and those who came arrived mostly from North Africa or southern France but remained under the radar. In 1877, there were about four hundred Jews in Spain. In 1916, the first synagogue in modern times opened in Madrid, the capital. In December 1924, Spain granted Sephardic Jews living abroad the right to reclaim the Spanish nationality and settle in Spain. Only a few took advantage of this offer. In 1968, when the Edict of Expulsion was finally annulled, the government encouraged Jews to return to Spain. Consequently, more Jews started to arrive. During the dictatorial rule of General Francisco Franco (1892–1975) (the "Caudillo by the grace of God"), some Jews, escaping the Nazi regime, were allowed into Spain but, as it was recently discovered, Franco also ordered that a list of all Jews be prepared for the benefit of the Nazis in order to deport them from Spain.

In 1982, The Federation of the Jewish Communities was established with its headquarters in Madrid, and since 1992 it has become the sole representative of the Spanish Jewish communities vis-à-vis the government. The Federation's Internet voice is Radio Sefarad (www.radiosefarad.com), which emits daily news about Jewish life in Spain and around the world. Even though the State of Israel was established in 1948, Spain recognized it only in 1986. Spain supports Casa Sefarad-Israel (http://www.casasefarad-israel.es), a cultural and economic consortium created in December 2006 by agreement between the Ministry of Spain's Foreign Affairs and Cooperation, the Spanish Agency for International Cooperation, and the municipality of Madrid.

The exact number of Jews living in Spain is not known. According to a report by the European Jewish Congress, dated August 28, 2012, there are about forty thousand Jews in the entire country. My impression is that this number is too high, and the reality may be around twenty thousand. Most Jews live in Madrid and Barcelona (about five thousand each) and the rest are spread out in different parts of Spain, including southern Spain, Galicia, and Asturias. The majority of these Jews came from North Africa and southern France, but recently a large number of Jews have arrived from South America, primarily Argentina.

There are about thirty synagogues in different parts of Spain today. Most Spanish Jews are Orthodox by affiliation, if not practice. There are Conservative/Masorti congregations in Alicante, Madrid, and Valencia. In addition to the two Progressive congregations in Barcelona (see below), there is one in Oviedo, one in Asturias (Beit Emunah), and one in Seville (Bet Rambam), which was recently established in December 2012. A few other Progressive groups are still in formation in places like Madrid, La Coruña (Galicia), and Ibiza. The congregations in Barcelona and Oviedo are affiliated with the European Union for Progressive Judaism (EUPJ). Bet Rambam of Seville is not yet affiliated.

Barcelona, Spain

Barcelona, with about five thousand Jews, has four different synagogues: Comunidad Israelita de Barcelona (CIB) is the largest Orthodox religious institution in the city, and has about three hundred families. Chabad has a small group and is not well organized. La Comunitat Jueva Atid de Catalunya (Atid, for short), the first Progressive congregation affiliated with the World Union for Progressive Judaism (WUPJ), was established in 1997, and has about 150 families. After worshiping in a downtown converted warehouse, it now has a fine building in the suburbs with a sanctuary and meeting rooms. Although it presently has no rabbi, it was served for some years by Rabbi Roly Zylbersztein and lately had the services of a visiting HUC student rabbi from Jerusalem, Tamara Schagas. Atid has been very active in Netzer (the WUPJ youth movement) and runs camps for youth and family gatherings.

La Comunitat Jueva Bet Shalom de Catalunya (Bet Shalom, for short), "my" synagogue, has about sixty families. In terms of liturgical practices, Atid is much more "traditional" than Bet Shalom, which functions like another mainline Reform congregation in the United States. There are two kosher restaurants in Barcelona,

Delicias and Restaurante Kosher Club. The only *mikveh* is affiliated with the CIB.

Bet Shalom, Barcelona

My primary connection with Spanish Reform/Progressive Judaism in Spain is through Bet Shalom in Barcelona. In 2008, I discovered Bet Shalom on the Web when a colleague, Rabbi Ariel Edery, now in Raleigh, North Carolina, posted information about them (I think it was on Ravkav). I contacted the leaders in Barcelona asking if there was anything I could do to help out. Not only did they welcome my questions but quickly invited me and Ines, my wife, to visit them as soon as possible. The fact that I could speak Spanish was of great advantage to them, because Spanish is one of the two languages spoken in Catalunya, the other being Catalan, which I understand but do not speak. So, in 2008, Ines and I spent the month of June in Barcelona, a beautiful city of about 1.5 million inhabitants located on the Costa Brava. I led religious services, taught Judaica classes, converted a non-Jew, and then married him and his Jewish bride in what was considered to be the first wedding of the synagogue. That year, I was also able to bring them a Torah scroll, which was generously donated to them by Temple Beth Israel of Sharon, Pennsylvania.

Bet Shalom is only eight years old, established in 2005 when it split from Atid. Since then, it has made tremendous progress. It is led by a charismatic leader, Jai (pronounced as Hai) Anguita, a Jew-by-choice himself, and his wife, Adele, with an energetic volunteer administrator, Rosina Levy, who comes from Uruguay. The congregation holds *Kabbalat Shabbat* services, observes all the holy days, sponsors an Introduction to Judaism class (taught by Jai) as well as Hebrew classes for adults (taught by another member who is Israeli). They maintain a website (www.betshalom.cat) and regularly communicate with their members by e-mail. Being a middle-age congregation, they do not as yet have a religious school or a youth group. They are, however, very visible in the community. They are enthusiastic, energetic, and highly motivated to lead a meaningful Jewish life in a country that does not always welcome its Jewish minority. Nothing happens in the Liberal Jewish community of Spain without Bet Shalom's leadership and involvement.

The membership of Bet Shalom is rather mixed. Some have come from Latin America and other parts of Europe, and others are Jews-by-choice, born in Spain, who have joined the temple as full-time members after their conversion. There are also just a few Americans and Israelis who either live permanently in the city or have come to live in Barcelona for a limited period of time, either to study or work.

Bet Shalom does not have a full-time rabbi, nor can they afford one. In the past, they were blessed with temporary services by Rabbis Ariel Edery, Gabriel Mezer, Sue Oren, James Glazier, and others who came for a short time. Once in a while, they welcome visiting rabbis from the United States and different parts of Europe. In the last five years, I have volunteered my time in Barcelona by spending about three weeks each year, usually in June, doing all their rabbinic work. I teach, lead religious services, officiate at their life-cycle events, carry out pastoral duties, and participate in community functions. When I am at home in Boston, I often talk to them by Skype and teach classes online—not only to the members of Bet Shalom but also to other Jews in the rest of the Progressive communities of Spain, such as Asturias, Galicia, and Andalusia, who wish to join in the conversation. I also counsel individuals via e-mail, phone, or Skype. Bet Shalom does not pay me a salary but covers my expenses. When there is no rabbi present, a lay person reads the Sabbath liturgy; a few members lead the singing and give a *d'var Torah*.

The dedication of Bet Shalom's lay leaders is commendable. They are able to attract young people in search of a liberal understanding of Judaism. In their crammed little space, they meet regularly every Shabbat evening and holy days and, after services, serve an elaborate pot-luck Shabbat/holy day meal for everyone in attendance. They hold High Holy Day services as well as Pesach seders at a local hotel, because they cannot accommodate all their members in one place. They also organize programs on women's rights in Israel, conduct Holocaust memorial ceremonies, celebrate Israel Independence, sponsor lectures by prominent speakers, and maintain a cemetery for their members. At the present time, they are involved in creating a Federation of Progressive Synagogues of Spain. Furthermore, one of their congregants, Dr. Felipe Ojeda, a prominent surgeon trained by me in Jewish law and customs, was certified by the Berit Mila Program of Reform Judaism in the United States in March 2010 as the first Reform mohel in Spain.

In June 2008, Bet Shalom was accepted as an associate member of the Federation of Jewish Communities of Spain, and in 2009, through the efforts of my colleague, Rabbi James Glazier of South Burlington, Vermont (who spent four months with them in early 2009), my personal contacts in the Jewish world, and their own list of achievements, the congregation was formally admitted into membership by the London-based European Union for Progressive Judaism.

Among the leaders of the European Region ER of the WUPJ (ERPJ) who have been very supportive of Bet Shalom are two individuals who merit special note: Rabbi Andrew Goldstein, rabbi emeritus of Northwood and Pinner Liberal Synagogue in London and the immediate past chair of the ER, as well as Dr. Leo Hepner, one of the prominent lay leaders of the Liberal Jewish community in London and, for the last few years, the secretary of the European *beit din* (who has even joined the temple as a new member).

Now that Bet Shalom is part of the EUPJ, a member of Bet Shalom's executive board has been tasked to take care of all the logistics of the European *beit din* that comes from London to Barcelona for the formal *giyur* (conversion) of candidates. It is made of three or four rabbis representing both the Liberal and Reform movements of English Jewry, a lay secretary, and me as "their Rabbi." Conversions approved by this *beit din* are accepted by the Jewish Agency for purposes of *aliyah*.

Customarily, we set up court in one of the local hotels and, after a careful examination, we formally admit prospective converts into Judaism by giving them either a Certificate of Conversion or a Certificate of Return (to those who prove they have a Converso background). In 2011, we welcomed twenty-nine Jews-by-choice; in 2012, the number was twenty-four. These candidates came from different places, such as Madrid, Asturias, Galicia, Sevilla, Valencia, and Barcelona. Most of them sought Judaism because they did not find Catholicism satisfactory; and some of them chose reaffirmation because they discovered that they had some Jewish family ties with Conversos in medieval times and were now curious and even eager to reclaim their Jewish identity for themselves. All of them had studied Judaism for at least a year or more, demonstrated that they were active in their respective synagogues, and all men underwent ritual circumcision in accordance with the requirements of the European *beit din*. Not having a *mikveh* of our own, we usually take them to the local beach for immersion (*t'vilah*). This is followed by a festive *Kabbalat Shabbat*, during which I give each Jew-by-choice his or her certificate and, next morning, invite them for an individual *aliyah latorah* during a Shabbat morning service that takes place in the Kal (perhaps, from *k'hilah*), reputedly the historic synagogue in the old city of Barcelona. (If this is not the exact building, it was perhaps in the same area, close to the cathedral.)

Judaism is a text-based religion and you need books to study it. Regrettably, educational material on Judaism written in Spanish or Catalan is sorely lacking in Spain today. Even though I could find a few books on Kabbalah and Israel in the only Jewish bookstore that existed until recently (it closed in 2011), I saw very little written on Jewish philosophy and religion. In 2012, in order to fill this gap, I published an introduction to Judaism, titled *Vivir Como Judio* (To Live as a Jew) (Palibrio, 2012), and made it available to Jews in Spain and others in Latin America.

Spanish Jews interact with non-Jews daily in commerce and other cultural matters. Even though the rate of interfaith marriages is very high, interfaith dialogues are almost nonexistent. This past year, I initiated official contacts with the Catholic hierarchy of Barcelona. In June, through the efforts of Jai and the good offices of UNESCO, I led, perhaps for the first time in many years, an interfaith dialogue, which was moderated by Dean Armand Puig I Tarrech at the School of Theology of Catalonia of the University of Barcelona. Before an academic audience, Dr. Eric Cortes, a senior Bible professor of the Seminary, and I discussed the impact of Nostra Aetate and Dabru Emet. In a country where the Palestinian cause is preferred in many circles, and where anti-Semitism, both violent and sub rosa, is palpable everywhere, to have a successful religious dialogue based on mutual respect is no mean achievement.

The Future

The future of Progressive Judaism in Spain is getting brighter. The EUPJ considers Spain a major priority and has, in the past two years, sent Rabbi Hillel Athias-Robles (born in Costa Rica, but until recently serving a community in London) to visit various cities in the country in an attempt to set up groups of Progressive communities. Galicia has a small group but is not ready to establish itself as a congregation. The same applies to Madrid. All Progressive congregations in Spain receive some help from the EUPJ, but, more importantly, get guidance and advice during the year from the leadership of Bet Shalom in Barcelona.

Bet Shalom continues to make progress but still faces many challenges. They need larger quarters to accommodate their members and their various activities; they have to institutionalize their operation and need to function with a better organizational structure; they also need steady rabbinic leadership, even on a part-time basis, which will provide liturgical and programmatic continuity. Though they have a weekly newsletter that informs their friends of upcoming events, they need an up-to-date Web page in order to reach a broader audience. They desperately need a revised prayer book for Shabbat and holy days; their Judaica library is meager and could use more books in Spanish, English, Hebrew, and other European languages. They need financial support from the world Reform Jewish community in order to carry out their multifaceted activities. This past year, the EUPJ has provided them with a student rabbi from London who came once a month for religious services and sundry rabbinic work. I hope this pattern will continue in the future. The relationship of Bet Shalom with the rest of the Jewish religious establishment is still tenuous. The Orthodox do not recognize them as legitimate, but contacts with Congregation Atid are starting to warm up, and that is good news for the Progressive community of Barcelona. My contacts with Atid have been limited. Last year, I finally established more cordial relationships with some of their leaders, volunteered to give a talk at their synagogue, and was welcomed by those who attended my lecture.

At the moment of this writing, Spain is in the midst of a major economic crisis. Unemployment has already reached close to 25 percent of the population. Everyone is affected by the downturn of the economy and there are a number of people at Bet Shalom who have lost their jobs or have taken major salary cuts. This obviously impacts on collection of dues and the planning of many life-cycle events, such as weddings and major anniversaries. The EUPJ is attempting to provide some relief to Spain but they too lack the necessary funds. In spite of all these problems, congregational life continues vigorously in all Progressive congregations of Spain. Those outside of Barcelona share programmatic information with one another and keep in touch through a Facebook page

(Comunitat Jueva Bet Shalom Catalunya) maintained by Bet Shalom of Barcelona.

It is not likely that the Jewish population in Spain will increase greatly in the foreseeable future, and there are a number of secular Jews in the country who have very little interest in an organized Jewish community. However, all Jews are concerned with the increase of anti-Semitism in the country and actively support Israel and other Jewish causes. I am convinced that many of them would opt for a more liberal approach to Judaism if they knew about its existence in the country. These individuals could be brought closer to the organized Jewish community by creative programming of a cultural nature. The Spanish government decries discrimination and there are small pockets of gentiles (the well-known journalist, Pilar Rahola, among them) who are becoming more sympathetic to Jewish concerns, including Israel. I have been approached by numerous individuals who, once they knew I was a rabbi, told me quietly that they have "Jewish blood" in them and wish to know more about the Jewish faith. That accounts for the numerous conversion ceremonies that I have officiated over the last few years, and the numbers, I expect, will continue to rise.

For me, the experience of working with Bet Shalom has been very rewarding. I have met some wonderful people who are eager to learn and who affirm their Jewish identity with pride. What more can a teacher like me expect? I am grateful for their friendship.

"All in the Family": What Binds Together and Separates Reform Jews Worldwide

Joel D. Oseran

While the term "Jewish Peoplehood" is at the heart of this cluster of articles, it is likely that many readers have different understandings of the term. By "Peoplehood" do we mean more than simply the particular group of people who are called Jews? Does the term suggest that people who are Jews have some kind of inherent connection or relationship, one to the other? If yes, then what exactly is the nature of that relationship? And is this relationship a conscious matter, explicitly felt and understood by each member of the people, or is it a relationship that exists in potential, but one that must be nurtured and developed in order to have meaning and impact upon the life of each Jew?

I suggest that the term "Jewish Peoplehood" can best be understood and appreciated by substituting the metaphor of family. Family suggests an inherent personal connection that binds each member of the family together. We love family even before we actually have had the opportunity to get to know them. Why? Because, a priori, these are people who are personally meaningful and important to our past, present, and future. We usually feel good when spending time with family, reminiscing about the past and about our common ancestry. And in a deeply profound way, we cherish the fact that our family will survive long after we individual members have departed. We learn to protect family with a fierce sense of responsibility and commitment. We provide help and support for family that we would never feel obligated to provide for nonfamily. The Sages said it best: "כל ישראל ערבים זה לזה"

RABBI JOEL OSERAN, RJE (NY76) is vice president, International Development, of the World Union for Progressive Judaism.

(loosely translated: "Each member of the family of Israel is responsible, one for the other").

Like in all families, we naturally gravitate to those members with whom we share the most in common, with whom we actually enjoy spending time, with whom we become friends as well as family. And we all have family members who live far away—distant relatives we call them—both referring to geography and intensity of the relationship. But in the end, our relationship to family runs deeper than it does to other friends or acquaintances: whether we particularly like family or not, choose to spend time with them or not, they are fundamentally a part of who we are and we are part of who they are.

The Torah affirms this approach as well, by using the term בני ישראל (Children of Israel) to refer to the progeny of Abraham and Sarah. The people of Israel are the descendents of the family that traces its roots back to Abraham and Sarah. Had we used the term "Family of Israel" instead of "Children of Israel" (children suggests something infantile and completely unrelated to me, an adult member of a group) from the beginning of Reform Judaism in the nineteenth century, our movement might not have strayed so far from recognizing the fact that Judaism, from its inception, is best understood as the intricately woven tapestry of beliefs and practices of a particular family (בני ישראל) in covenant with their God (what Mordecai Kaplan refers to as a religious civilization).

An additional reason why the metaphor of family helps us to better understand the deeper implications of Peoplehood relates to the fact that a family lives in a home. We often attach inordinate importance to the physical home in which we grew up and in which we developed our primary relationships with our nuclear and extended family. Within the walls of our home, our family experienced the most profound moments of time, joyful as well as tragic. Our home was the focus of our historical memory as a family, helping us to preserve for the future those events that shaped who we are and who we might become as a family. And as life changed and we moved from one home to the next, the special feelings and relationship we developed towards the home in which we grew up (our ancestral home) was rarely surpassed by other homes in which we lived.

The Jewish People is that family that grew up in its own Home-Land (written this way to suggest both Home and Land),

Eretz Yisrael, a land sanctified and promised to the family by its God. On that Home-Land, our family created and developed its own civilization and established roots that have remained intact for nearly four thousand years. Over those centuries, and in spite of the fact that the family journeyed (or was exiled as the case may be) to other lands, built other homes, and developed relations of various degrees with other world families, it never forgot its historic bond to its ancestral Home-Land. Shared memories of the formative years of the family in its own Home-Land were preserved and recounted in the family archive: the Torah.

Dispersion and life outside the Home-Land meant a weakening of the family connection. We lost contact with parts of the family who traveled and settled far from where we lived and whom we never met. Yet, our shared history and memories preserved by family chronicles as well as religious teachings that set us apart and reminded us of the importance of our Home-Land have kept the family intact. Some would argue that the hostility of the world towards our family, its refusal to see us as equals and to integrate us into the societies in which we lived have also contributed in keeping the Jewish family intact.

The establishment of the State of Israel in 1948 represents the return of some of the family to our ancestral Home-Land. Most of those who did return then and who have since returned to Israel did so either because they had no other home to go to or because Israel represented the potential for a better future for themselves and their children. Some, but not many, returned Home because it was the will of our family God that all the family must live at Home and on the Land and this part of the family took God's word literally. At this early period in the twenty-first century, and for the first time since the establishment of the State of Israel, more of the family lives in the Home-Land than lives in North America. In another few decades, according to demographic studies, more family will be living in the Home-Land than in the entire Diaspora. The family is finding its way back to the Home-Land.

What does this trend suggest for that part of the Jewish family that identifies as Reform? (Reform is used interchangeably with Progressive and Liberal in this article.) To what extent do Reform Jews see themselves as part of the Jewish family (Jewish Peoplehood)? And to what extent do Reform Jews, as members of the family, relate to the modern State of Israel as their family inheritance, as their ancient/modern Home-Land?

A Closer Look at the Reform Jewish Family

The Reform Jewish family, numbering approximately 1.8 million of the total 13 million Jewish family members in the world today, is spread out in forty-five countries and joined together administratively by the World Union for Progressive Judaism (WUPJ) in seven regions: North America, Europe, Former Soviet Union (FSU), Australia/New Zealand/Asia, South Africa, Latin America/Central America/Caribbean, and Israel. As the center of our world movement and site of the WUPJ headquarters, Israel is unique among the nations and merits its own status as a separate region.

While our Reform family today reaches every corner of the world, it is fascinating to remember that the vast majority of us emigrated within the last two to three generations from nearly the same communities in Central/Eastern Europe and the FSU. The historic emigration of over a million of our Jewish family from Central and Eastern Europe (including what is today the FSU) in the nineteenth century gave birth to Jewish communities in North and South America as well as strengthened Jewish communities that had evolved in Western Europe (including England) from medieval times on. The aftermath of the Holocaust and the emigration of thousands of survivors to far away continents of South America, Australasia, and South Africa as well as to England and other Western European countries (America was closed to many Jewish refugees after World War II) continued the migration of European Jewish family roots across the globe.

Some of the family relatively quickly assumed the language, dress, cultural mores, and idiosyncrasies and inherited the political legacy of the countries to which we emigrated and which became our new homes. While those family members who gave birth to Reform Judaism in the nineteenth century came primarily from Central Europe (Germany in particular), it was in North America in the twentieth century that Reform (and Conservative) Judaism blossomed and became the dominant Jewish approaches. Reform Judaism, for the largest number of members of the Reform Jewish family in the world, developed in a uniquely American context.

Others in the family, those who remained in Eastern Europe (including the Pale of Settlement) primarily preserved and maintained their traditional family ways and relationships to the outside society. In these parts of the world, Reform Judaism, though a presence in some select communities in the nineteenth and twentieth centuries, did not become the mainstream family way as it did in America. It is only in the last few decades that Reform Judaism has become a viable Jewish option for those in the Jewish family who survived the horrors of the Shoah and subsequent Communist repression.

The first Reform congregation in the FSU, congregation Hineini in Moscow, was welcomed into the WUPJ in 1990 at the WUPJ biennial convention in London. Six indigenous rabbis, trained by movement seminaries in London and Jerusalem, lead the Reform Movement in the FSU today, which includes over fifty congregations (with newly established WUPJ multipurpose centers in Moscow, St. Petersburg, Kiev, and Minsk), a vibrant youth movement (Netzer Olami), and summer and winter camps that attract over one thousand youth each year.

The Case of Greatest Divergence

Tracing the growth and development of Reform Judaism in different regions of the world gives us an interesting vantage point from which to compare the relationship of Reform Jews to the Jewish family. Perhaps the case of greatest divergence in how Reform Jews perceive their Jewish identity and connection to the Jewish family is the contrast between Reform Jews in America and in the FSU.

For most Reform Jews in America, Judaism constitutes a religious approach to living and identifying as a Jew—parallel to what Christianity and other religions represent on the American scene. As Reform Jews, we come together in our temples and synagogues to worship God, study our ancient texts, celebrate as a community Shabbat and holidays and practice mitzvot, which we more comfortably describe as doing works of *tikkun olam*. And yes, at special times during the year, we pay respect to the tragedies that befell Jews in the past—foremost among them the Holocaust—and we pay tribute to the "miracle" and accomplishments of the modern State of Israel.

Consequently, Reform Jews in America, for the most part, are Americans by nationality whose religious identity is Jewish. As American Jews, Reform Jews in America are loyal, first and foremost, to America (the fact that the Jonathan Pollard case failed to mobilize American Jewry may suggest that most American Jews are still concerned by the potential charge of dual-loyalty). Little wonder, therefore, that the term "Jewish People" may have less meaning in today's America than ever before. Reform Jews in America are so thoroughly integrated into American society and feel so totally at home in American society that the very idea they might actually constitute another separate Peoplehood (ethnic/national grouping—family) with their own Home-Land (Israel) is not even a realistic consideration.

We do find a different orientation to the concept of Jewish family when looking at different Orthodox Jewish communities in America. Orthodox Jews, for the most part, do place considerable importance in preserving distinctions between themselves as Jews (members of the family, or as is often said with a touch of humor, members of the tribe) and the non-Jewish environment that surrounds them. Practicing traditional mitzvot adds to their separation from non-Jews and counters their assimilation into American society. For the most part, Orthodox Jews, as a result of Jewish traditional teachings, maintain a closer attachment to Israel and, in greater numbers than other Jews in America, make *aliyah* to Israel as the fulfillment of the mitzvah to live in the Land.

When we contrast the American Reform Jew's sense of "at-homeness" and national identification with America to that of our Reform Jews in the FSU and Eastern Europe, we see a substantial difference. Jews in the FSU, whether they are Reform, Chabad, or assimilated but maintaining a Jewish identity of some kind, have little to no sense of identification with the Russian, Ukrainian, Belarusian, or any of the other national groupings in what once constituted the Soviet Union. A Jew in Russia is a Jew by nationality and not by religion. In fact, until the fall of the Soviet Union (the end of the 1980s), included in identity cards was the category "nationality," which meant Russian, Ukrainian, Belarusian, etc., or Jew. Being Jewish meant being part of the Jewish People (family). It was not a religious identification but rather a national/ethnic identification.

Even in today's FSU, where Jews are no longer identified by nationality but are listed in their identity cards as citizens of their respective national country or republic, they still, for the most part, maintain a separateness and "otherness" when it comes to identifying with their national country. And no less significant, Jews are still seen as the "other" in the eyes of Russians and other nationalities in the FSU. At a recent funeral service in Belarus, when non-Jewish friends of the deceased (who was Jewish) drank toasts to the deceased as is the local custom throughout the FSU, many characterized the deceased as follows: "He was a wonderful man, even though he was a Jew." (In that light imagine how bizarre/ shocking it must be to Jews from the FSU who, after *aliyah* to Israel, are referred to by Israelis as "Russians.")

Interestingly, there appears to be little difference between Reform and Orthodox Jews in the FSU in their relationship to the Jewish family. All Jews who identify as Jews (or who are identified by general society as Jews) assume the identity of the "other" and relate primarily as being part of the Jewish group/nation/family.

This contrast between Reform Jews in America and in the FSU is further demonstrated by their respective relationship to Israel. Notwithstanding the declarations by Reform Jewish leaders in America (and the dedication and commitment of many active ARZA-WUPJ supporters of Israel) that Israel must be a major component of Reform Jewish identity and Reform Jews must strive to build a pluralistic Israel that recognizes Reform Judaism, the rank and file of Reform Jews in America are far less concerned with, or personally connected to, Israel than they are with many other issues in their congregation. Less than 10 percent of American Reform Jews are members of ARZA, and fewer Reform Jews visit Israel each year than their counterparts in other Jewish religious denominations (other examples of this distancing of American Reform Jews from Israel are unfortunately all too available).

Many American Reform Jews feel alienated from an Israel that denies recognition to Reform Judaism in Israel and that denies recognition to Reform converts. Continued limitation of women's rights in public spaces, symbolized by the Women of the Wall issue, creates an ever-widening gap between Israeli society and the religious values of Reform Jews in America. And as the number of Jews-by-choice in the American Reform Movement increases (along with the number of non-Jews who represent a growing number of participants in American Reform congregations), the inherent personal connection to the Land and People of Israel (the family connection) can no longer be taken for granted. Add to these reasons the primacy of religious identity over identification with the Jewish family and their near total integration into American society, it is little wonder that most Reform Jews feel ambivalent at best towards their relationship to Israel and the Jewish People.

The meaning of Israel for Reform Jews in World Union congregations throughout the FSU is quite different. The impact of generations of forced isolation from mainstream society (under the czars as well as under communism), coupled with a strong national identity (Peoplehood/family) all reinforced by Israel's dramatic victory in the Six-Day War in 1967, strengthened the ties of Jews in the Soviet Union and later in the FSU to Israel. It is important to note that during the dark days of the Communist regime, the lifeline to Jews in the Soviet Union (even taking into account important public demonstrations in the Diaspora to Free Soviet Jews) came from Israel and the underground work of the Israeli government—through the Lishkat Hakesher division. Jews from the Soviet Union and later from the FSU immigrated in great numbers to Israel and established a major presence in the life of the country. One out of every five Jewish Israelis in Israel today is a native Russian speaker.

For Reform as well as Orthodox Jews in the FSU today, and for the larger number of Jews who remain unaffiliated religiously but connected in one way or another to Jewish life, Israel is an important component of their Jewish identity. There is hardly a Jewish family in the FSU that does not have either a relative or friend living in Israel. Travel between Israel and the FSU is relatively simple and inexpensive, with tourism (including Jewish tourism) breaking records each year. And notwithstanding the fact that approximately three hundred thousand Jews from the FSU who have emigrated to Israel are not recognized as Jewish according to the chief rabbinate (and consequently are not entitled to be married or buried as Jews in Israel), the importance of Israel and the connection to the People of Israel among Jews in the FSU remains strong. Reform Jews might continue to live in Moscow, St. Petersburg, Kiev, and Minsk—and they might even be benefiting from newfound economic opportunities— but very few Jews in the FSU who maintain a Jewish identity feel fully integrated into the larger social order and feel secure that their future as Jews is protected and ensured.

The Global Perspective

Growing up in America, as I did, I was totally unaware of how significant the impact of Europe was on my family's Jewish identity and observance. Like most Americans, Jews had little interest in holding on to and identifying with their European (family) roots. My Judaism was American Judaism, made all the more American by the fact that my grandparents and to an even greater extent my parents, wanted nothing more than to rid themselves of their European roots: languages, family/cultural mores, and old-world religious traditions as well. Ask any Reform Jew in America under the age of fifty in what city were his/her grandparents born, and it is likely they will not know such a basic fact of their family history.

This was not the case with Jewish family migrations to other continents such as South America, South Africa, Australia, and even westward migrations to England (which has the second largest concentration of Reform Jews after North America). In our WUPJ congregations in these continents, the memory and impact of Europe, including the memory of the Holocaust, which touched the lives of many Jews who found refuge in these countries, remains strong and compelling. Jews in these communities have preserved the family memory of their European roots to a greater extent than have most Reform Jews in America (linked to the fact that these host societies were not as open to integrate the Jew as was America). Moreover, for the most part, Jews in these communities (South America, South Africa, Australia, and Western Europe/England) have established a closer relationship to Israel and world Jewry in general than their fellow American Reform Jews.

It is important to note that Canadian Jews (from all denominations), unlike American Jews, have more closely preserved their connection and relationship to their European roots (clearly reflecting the fact that Canada remains far more connected to Europe than does America). Canadian Reform Jews, for the most part, and in contrast to their American co-religionists to the North, see themselves more comfortably as connected to the Jewish family and are more connected to Israel on many levels.

Special mention should be made of the fascinating story of the return to Jewish life in Central and Eastern Europe after the fall of Communism in the late 1980s. There are today Reform congregations in Budapest, Prague, Warsaw, Krakow, and a major Reform

Movement presence in Germany (with a Jewish population of approximately 180,000, mostly emigrants from the FSU). Reestablishing Jewish religious life in countries where Communism so aggressively impacted on the spirit of religion in general has been a huge challenge. The development of Reform Judaism has been particularly thwarted by the fact that in most of these countries, the organized Jewish establishment has been co-opted by various Orthodox groupings that have refused to recognize WUPJ congregations as part of the larger Jewish community (lack of recognition means no communal funding to support rabbinic salaries, no return of Jewish property to Reform congregations, no programmatic budgets for developing Jewish education, etc.).

The fact that these Reform congregations are so small and carry so little political weight within the larger Jewish community (and in the general society as well) has been a clear obstacle to the growth of Reform Judaism in these countries. As a result, the WUPJ together with its European affiliate (EUPJ) have played a critical advocacy role in representing the interests of these Reform communities to receive recognition from both the Jewish establishment and from the national government. This is an excellent example of how the fundamental meaning of Jewish Peoplehood plays out in modern Reform Jewish history. The WUPJ appeals to governments and Jewish communal structures on behalf of 1.8 million Reform Jews worldwide, bringing with it the political clout of the largest Jewish religious movement in the world. Successes in Germany, Czech Republic, Hungary, and even in Poland indicate the need to increase this type of advocacy support.

The Expat Variable

The spread of Reform Judaism around the world in the twentieth and now in the twenty-first century can often be attributed to the important role played by the expatriate citizens who leave their country of origin to relocate to other countries—often on a temporary basis for business purposes but sometimes permanently. Expats who grew up in a Reform congregation and who relocate to countries where there are no (or only underdeveloped) Reform communities have often been responsible for establishing new Reform communities in their new home. This has been the case in countries as diverse as Costa Rica, El Salvador, France, Germany,

Australia, New Zealand, India, Hong Kong, Beijing, Singapore, and Shanghai.

Expats bring with them the essential ingredient required to establish any new Jewish congregation: their personal need to have a Jewish communal experience. This goes back to the very meaning of Jewish Peoplehood: the need to have and be part of a family experience. Where there is no actual family, the expat must therefore create family—and hence many Reform Jewish congregations have been established around the world because one or two expats made the commitment to do so.

To what extent do expats influence the indigenous Jewish character of the congregations they help establish? In most cases the answer depends on the ratio of expat to indigenous membership within the congregation and the length of time key expat leaders spend in the community. The expat influence is largely felt at the beginning of the life of the congregation. Expats (especially those from North America, the UK, Australia, and to a growing extent from Israel as well) bring with them a first hand, personal experience of how Reform Jewish life can be. Expats also bring with them the initiative and can-do attitude that is required to create new communities (this is especially true with North American expats). Over time, there is a natural blending of expat and indigenous membership—where there is an indigenous community to begin with. Expats are most influential in developing congregations when they are rooted in the community and remain there for an extended period of time.

Hong Kong is a fascinating case study in how American and British expats (together with a few Australians and other Western Europeans) joined together over twenty years ago to create a Reform congregation in a city where the only Jewish option was Orthodoxy. Expat Jews who grew up attending synagogue as youngsters, and who learned some Hebrew and how to sing some of the prayers, found themselves in a position where they could truly make a difference in creating a Jewish community for themselves and others. Expat parents are even more influential since their commitment to providing Jewish education for their children is often a powerful motivator in establishing a Jewish community. The United Jewish Congregation of Hong Kong, proud member of the WUPJ, recently celebrated its twentieth anniversary year—with close to two hundred members, a rabbi, educator, and active Jewish life program.

The meaning of Jewish Peoplehood for groups like the UJC, and many others where the expat variable is at work, is fundamental.

Are We All in the Family?

Throughout Jewish history there have been marked differences between those Jews who identified with Judaism primarily through religious principles, ideology, and practice (mitzvot), and those who identified primarily through the national, peoplehood (family) connection. The challenge facing Reform Judaism from its early roots in the nineteenth century to the present moment has been this same challenge—are we American, German, Russian, British . . . nationals of the Mosaic persuasion (the popular term for religion used by the early Reformers) or are we a nation (people-family) infused with religious beliefs and principles? Mordecai Kaplan's teaching that Judaism is best understood as a religious civilization was an attempt to integrate both elements of religion and nationality (family) into one organic whole. Reform Judaism internationally has officially incorporated Kaplan's synthesis into its platforms, pronouncements, and organizational affiliations. In practice, however, Reform Jews, especially those in America, continue to struggle with balancing these two elements of Jewish identity: the religious and the national.

The fact that most American Reform Jews are less connected to the Jewish family than are Reform Jews in most every other region in the world is potentially devastating for the future of Reform Judaism in America, in Israel, and around the world.

Even though the entire Reform Jewish family has an impressive membership of approximately 1.8 million, over 80 percent of the family is American Reform Jews. The irony is inescapable: at this time in history when American Reform Jews are the largest branch of the Reform family in terms of number, aggregate wealth, and political clout, they are also the least connected to the wider Jewish family, and the family's Home-Land, Israel.

The Reform Jewish family worldwide, especially those family pioneers creating Reform Judaism in Israel, are in desperate need of the support, both material and human, that their American Reform family can provide. And while some Reform Jews in America, lay and professional alike, are deeply committed and give generously to Israel and world Jewry (to the family), there are just too few who do. There are too few rabbis and congregational board members in America who insist that financial support for Israel and world Jewry must be a top priority in their congregation, no less a priority than meaningful worship services or critical *tikkun olam* projects. There are too few rabbis and congregational board members who insist that members get out of their American comfort zone to meet, understand, and connect to those family members who never left Eastern Europe or the FSU and who look to their American Reform family for relationship and support.

American Reform Jews are on the way to establishing a uniquely American Jewish religious denomination that is detached from the larger Jewish family and our family's ancestral Home-Land. Without the grounding of family and Home-Land, American Reform Jews, not unlike Americans in general, are liable to drift away from the rest of the world and become an island unto itself. A strong island, perhaps, where the creative impulse based on American realities forges ever new religious meanings and experience; but those who live on an island become insular and will eventually disconnect from their family and ancestral Home-Land. All of us in Reform communities worldwide must hold tight to one another and stay firmly together in the Jewish family. In the end, it is all about the family.

Reform Judaism in the South Pacific

John Levi

In 1959, the year before my ordination, I asked Dr. Jacob Rader Marcus, the formidable Hebrew Union College professor, whether I could be excused from attending his compulsory course on the history of the Jews in North America. After all, I was an Australian who would soon be going home. After five years at the College, the professor's resounding refusal was not unexpected. "My boy," he explained, "Jewish history is the story of seas and oceans. It began in the Kingdom of Judah and Israel close to the Dead Sea and the Sea of Galilee. It then embraced the Mediterranean. It followed the rivers of Europe and the Middle East. The Atlantic Ocean was the next focus that linked the Jews of the Old World with the New. Now the Jews of America are moving westwards and the Pacific Ocean would undoubtedly emerge as the new center of the Diaspora. Clearly Australia will share in that regional transformation." Dr. Marcus proved to be prophetic but in our wildest dreams neither of us could guess that by early 2013, China would have overtaken the United States as the largest economic power in the world. With his eyes fixed on me, the professor declared meaningfully, "Someone, sooner or later, will have to write the story of Australian Jewry."

And so it has come to be. The countries surrounding the Pacific Ocean are undoubtedly emerging as the dynamic center of the world. The Pacific Rim and Australia, with its stable democratic system and its vast mineral resources, is part of this economic revolution. In 1960, the Jews of Australia numbered 30,000. That

JOHN LEVI (C60) served as rabbi of Temple Beth Israel for thirty-seven years. He is a member of the Order of Australia and has a Ph.D. from Monash University. He is a member of the Executive Council of Australian Jewry, the author of five history books, a creator of an Australian Haggadah, and a researcher and compiler of a double-CD recording of the Music of the Berlin Reform synagogue. He has founded Progressive synagogues in Australia, New Zealand, and China.

figure has now quadrupled to 120,000 and we have become the fourteenth largest community within the Jewish Diaspora.

Extraordinarily, five of the most prominent Australians have been proud Jews. General Sir John Monash, whose uncle by marriage was the historian Heinrich Graetz, became the commander-in-chief of the Australian Military Forces in France in 1918 and won the battle of Amiens. His portrait is on the $100 banknote and a university bears his name. Sir Isaac Isaacs was chief justice of the Commonwealth of Australia and the first Australian to be appointed governor general. Sir Zelman Cowen became governor general and served in that office with such distinction that Australia's most serious constitutional crisis was averted. The central building containing the Public Lecture Theatre at Monash University is named in honor of the Australian born moral philosopher Samuel Alexander. The great Jewish encyclopaedia of 1901 was edited, and in large part written, by the Sydney born scholar Joseph Jacobs.

European settlement of this vast dry continent began on January 26, 1788. The British government had scooped up 759 convicts from the overflowing prisons of London and hurriedly dumped them on the shores of Sydney Harbour, effectively forestalling French colonial expansion in the South Pacific. Among those prisoners were at least 14 Jews. It was not exactly the arrival of the Pilgrim Fathers but it has given Australia a character of its own. Among the 150,000 convicts to be sent to Australia during the next 60 years there would be more than 1,000 Jews. Most of these enforced exiles would stay on "for the term of their natural life." Only the discovery of gold in the 1850s brought that strange and expensive experiment in mass migration to an abrupt end.

For many Jews, transportation from the slums of East London to the expanding townships of Eastern Australia brought wealth and a hitherto unimaginable degree of social status. News of the success of these former convicts brought scores of cousins and siblings to this free new world. "On 22 February 1854 five hundred Jews crowded into the newly built Melbourne Synagogue to protest against a proposed Constitution Bill which forgot to mention the existence of a Jewish community. To thunderous applause the shopkeeper Michael Cashmore declared the Jews asked 'neither for tolerance in a Colony where all Her Majesty's subjects are upon an equality nor favour from those who are bound to mete out justice for all, they claim as a right being good citizens and loyal subjects, that they not be excluded!'"[1]

A brief political struggle resulted in land being granted for synagogues and for Jewish cemeteries. The chief rabbi in London was the source of their respectability. He was understood to be a version of the archbishop of Canterbury, and his desultory rulings regarding conversion to Judaism and the Jewish status of locally born children were accorded a reverence far beyond their real worth. After all, twelve thousand miles separated the Dayanim of London from the Jews of Australia.

And so, by the beginning of the twentieth century, Australian Jewry was more British than the British. Never numbering more than one half of one percent of the general population, the Jewish community brought out its "ministers" from England. They wore the garb of the Anglican clergy complete with ecclesiastical "dog collar" and black pulpit gown. Synagogue office bearers customarily wore top hats. The mode of prayer was Anglo-Jewish. The only English heard from the pulpit was the prayer for the royal family intoned in that strange sing-song tone that is (or was) typical of the Church of England.

It is a miracle that Jewish life in Australia survived. In fact, it almost didn't. The community was very small and interrelated. Sadly, during World War I, the young Australian Jewish men enlisted en masse to fight the Great Patriotic War against Germany; so by the time the war ended, a whole generation lay buried on the cliffs of Gallipoli and in Flanders Fields. Many of those who returned from the battlefields had no wish to be part of the community of their youth. Intermarriage was overwhelming, and the Jewish community was dying.

A few valiant attempts to reform the synagogue in nineteenth-century Australia had all but failed. In 1929, while on a visit to London, Mrs. Ada Phillips, a feisty and elderly Melbourne woman, attended a service at London's Liberal Jewish Synagogue and met the equally dogged Hon. Lily H. Montagu. Ada had a problem. One of her sons had fallen in love with a non-Jewish girl and there was no way in which a conversion could take place. And the Hon. Lily was an empire builder. She was the daughter of Samuel Montagu, a member of parliament who became the 1st Baron Swaythling. Her younger brother, the Rt. Hon. Edwin Montagu, became the secretary of state for India. Lily Montagu's empire became the

World Union for Progressive Judaism, which she personally managed from her home in Bayswater. Ada Phillips enlisted her family
and friends to start a Liberal synagogue in Melbourne. Lily Montagu told her to contact Rabbi Julian Morgenstern, president of the
Hebrew Union College in Cincinnati, in order to find an adventur-
ous rabbinic candidate.

As Rabbi Jerome Mark of Selma, Alabama, arrived in Australia,
the Great Depression set in and the one hundred members of the
new congregation began to waver and then disappear. A second
rabbi was sent from Cincinnati. He too failed, even though he was
a Canadian and therefore, it was thought, would be able to cope
with fellow Jews from an outpost of the British Empire. In spite
of the Depression, the congregation tried a third time. Each rabbi
brought to Australia the classical Reform practices of the American
Midwest. In the course of a cozy afternoon tea, Mark had unwisely
confessed to the editor of the local Jewish newspaper that he was
very partial to fresh Australian oysters. It was grist to the mill. As
the wiley editor wrote, ". . . we took him in."[2]

In 1936, the Hon. Lily Montagu sent Melbourne its final rabbinic choice. The twenty-six-year-old Rabbi Dr. Herman Sanger
had grown up in Breslau and had studied at the Jewish Theological Seminary there. He was a seventh generation rabbi and
served his apprenticeship at the Oranienburger Strasse Synagogue in Berlin. Fluent in French and English, he had worked
as the roving emissary of the Berlin community until one night
an anonymous telephone call told him it was time to catch the
next plane to London. He did so. Within months he found himself in Melbourne.[3]

Sanger brought European Liberal Judaism to Australia. Within
a week, the men in the congregation covered their heads at services. Prayer shawls appeared. The English hymns of the American *Union Hymnal* vanished. And Sanger was a fervent Zionist.
The community took a deep breath and within a year the tide had
turned. There was now an expression of Judaism they could understand. By 1938, Jewish refugees from Germany and Austria began to arrive and Sanger was literally there on the wharf welcoming them to their new, and often baffling, English-speaking home.
Among the refugees was a dentist who was also a trained cantor.
And from Berlin, Sanger rescued Dr. Herman Schildberger, the director of music at Berlin's Reform congregation. From services in

a rickety parish hall to a new temple took the congregation little more than a year. By the time the war had ended, Temple Beth Israel was the largest synagogue in Australia and High Holy Day services had to held in hired city halls. The American *Union Prayer Book* was now used by the congregation with as much Hebrew as it could provide. A supplement was eventually published in Australia for the Afternoon Service of the Day of Atonement, and the long, rather lofty English texts were replaced by the great musical compositions of Lewandowski and Sulzer.

In 1940, by great good fortune, a nascent Liberal Jewish group in Sydney imported Rabbi Max Schenk and his wife, Faye, from New York. Literally, within months, the new temple was able to boast that it had one thousand members. The ghosts of the past still haunted Australian Jewry, and in 1948, as a guest of a rural rotary club, Max Schenk committed the inexcusable sin of mildly criticizing the conduct of Great Britain in Mandatory Palestine and was dismissed from his post.

Huge changes have shaped Australia and Australia's Jewish community since 1948. The community doubled in size when thousands of survivors of the Shoah arrived as part of the country's decision to "populate or perish." They have been followed by arrivals from Hungary, the Former Soviet Union, South Africa, and Israel. The community doubled again. The Jewish community remains strongly Zionist, and Australia itself has a tradition of sympathy for Israel, as it remembers the warmth its soldiers received from the Yishuv in two world wars. Netzer, the Reform Movement's international youth organization, was born in Australia. A remarkable 70 percent of the community's young people attend Jewish day school and our own King David School currently educates eight hundred students ranging from kindergarten to year twelve.

Surprisingly, the Jewish landscape has changed. Nowadays, it is either "them or us" because the moderate Anglo-Orthodox expression of Jewish life has almost entirely vanished and people must now choose between Chabad and the Progressive Movement. Do we interact religiously? Not at all. However, the community functions through a secular umbrella: the Executive Council of Australian Jewry, at which Liberal and Orthodox Jews comfortably, and for the most part, happily meet and unite to speak on behalf of the entire Australian Jewish community.

The Australian Constitution mentions God in its preamble bluntly and carefully separates Church and State. There is therefore no established church or religion in Australia and no national cathedral. Parliamentary sessions begin by the Speaker of the House reciting the Lord's Prayer and even this has now come under question. Unlike Israel and various European countries, we have no chief rabbi to represent us at special occasions and no legislative backing to halachic rulings. For that this writer gives profound thanks.

We are now big enough, and old enough, to have begun to develop our own modes of worship. When the CCAR produced *Mishkan T'filah*, we obtained permission to produce our own "World Union Edition." Some of the changes we made are linguistic. We were uncomfortable with the use of *Adonai* in the English text. It seemed unduly sexist. Some phrases and poems sounded strange and florid to non-North American ears and were reedited or removed. The prayer book didn't need to conclude with the anthems of Canada or the United States. Australia's climate, and its place in the Southern Hemisphere means that seasonal references are not relevant. For Jews in our part of the world, Rosh HaShanah and Sukkot occur in the spring. And how do you pray for rain in the winter season when, during the tropical cyclone season, it literally pours during summer?

One of Australia's most perceptive historians, Geoffrey Blainey, wrote about "the tyranny of distance" that has shaped the way we live.[4] Distance is certainly a major factor in our lives. Our congregational union now includes constituents from around Australia, New Zealand, and Southeast Asia. The distance between Perth in Western Australia and Dunedin in the South Island of New Zealand is far greater than the distance from London to Moscow. And, I know this may come as a shock, but for us, our closest, largest, and most influential Jewish community is Los Angeles. It is "only" a single plane ride away. At the same time, as Israel's Jewish population grows, the existence of the World Union for Progressive Judaism in Jerusalem is our congregational and communal anchor and the policies of the Israel Movement for Progressive Judaism are vital for our future.

Every four years a detailed census of the Commonwealth of Australia is held and one of the sections of each census deals with the ethnic and religious affiliation of the populations. The Centre for

Jewish Civilisation at Monash University has conducted a much closer look at the Jewish community, identifying Jewish religious affiliation, attitudes toward intermarriage, conversion, the consequences of Jewish day school education, visits to Israel, and the long-range impact of membership in Jewish youth movements. The reports are available at www.artson-line.monash.edu.au and are well worth reading. They are certainly relevant to North American Jewish communities and the Reform Movement in particular.

In New Zealand, just over 33 percent of the Jewish population said they were Progressive, another 9 percent said they were Conservative, and 20 percent said they were Orthodox. Australia, with its much larger population of Shoah survivors and their children, reported that 58 percent were Orthodox or Chasidic while 24 percent were either Progressive or Conservative. The Jewish communities in both New Zealand and Australia are therefore quite distinctive. For one thing, the Jewish population is growing even though the rate of intermarriage is high. The word "marriage" is actually an exaggeration as many of these couples choose to avoid any ceremonial commitment ceremony as part of their relationship. It should be said that Jewish day school education often helps to anchor the children of these intermarried couples into the community. The Progressive community recognizes the children of one Jewish parent who have a meaningful Jewish education as potentially Jewish. The Progressive rabbinate in the region has its own rabbinic association (Moetzah) and brings together the twenty or so rabbis to unify modes of practice and *minhag* by common consent. Most of its members are graduates of the Hebrew Union College in Israel and in America and, for that fact, we are deeply grateful. The vision of Professor Marcus has come true.

What of the future? For two hundred years, immigration to Australia has replaced the loss of Jewish individuals. Invariably, on giving a speech about Judaism anywhere in Australia, someone from the audience will come up to me and say "My grandmother was Jewish." I never know how to respond. *"Mazal tov"* seems inappropriate. And I know that timidly mentioning a Jewish grandparent makes that claim on a half forgotten, vague identity "safe." However, each census reflects a growing and changing Jewish community. It is true that we lose Jews and there is always a residue of anti-Semitism somewhere, although mainstream church attendance is continually dropping. For better or worse, nobody could now claim that Australia is a Christian country. But being Jewish in an aggressively secular environment that is increasingly culturally diverse can be a real advantage. We are given credit for our sense of identity and commitment to important concepts that have shaped the world.

Is there a distinctively Australian expression of Judaism? Not yet. But there will be. And it will be created with our day schools, our youth movements, and our synagogues. It will be created by common sense. Our traditional neighbors are bedevilled by the role of a dead *Mashiach* and their rigid separation of men and women, which has apparently led to a series of abusive sexual scandals in the schools they run. We accepted woman rabbis more than forty years ago and the sky did not fall in. We have printed our own prayer books. And then, as so often happens, we know that our Liberal Jewish initiatives will be copied by our more traditional neighbors. And, I suspect, they know that too.

Notes

1. John S. Levi and G. F. J. Bergman, *Australian Genesis, Jewish Convicts and Settlers 1788–1860* (Carlton: Melbourne University Press, 2002), 295.
2. Geoffrey Blainey, *The Tyranny of Distance* (Melbourne: Sun Books, 1966).

Progressive Judaism in Britain:
A Personal View

Julia Neuberger

I am very privileged to be senior rabbi at West London Synagogue, the oldest Reform synagogue in the United Kingdom, founded in 1840, where I grew up and where my father was a warden, so very much back to my roots. For the record, its history is an interesting one. It was essentially a breakaway from the two great Orthodox communities: Sephardi—Bevis Marks, on the edge of the city of London; and Ashkenazi—the Great Synagogue, no longer in existence, in the East End. At least one of the reasons—but by no means the only one—for its creation was the number of Jews who had moved to the West End, a more salubrious area of London, and who did not want to walk the six miles or so to the synagogues in the East. Had those synagogues been willing to set up new branches further west, the great split, and indeed *cherem*, might never have happened. And Reform would have come to these shores a great deal later.

The congregation called itself the West London Synagogue of British Jews (still its name) because it wanted to make it clear it was neither Ashkenazi nor Sephardi, but much of its ritual, its early prayer books, and its style was more Sephardi than Ashkenazi, and some of that remains the case. It hired the remarkable David Woolf Marks, who was assistant reader in Liverpool and professor of belles lettres at Wigan College. He was already known to be sympathetic to Reform, then creeping across from Germany and indeed from the Reform rumblings in the United States, in Charleston, New York, and Baltimore. Marks had already refused to read Torah on the second days of festivals, and his reputation came to the notice of the great men (no women at that time)

JULIA NEUBERGER (LBC77) is senior rabbi at West London Synagogue, a cross-bench (independent) member of the House of Lords, and a trustee of several charities.

who founded West London, and thus Reform in the UK. He was elected, at the age of twenty-nine, minister of the West London Synagogue of British Jews, where he remained for sixty years! He was passionate about improving decorum in worship, something that has remained key to how West London functions and is an enormously important part of Reform and Liberal Jewish thinking in the UK and worldwide, and he was also a considerable scholar, holding the chair of Hebrew at University College London, from 1848 until 1898.

So my particular community, along with other Reform and Liberal communities in the UK, feels very well rooted in British society. We have been around a long time. We can claim between us several members of both Houses of Parliament, many well-known business people, academics, senior lawyers, senior judges, actors, musicians, authors, and others. On the whole, the Anglo-Jewish community—at the Progressive end—is not unduly worried about anti-Semitism as such, and indeed several Reform and Liberal synagogues have a very good relationship with neighboring Christian and Muslim communities, and a few have close relationships with Sikhs and Hindus as well. However, there is real concern amongst members of the progressive community of all shades of political opinion, from doves to hawks, about the strength of anti-Israel feeling in the UK, and indeed the way that anti-Israel rhetoric can, and sometimes does, turn into anti-Semitism.

As I write this, within recent days there has been an outburst just before Holocaust Memorial Day by one Member of Parliament, David Ward, whose strong reprimand from the Liberal Democrat leader and the Whips in the House of Commons did not lead to any guarantee that he would not offend again. He perpetuated the "link" between the Shoah and what Israel's forces (and settlers) are doing in the West Bank. However constructively critical many members of the Anglo-Jewish community are of the actions of the Israeli government, and of the settlers, the two are clearly not comparable. This was exacerbated by the suggestion that Jews should somehow have learned from the Holocaust experience not to inflict such things on others—with no sense about who were victims and who were perpetrators in the Shoah.

And there are more such incidents, some a great deal more serious than others. That same Holocaust Memorial Day, Gerald Scarfe, a cartoonist known for making everyone of whatever opinion or grouping uncomfortable, published a highly critical cartoon in the *Sunday Times* appearing to depict Israeli Prime Minister Benjamin Netanyahu building a brick wall containing the blood and limbs of Palestinians. Rupert Murdoch has apologized for this "grotesque, offensive" cartoon that led to complaints of anti-Semitism, as has Scarfe himself, especially regretting its publication on Holocaust Memorial Day.

These are just a few of the examples that make some members of the Anglo-Jewish community uncomfortable. But despite assertions to the contrary in much of the U.S. press, anti-Semitism is at a relatively low level in the UK, and that is obviously so to those of us who travel to France, where it seems widespread, and other European countries. So the view that is held pretty much across the Reform and Liberal community in Britain is that we should be watchful, aware, but also very welcoming of non-Jews into our communities, and we certainly pride ourselves on inviting non-Jews to give sermons and addresses from our pulpits.

Meanwhile, assimilation goes on apace. All our Reform and Liberal communities have many members in interfaith relationships, for whom we have been able to do far too little in terms of recognizing those relationships. Only very recently has the Movement for Reform Judaism in the UK agreed to some kind of religious service of blessing following an intermarriage, something that Liberal Judaism, rightly, has allowed for many years. Children of interfaith couples have an additional road to negotiate beyond what their religion school classmates who have two Jewish parents have to deal with, and including the non-Jewish parent fully into our bar and bat mitzvah ceremonies and other life-cycle events is of huge importance. I still feel that we could all go further in inclusivity and that there is still something of a reluctance felt by some senior members of both Reform and Liberal synagogues, because of their fear of assimilation, to include non-Jewish parents in our services. There is a clear and forceful argument to be made the other way, however, which argues that these non-Jewish parents have made a supreme effort to support their Jewish spouse or partner in bringing up the children as Jewish. For me, this is an enormously generous thing to do, and I believe we could and should be both more gracious here, and more grateful.

I also think that, at some stage in the near future, the Movement for Reform Judaism needs to tackle the issue of equilineality, something that the youth of the Reform Movement support strongly. Sticking to the halachic line of only accepting Jewish status through the maternal line is nonsense in an age of genetic testing, and absurd given Reform Jews in Britain recognize as Jews for the purpose of synagogue membership (and all that goes with it) anyone in good standing as a member of another constituent member of the World Union for Progressive Judaism (the so-called gentlemen's agreement), which means accepting members from Liberal communities who are patrilineal and many people from the United States who are patrilineal Jews by descent. Liberal Judaism in the UK and Reform Judaism in the U.S. made the right decision about patrilineality early on in their history, and British Reform Judaism needs to be braver in asserting that it does not matter which parent is Jewish, but a Jewish upbringing, and a sense of peoplehood, is what makes a person Jewish.

This question of interfaith families is of course only a part of how the community interacts with the non-Jewish world. Almost all children in my own congregation—unlike many others in the Reform and Liberal communities—go to non-Jewish schools. Their social lives are mixed. They have masses of friends who are not Jewish, as we see with the assembled ranks of children in synagogue for their friends' *b'nei* and *b'not mitzvah*. Social life is mixed for most—but not all—of our members, and there is real pride amongst our members in bringing their non-Jewish friends to our beautiful and historic synagogue. People at West London love the building and are amused by the apparent contradiction of rabbis wearing gowns, wardens wearing morning dress, and a clear insistence on a certain style and formality in services with the fact that we have three women and one male rabbi, and that one male is openly gay. There is enormous pride in the extent to which West London has become the congregation of choice for many male gay Jewish couples in London, and a feeling of openness and inclusivity that is admirable. Meanwhile, there is a congregation that is by and large gay in London, a total acceptance at most Reform and Liberal synagogues of gay couples, and an increasing desire of Reform and Liberal rabbis to conduct blessings after a gay civil partnership, and when the legislation is passed, to officiate at gay marriages. It is not yet universal, but is by far the majority.

On the other side, one in four Jewish children now goes to a Jewish school in the UK (these schools are mostly free-funded by the government under our "voluntary aided" system), and that includes a significant proportion of the children who belong to Reform and Liberal synagogues. We have our own Reform Jewish day schools (though not all of us are supporters of them, given we do not necessarily think it right to separate our children from people of other faiths, and none, during their school days), and we now have one cross-communal secondary school, which has many of our young people attending it. So we are increasingly educating our children separately, whilst maintaining that we are open and universalist, something that still needs further teasing out within our communities and rabbinic debates. The argument in favor of Jewish schools is that the children will know more about Judaism, be more Jewishly competent, and are less likely to marry out. The evidence is unclear about the latter, but whilst admiring the desire for our children to be Jewishly more competent, there is a strong Enlightenment-influenced view in Reform and Liberal Judaism that encourages us to grasp the outside world with both hands—which retreating into single-faith schools really does not encourage.

There is clearly a strong sense of peoplehood in the UK community, as the Jewish schools attendance makes clear, but it is a porous peoplehood. There is, across Reform and Liberal synagogues, a desire to welcome in and to include, and we have large numbers of people coming forward for conversion. Some come for reasons of marriage, but a large number come for its own sake or because they find that, somewhere in their background, there lurks a Jewish grandparent or great grandparent, and they feel that is a significant part of who they are. The increasing popularity of TV shows such as *Who Do You Think You Are?*, let alone Internet genealogical searches, have a lot to answer for!

Meanwhile, within Progressive Judaism, attitudes to belief as we understand it are very mixed, peoplehood notwithstanding. There is a proud theological tradition within Reform and Liberal Judaism, with perhaps the strongest input coming from the Masorti Movement, with Rabbi Dr. Louis Jacobs's *z"l* enormous contribution to theological understanding and his great contribution to teaching a whole generation of rabbis at Leo Baeck College. But of course historically we have had Claude Montefiore, one of the founders of the Liberal movement in the UK, whose contribution is being recognized once more for its incredible significance, not to mention Israel Mattuck, Ignaz Maybaum, and others. Yet theological debate leaves many of the members of our communities cold. A considerable number of Reform and Liberal synagogue members (and possibly Orthodox as well, though it is harder to know) say firmly that they hold nothing, or very little, in the way of religious beliefs, but they feel they need or want to belong to show their association with the Jewish people. How that will be affected in coming years with the opening later this year of the first JCC in London that is equivalent to U.S. JCCs, entitled JW3 (it is in the NW3 area of London), remains to be seen. It is becoming easier in the UK than it used to be to be actively Jewish by peoplehood and association without belonging to a synagogue, with Jewish Book Week a huge event these days, and the Jewish Film Festival a must-attend series of screenings and talks. Synagogues have clearly got to up their game to be attractive enough to people whose first Jewish priority is neither prayer nor religion school. The radicalism of a Claude Montefiore and the Jewish Religious Union once brought people back into the fold, back in the early years of the twentieth century. It is not clear yet what movement, or philosophies, will have the same powerful effect in the early twenty-first century.

Israel and Israel-related activities may be a part of that. They are enormously important. For example, last year at West London we hosted a musical performed by young people from Ein Mahel High School and the Leo Baeck School in Haifa, with our families hosting all the young people, attended by many members of other Reform and Liberal synagogues. We all tend to have regular discussions around Israel themes, and many of us link with the Israeli Embassy in London for a variety of events. For instance, both the Israeli and Czech ambassadors to the United Kingdom attended West London for Holocaust Memorial Day 2013, along with many members of other Progressive synagogues, and we watched a remarkable performance of the Czech play, *The Good and The True*, recounting the experiences of two Czech people who had experienced concentration camps and survived. Hana Pravda—who died in 2008 aged ninety-two—suffered extreme brutality in the Nazi death camps, including beatings, starvation, and other horrors that she said were too painful to record in her wartime diaries. She was portrayed by her own actress granddaughter, Isobel Pravda. The other character in the play, Milos Dobry, a sportsman, was played by Saul Reichlin, a well-known actor in the UK, and the whole was followed by short speeches from both the Czech and Israeli ambassadors, for both of whom this related to family history. The synagogue was packed with Jews and non-Jews, and, most remarkably, a large party came from the Christian Friends of Israel, including their archbishop. So links with Israel, and a strong belief we are free to both support and criticize constructively, is a key part of how the Progressive Anglo-Jewish community functions. And a profound sense of history, and a bonding to those who perished in the Holocaust and those who survived it, as did many of our parents and grandparents, is an important part of who we are. But that sense of links with other countries and other times also manifests itself in our relationships with the United States in particular, from where we get so much of our Reform input, musically, intellectually, and simply in terms of pure confidence. It is easier to be Jewish in the United States—at least on either coast—than in the UK, and many of us travel there frequently to get a sense of the possible, and a reinvigorated sense of can-do. Many of our constituent synagogues also have large numbers of U.S. members, although they are now being challenged in numbers by people coming from France and Turkey. All Reform and Liberal synagogues actively welcome visitors from all over the world to our services, Jew and non-Jew alike. In most Progressive synagogues, we are proud of our international links, and for some of the older Reform and Liberal communities, that sense of pride goes back to before World War II, where some—but not all—gave a huge welcome to refugees from Nazi Germany, Austria, Czechoslovakia, and Hungary. And, of course, the numbers of Reform rabbis reaching British shores as refugees was an important part of strengthening Progressive Judaism in the UK in the 1950s and 1960s and beyond. In the wake of that, a sense of obligation to reach out to asylum seekers and refugees remains a core part of many of our congregations' thinking, as is made clear by drop-in centers run by several synagogues for asylum seekers on a monthly basis, homeless shelters (sometimes in association with local churches), food distribution networks, and literacy programs.

But there is also interfaith work, which all Progressive communities take great pride in. We offer our pulpits to people of other faiths on a regular basis, we take part in interfaith activities, and we host many such activities within our buildings. In West London's case, pride of place must go to our program for teenagers, post bar and bat mitzvah, entitled Peace by Piece. We run it with the An-Nisa Society's Supplementary Muslim School, and bring together Jewish and Muslim students, to learn how to express their own faith traditions to others with confidence and learn how to begin dialogue and get to know, and learn from, each other. The group then works together on a joint social action project, before traveling to Morocco together, exploring Jewish and Muslim coexistence.

Links with other sections of the Jewish community are mixed for all of us. Our relationships across the non-Orthodox community are excellent, including Reform and Liberal, who work as one on some issues, Masorti (Conservative) and independent non-Orthodox. Our relationship with Sephardi communities has tended to be good, and we share cemeteries with them. Our relationships with individual Orthodox congregations have often been excellent, but officially our links are limited, and even though many Reform and Liberal communities have several members who belong to both Orthodox and Reform, we see little collaboration, other than with the Chabad minyanim at some Orthodox synagogues. We are well represented at the cross-communal level, however, and where the issues are not "religious," we work well together, as has been the case for many years. We have members of our congregations represented on the Jewish Leadership Council and our Reform and Liberal congregants are strongly involved in many cross-communal charities.

But much more interesting is what the future holds and the direction of travel. I am quite clear that we need to be as inclusive as we possibly can, of interfaith couples, gay or straight, of the demi-semi Jews who are not sure of their identity, where we can help them find it, and also of those who are looking for more traditional expressions of Judaism, and less formal services. At West London, we are piloting a whole variety of services, some effectively more happy-clappy,[1] some more like egalitarian Orthodox, and one that is a curious mixture of happy-clappy and traditional organ and choir. Other Reform and Liberal congregations are also experimenting. This is hard for many of our people. The majority are familiar with the old services and are fearful—and even sometimes resentful—of anything new. The larger congregations can offer alternatives, whilst continuing with the "traditional" Reform or Liberal service. Smaller congregations find this more difficult, but are attempting to do it nevertheless, knowing that attendances at services will otherwise fall away.

My own view is that Reform and Liberal Judaism can grow and prosper in the UK. That growth will require an intellectual shift towards outreach and inclusion and a recognition that, for many people, religious services are not all, or even the majority, of what they are looking for. As synagogues reinvent themselves, we should be able to grow, to work closely with our non-Jewish neighbors, to open our doors and our hearts. I believe that we will thrive, and I also believe that, although anti-Semitism is greater than when I was a child, the institutional anti-Semitism of quotas in schools and colleges, and within the professions, has gone, and that we can thrive, overcome, integrate, but not assimilate. And the evidence is still slight, but our growth in marriages and civil partnership blessings, plus our general growth in membership, suggests to me that, for some young Jews at least, and some older ones, we are on the right track. At some point, the vexed issue of two Progressive movements in the UK (Reform and Liberal) will need to be tackled again. Freeing resources to do more outreach would be a wonderful justification for cutting back offices and administration, and thinking through how to reinvent the synagogue might bring all of us closer together. Until that point, the future still looks pretty rosy for Progressive Judaism in the UK. We are attracting good people to study as rabbis, we have strong lay leadership, we have fine buildings and an impressive presence on the national stage. We punch above our weight in national affairs. The question is whether we have the strength of will and utter conviction to continue that journey, and to be a truly progressive force amongst religious organizations in our country. For that, only time will tell.

Note

1. Ed. Note: This term is the British equivalent of "touchy-feely."

"We Were Only a Handful, and We Had a Dream of Rejuvenating Religion in the State of Israel"

Ada Zavidov
Translated by Evan Cohen

(Some minor details regarding families mentioned have been altered to preserve their anonymity.)

She's very intelligent. Well-educated. A nice person. She works in a respected profession for one of the best employers in Jerusalem. She's a single parent, impressively raising her two children on her own. Two years ago, her first-born daughter held her bat mitzvah here at Har-El, and now she has returned with her younger son. As always, with returning families, the atmosphere during this meeting with me is much more familiar and relaxed. There is a sense of trust since we've already gone through the process and the experience they had previously was a positive and meaningful one. Now, since we already know each other and have built a connection, we meet, this mother and I, to set a date for her son's bar mitzvah. As we open our calendars, we see that the Shabbat morning immediately following her son's birthday was already taken. (What can you do; there's a lot going on at the synagogue.) She begins to get concerned, and so I try to calm her, explaining, "No problem, we can just choose another date after his birthday. It's really OK! Moreover, it's even preferable since it will give your son more time to be well prepared for the ceremony." Yet for some reason, she's still not at ease. She then mumbles something about

RABBI ADA ZAVIDOV (J99) serves Kehilat Har-El in Jerusalem and is former chair of MARAM (the Israel Council of Progressive Rabbis). She is grateful to Cantor Evan Cohen of Kehilat Har-El for translating this article into English.

CANTOR EVAN COHEN serves Kehilat Har-El in Jerusalem and is a graduate of the Tel Aviv Cantorial Institute.

"tradition" and asks what's "customary." From this I realize that I now need to explain in this direction: "It's also fine according to Jewish tradition as well. Don't worry! It's not customary to hold a bar mitzvah early, but to hold it a little after the boy's thirteenth birthday is OK as well." We end up setting two tentative dates, and conclude that she will think it over, check the dates with the rest of the family, and then get back to me with her decision.

Two weeks pass and we meet once again. She enters my study wearing a big smile, saying, "That's it. We've decided. We'll delay the date of the bar mitzvah even more than you suggested!" I am happy, though curious to know what changed her opinion. "I have an ultra-Orthodox friend of mine at work, and she told me that it's absolutely fine to celebrate a bar mitzvah any time after the son's birthday." Well, this is what placated her: her ultra-Orthodox friend at work, and not me, the Reform rabbi.

Dear readers, please meet the typical "secular-Orthodox" Israeli. A classic example. I've met and continue to meet so many Israelis like her. They live completely secular lifestyles, but *think* like Orthodox Jews. They are uninvolved Jewishly, and their level of knowledge regarding Jewish sources is very basic. (What you learn about Judaism in a secular school in Israel is very little, believe me.) If you ask them, they would even say that they keep their distance from any synagogue, with some of them truly hating the ultra-Orthodox who don't serve in the IDF, etc. However, despite this revulsion for them, they also say about the ultra-Orthodox that "*they* know, *they* represent authentic Judaism." This perhaps is the primary reason that the Reform Movement in Israel still struggles for its place in society and in the public sphere, despite its extensive and praiseworthy activities these past few decades.

Many families contact us regarding the possibility of a bar mitzvah through Har-El (and here I mean only ceremonies for boys; *b'not mitzvah* are few and far between, and those who do come are already quite egalitarian), but at the same time they are hesitant, indecisive, and struggle with this option: What will our Orthodox grandfather say? What will our ultra-Orthodox family do? Will they agree to even enter a Reform synagogue? There's no *m'chitza*, there's musical instruments (our cantor plays the guitar), and "worst" of all, there's a woman rabbi who wears a *kippah* and a tallit! Certain families even try to hint that perhaps the ceremony could be led by our male cantor, without the female rabbi, which would then be preferable to the family. We of course reject this out of hand. Only recently we experienced a bar mitzvah where the ultra-Orthodox grandparents almost boycotted the service. In the end they did come, albeit late, sitting at the rear of the sanctuary and, of course, not participating in the service. How much stress and anguish they caused their son, the father of the bar mitzvah boy. In contrast, the great grandparents, themselves ultra-Orthodox but much more tolerant and open-minded, sat in the front row, close to the bimah, received an *aliyah* together (!), and at the end of the service, full of emotion, approached the cantor and me to thank us and share that they never had such a positive experience like this one. Incidents like this happen in our complicated reality as well.

Regarding weddings, my female rabbinic colleagues in Israel can testify to the following scenario in quite a number of instances concerning couples contacting our movement: They come and say that they want an "egalitarian Reform wedding," but wait, with a woman rabbi?! "That's already too much for us. A Reform wedding will be difficult enough for my family, but with a woman rabbi it's not an option at all." *Yishar koach* to all my male rabbinic colleagues who refuse to officiate at weddings for couples like these.

So here are the challenges facing us here in Israel:

How do we overcome the complicated and complex love-hate relationship between the secular and the Orthodox (and ultra-Orthodox) in Israel? This connection prevents Israelis from joining our movement en masse. How do we penetrate their hearts and present a convincing, brave, and worthy alternative to both secularism and Orthodoxy?

I will never forget how in the last year of my rabbinic studies at the HUC in Jerusalem (in 1998), I traveled to the United States for two weeks at the invitation of the American Jewish Committee as part of a delegation of Israeli leaders. Participating in this group were representatives of the different streams of Judaism in Israel: secular, Orthodox, a Conservative rabbi, and me, representing the Reform Movement. It was truly shocking to see how, in such a very short time, the secular and Orthodox representatives bonded so strongly, like two long-lost brothers who found each other, while we, the Conservative and Reform representatives, were ignored, falling between the cracks. It was truly a difficult experience.

How do we deal with the multiplicity of prejudices and ideologies in our society that view everything as either black or white, without any shades of color in between? I can't count how many times in the past twenty years I've heard, "Oh, you use a car on Shabbat? Then you're not religious!" There is something very deep in Israeli society that is not open to the liberal, individual, or feminist ideology of our movement. I encounter this barrier on every step: with the *Y'rushalmi* taxi driver, with the IDF officers to whom I speak from time to time about our movement, with the girls whose older brothers held their *b'nei mitzvah* at Har-El but they themselves refuse to hold a bat mitzvah when their turn comes, for what can you do, it's still not accepted practice for Israeli secular girls to be called to the Torah. "It's only for boys," they tell me, and my heart aches.

Yet, alongside these many challenges, we cannot close our eyes to our many and impressive achievements in Israel. I remember my time as a rabbinic student in the beginning of the 1990s. Just by mentioning to those interested in what I was doing that I was studying to become a Reform rabbi brought forth responses of surprise, negation, and antagonism. Today, however, no one makes a big deal about this anymore since there are already now many women rabbis, thank God. And despite all the barriers and the Orthodox monopoly in the State of Israel, we recently had a major legal victory regarding my friend Rabbi Miri Gold of Kibbutz Gezer. (*Yishar koach* to Miri and the Israel Religious Action Center!) Likewise, many families do indeed choose to have a bar or bat mitzvah at our synagogues, and many couples do get married under our auspices despite the fact that the state doesn't recognize Reform weddings. Most importantly, we have many established congregations stretching from the north to the south, and many *chavurot* and minyanim from which new Reform congregations will grow and flourish. We shouldn't despair and give up!

I have the privilege of serving as the rabbi of the oldest Reform congregation in Israel, Kehilat Har-El, in the heart of Jerusalem. Recently, on Shabbat *Parashat Bo*, this past January 2013, we celebrated fifty-five years since the founding of our community. The intellectuals who founded Har-El, led by Professor Schalom Ben-Chorin z"l, believed that for the people dwelling in Zion, the majority of whom are "traditional" (i.e., neither Orthodox nor secular), the Reform Movement would fit like a glove. These pioneers hoped that with bearing the flag of religious renewal, "a new type of religious person" would arise here (Prof. Schalom Ben-Chorin, Tishrei 1942). Till today, Avital Ben-Chorin, widow of Prof. Ben-Chorin, doesn't understand how is it that the Israeli masses aren't banging down our doors: "For our services are so beautiful and our message is so suitable for Israel."

I would like to conclude my words with the poem that Avital wrote in honor of Har-El's fiftieth anniversary, a poem that expresses our hope that despite all the challenges and difficulties, we will succeed!

שיר ליובל של הר־אל
מאת אביטל בן־חורין (ממייסדי הר־אל)

קומץ היינו וחלמנו חלום
על תחיית הדת במדינה,
הוי צפינו לפרוץ בעקבות אותו יום
בו ערכנו תפילה ראשונה.

היה זה ערב חורפי מלא־רוך,
התכנסנו לקבלת השבת.
בלבנו תקווה שכולה אך זוך
ובגופי נעה זעה . . . הבת.

"יובל היא קודש תהיה לכם"
כך צווינו בתורה.
אנא כל אחד ואחת מכם
התקדשו ובשרו הבשורה!

קומץ היינו — כלום קומץ נהיה?
נתעורר, נתאושש ונגשים.
נמשיך לחלום, גם למאבקים נצא.
עם אמונה בלב כל משימה נרים.

מפה לאוזן את שמנו לוחשים
בהגיע בן למצוות.
הבנות מהססות, אך רבים האורחים
הפוקדים את "הר־אל" בשמחות.

"הר־אל" עתה בת חמישים.
לאישה בימינו זה גיל צעיר,
במיוחד כשאת גילה משווים
לגיל של ירושלים העיר.

חמישים חורפים חלפו לי כחלום.
אמנם קצת בגרנו, אך שרד התום.
עתה נבקש פה ברכה ממרום
לפריצת הדרך, צמיחה ושלום!

A Poem for Har-El's Jubilee
Avital Ben-Chorin (one of the founders of Har-El)

(The original Hebrew rhymes in couplets.)

We were only a handful, and we had a dream
Of rejuvenating religion in the State of Israel,
We hoped for a breakthrough as a result of that day
That we held our first service.

Though it was a wintry evening, it was warm inside;
Gathering together for *Kabbalat Shabbat*.
In our hearts there was a hope that was pure and innocent,
While in my belly, moving to and fro, was a baby girl.

"The Jubilee shall be holy for you"
So commands the Torah.
So please, each and every one of you,
Purify yourselves and spread the word!

We were only a handful, but a handful shall we remain?
We will awaken, recover, and make it come to fruition.
We will continue to dream, and fight the good fight.
With faith in our hearts, anything is possible.

Through word of mouth our name is whispered
When a boy turns thirteen.
Though the girls are reluctant, our guests are many,
Attending Har-El at happy occasions.

Har-El is now fifty years old,
For a woman of today, fifty is still young,
Especially when comparing her age
To that of our city, Jerusalem.

Fifty winters have passed me by like a dream.
Indeed we're a little older, but the innocence remains.
Today, here let us ask for blessings from above,
To finally break through, for success, and for peace!

"First We Take Manhattan, Then We Take Berlin"

Meir Azari
Translated by Baruch Geffen and Adam Azari

Thus sang the legendary Leonard Cohen.

An influx of Israelis who have decided to continue their life's journey in New York City or who are temporarily working or studying in the Big Apple has created a vibrant presence in the city's five boroughs. There is an impressive volume of local Israeli papers, Facebook groups, restaurants, and cafés. Our friends and children who made NYC their home are finding their places in this melting pot, but many also wish to preserve their Israeli spirit, to have a home away from home. Such groups and communities of Israelis also exist in other American cities such as Boston, LA, San Francisco, and Miami. Similar trends can be seen in Europe, with Berlin being the most recent magnet for young Israelis. After bringing their tasteless Elite instant coffee and the more sophisticated Aroma and Max Brenner cafés to Manhattan, many of them are now taking Berlin.

It is believed that some one million Israelis and their offspring presently live across the ocean. Researchers have been studying this phenomenon and its causes. The data is complex and irregular, but clearly—even if fewer than a million Israelis presently live abroad, and even if many of them eventually return to Israel—the scope and power of this phenomenon requires that Israeli and Diaspora leaders give it some serious thought.

Similarly, the leaders of Reform rabbinical organizations must study the phenomenon and come up with action guidelines. Clearly, the Reform Movement would be wrong to ignore it and the challenges it poses. Our movement has always excelled in

RABBI MEIR AZARI (J92) is head of the Daniel Centers for Progressive Judaism in Tel Aviv–Jaffa. He is a former director of the Israel Movement of Progressive Judaism and former chair of MARAM (the Israel Council of Progressive Rabbis).

discerning and addressing challenges. We were among the first to actively address and promote the changes in the status of women in temples and communities, the struggles for gay rights, and other *tikkun olam* initiatives. Yet, in some recent cases—such as the development of Massah and Taglit programs—we failed to respond and become the leaders we should have been.

And so, we have a new challenge. Are we blind to the presence of Israelis who live next to our communities? Now, after organized Jewry has been rattled and the first shockwaves of the economic crisis are over, should we not sharpen our senses, step out of our cozy and familiar communities, and seek out our brothers as Joseph did before us?

If we add to the Israelis we just mentioned a vast number of Jewish immigrants from the Former Soviet Union, we have over a million first- and second-generation Jewish immigrants in North America. But despite many efforts, our movement has never done enough to bring them closer to our communities. Of course, the immigrants themselves were never really interested, possibly because they were unfamiliar with the special experience of Diaspora community life or because they were busy settling in and did not give much thought to identity questions.

When it comes to Israelis living in North America, both sides are on the losing end here: We fail to add the critical mass required to our weakening and dwindling communities, while they slowly discover that the Diaspora tends to erase their Israeli identity. Reminiscing over the quietness of Friday afternoons in Tel Aviv, Shabbat meals in the kibbutz, the sun and beach of central Israel, military service, Arik Einstein's songs, or the taste of cottage cheese and Abu Shukri's hummus in Jerusalem will not preserve the Israeli identity of second-generation immigrants. It seems that "Israeliness" is not sustainable for long without proper connections with Judaism.

Studies have pointed at that. In an excellent paper that the Jewish People Policy Institute presented to the Israeli Government, Yogev Karasenty wrote: "The Israeli identity is closely associated with the national and geopolitical realm of the State of Israel. When the two are apart, people discover that the state can no longer serve as a central and authentic identity framework, particularly for individuals who lived in Israel for a short period as children, or not at all. Thus, the Israeli identity of second-generation Israeli immigrants is constantly weakening in comparison to their newly assumed identities, sometimes to the point of vanishing."[1]

Studies have shown that, while losing their religious and national identities, first- and second-generation Israeli immigrants did significantly better economically than their American counterparts of similar social groups. Researchers Cohen and Haberfeld argue that while the economic assimilation process of immigrants normally lasts more than one generation, former Israelis did that in under a generation. Thus, while the Israeli ethnicity does not impair on their assimilation into North American societies as a whole, it does not offer a long-term preservation guarantee.[2]

Many of us still remember how the late Yitzhak Rabin lashed at and insulted the Israelis who chose to emigrate. He must have ignored or failed to understand the growing globalization phenomenon, which has profoundly affected the Jewish world and has changed Israel's demography. Coupled with the nature of Israel's hi-tech-based economy, globalization sent many Israelis around the world and many of them were enchanted by the big and vibrant cities and the economic opportunities that the world has to offer. But besides greater economic and employment opportunities, Israelis also found broader cultural and educational horizons abroad. Just consider fashion designer Alber Elbaz or Nobel Prize Laureate Daniel Kahneman: Could they have touched so many hearts had they resided in Israel? Perhaps they could, but their journey would have been much harder and more challenging. The vast and vibrant American and European markets are tremendously appealing for people who come from small and difficult countries. Potential success in these markets is greater and more tempting. As the world is becoming increasingly more globalized and accessible, temporary relocation is now much easier. Many immigrate for a while, to study, expand their horizons, or find better jobs and economic opportunities. This is a beneficial option these days.

While many Israelis go on their long, post-army trips to the Far East or South America, Western Europe and North America are an attraction for Israelis who seek an education or a new way of life altogether. Their mentality, language skills, and general appearance help them blend right in.

The Israeli establishment, which used to frown upon emigrants, calling them *yordim* (as opposed to *olim*), must presently address this new phenomenon and is slowly forging a new and different policy. To their credit, I must say that the Israeli government and Jewish organizations have been slowly grasping the need to change their attitude towards and mode of dialogue with Israelis abroad. The Israeli establishment has recently started offering more options than just talking about returning to live in Israel. A Canadian conference—held some two years ago and attended by an Israeli cabinet member and local Israeli community leaders—discussed the relationship between Israelis abroad and the State of Israel. Interestingly, the participants even discussed ways to bolster Israeli communities abroad.

It seems that there are many reasons for this change of attitude towards Israelis abroad. Some would say that it is quite impossible to resist the global temptations that attract many of our children and that we should learn to live with this phenomenon, which, incidentally, Israeli middle and upper class families are familiar with. Others may argue that the State of Israel consciously holds itself responsible for the Diaspora and cannot ignore the dramatic decline in the number of Jews worldwide or the interesting option of Israelis who have homes in both Israel and Europe or North America. These large immigrant communities that the Israeli government has so far ignored for ideological reasons are suddenly being prioritized because it benefits Israel. Hundreds of thousands of Israelis abroad and the large Jewish groups from the Former Soviet Union (although there is a difference between these communities) are currently being viewed as both legitimate and challenging. It has also been argued that there is strategic value in supporting Hebrew- and Russian-speaking Jewish immigrants abroad and helping them form true and organized communities.

Israeli communities abroad grow slowly, from the grassroots up, and, just like any community of immigrants, Israelis enjoy each other's company. They want to feel Israeli tastes and smells, but also seek Hebrew-based social relationships and make efforts to teach it to their children so as not to shame grandma and grandpa when they travel to Israel for their bar mitzvah. Furthermore, many of those immigrants still dream of returning to Israel one day or want their children to feel at home there. Many secular and liberal Israelis abroad do not find a home in local Jewish communities.

The communities are often based on religious establishments where synagogue and federation are paramount. Israelis are not familiar with that. Israelis who set foot in a temple when invited to life-cycle events of their acquaintances—even if they are impressed by the mixed seating, open-minds, and novelty of liberal communities—have a hard time adjusting to the local siddur, to praying in the local language, and even to membership fees. This has kept Israelis away from Reform and Conservative communities. Secular Israelis find it even harder to join such communities.

We believe that this presents Reform rabbis and community leaders with yet another important task. We must extend our hand to our Israeli brethren who live, permanently or temporarily, in our towns and cities. Both parties will have to lower their barriers, find new means of communication, accentuate the things they share, and mainly assert their ties with Israel. Too few of our communities have done that so far.

Rabbi Andy Bachman and his Brooklyn community are an example of finding ways to create an Israeli framework in a veteran and observant Reform community. Rabbi Ammiel Hirsch of the Stephen Wise Free Synagogue in Manhattan has recently launched a program based on opening community doors to Hebrew speakers who inhabit the Big Apple while finding their way in the American worlds of economy, science, and art, all the while having one foot strongly rooted in Israel. Personally, I am proud to be part of this pilot project that is being launched these days. It intends to create a community of Israelis that both acts as a space for Israelis to interact with each other as well as promoting bridges with the local American community. We expect the host community and the Israelis to establish a warm and vibrant home and find ways to cooperate and create a meaningful partnership.

There is no doubt that communities need to create additional room for activities in Hebrew. Many Israelis want their children to learn Hebrew at a higher level than is currently offered at Hebrew schools and Sunday schools. We must offer Torah and Judaism studies in Hebrew, as well as Hebrew language story time for kids. We mustn't forget that Israelis bring with them a very specific cultural heritage and—consequently—some very specific cultural needs that the average Diaspora community isn't currently equipped to satisfy. The Israeli parent, for instance, wants his/her child to know Lea Goldberg's children's verse, something that the

Diaspora is yet unfamiliar with. Israeli musical preferences are different as well. A community that wants to engage Israelis needs to open its ears, or at least provide Israelis with some autonomous space where musical activities could take place. A good example of this is Rabbi Bachman's community in Brooklyn, which offers monthly Friday night Israeli-style services. Our congregations should be aware that the Israeli calendar has several special dates that need to be part of synagogue life (e.g., Israeli Memorial Day/Independence Day).

Israelis also find it difficult to understand the concept of membership fees. We need to develop special methods that will enable us to financially support the activities mentioned. In our community in Tel Aviv we have discovered that Israelis are willing to pay for services that they receive from the congregation. I believe that a transitional fee-for-service option should be devised until the Israeli members find their way into the community. Our communities in the Diaspora, some of which are more than a century old, must understand that if they want to continue leading, they must embrace the Israelis who live among us. These Israelis must be approached outside the traditional Reform temples, particularly those that are justly based on the American spirit and way of life. Our communities have to develop frameworks of Israeli nature, embrace their leaders, and cooperate with them while bridging the various groups together and forming new diverse communities. At first, most Israelis might feel uncomfortable sitting in egalitarian temples. Yet, they will soon find out—as many in Israel have found in recent years—that progressive Jewish communities offer numerous advantages. We must understand that many Israelis would rather speak and pray in Hebrew and that the nature of their prayers and needs will not always match the adopting community's needs. Community structures and the nature of memberships will be tested too, but they are tested daily anyway. We need to realize that Israelis abroad are a yet-untapped human reservoir that the Reform Movement can draw on. The majority of these Israelis are secular, traditional, and modern, but if we examine them a little more closely, we will find they are Reform, only they don't know it.

Many of those Israelis find a home in Chabad frameworks. Though we may sharply criticize their views, the Chasidim open their doors generously, ask no questions, and collect no fees from

Israelis who seek a community. I believe that Reform, advanced, and egalitarian communities, which are sensitive to the LGBT community and to non-Jews, could offer a more natural and fitting home for emigrant Israelis.

Time and patience are required to build the foundations for the rejuvenation of existing communities, at least in cities with large concentrations of Israelis. Many Israelis will find that Judaism is not a frightening and intimidating establishment, but a positive experience that can empower and bolster their fate and identity in this vast ocean of identities. Bolstering our ties with immigrant communities in the Diaspora will necessarily help tighten the weakening ties between our Diaspora communities and Israeli society.

Notes

1. Yogev Karasenty, "Policy Recommendations for Strengthening Jewish-Israeli Identity among Children of Israelis and Their Attachment to the State of Israel and the Jewish Community," Jewish People Policy Institute (March 2012).
2. Yogev Karasenty, "A New Policy for Dealing with Israeli Emigrants —Helping Israelis Remain Jewish" (in Hebrew), Jewish People Policy Institute (2012).

Additional Articles

The Tent Peg Business, Revisited

Lawrence Kushner and Noa Kushner

A. Almost thirty years ago (1984), when I wrote "The Tent Peg Business" for the first issue of New Traditions (it went belly-up after the third), we were pretty clear about who was a Jew (Jewish mother, conversion); we knew who was a rabbi (HUC, JTS, yeshivah—Recon was just an infant); and we knew what a congregation was (building, dues, rabbi). Now we're unsure about how to define any of those categories. Indeed, even a print media journal like this may be on the way out. But, if you think that's challenging, try living in San Francisco. Here, nine out of every ten Jews are unaffiliated. At The Bagelry near my home, the young woman flips the bacon with chopsticks. We ain't in Kansas anymore.—LK

B. When some board members and I started The Kitchen as a place for disconnected Jews, everyone told us to avoid religion. "Too loaded," we were told. They suggested we find something cultural, something "easier" for those who were already disconnected from organized religious life. They were right about religion being a tough sell: There is no larger acceptance here for signing on to an organized, Western religion. Yoga? Sure. Buddhism? Of course. Jewish and religious? Totally countercultural, and not in the good way. This doesn't mean that we cannot still succeed. I think we rabbis have always been translators; in 2013 our work just takes a new turn.

In fact, I think the changes in the world make these parts of my father's original "Tent Pegs" more relevant, not less. "Tent Pegs"

RABBI LAWRENCE KUSHNER (C69) is the Emanu-El scholar-in-residence at Congregation Emanu-El, San Francisco, and teaches an annual, two-week seminar at HUC in LA. He has written eighteen books on spirituality and Kabbalah, and has oil paintings in two galleries in San Francisco.

NOA KUSHNER (NY98) is the founding rabbi of The Kitchen (www.thekitchensf. org): One part indie Shabbat community, one part San Francisco experiment, one part tool kit for DIY Jewish practice.

was unabashedly in favor of making places for serious religious life. Its message still strikes me as honest, necessary, easy to say, and hard to do.

We edited the original list, removing items that no longer hold, and put what remained in bold. Then we wrote some new items that respond to the current Jewish reality and added them to the list. Some of these are fairly general and some describe my specific experience with The Kitchen. We added a few headings to help guide readers along.—NK

Building Jews

1. **If synagogues were businesses, their product would be Jews. The more Jews they could manufacture from otherwise illiterate, assimilated, and un-self-aware members, the more successful they would be. That is (to continue the metaphor) the bottom line. Simply getting together with other Jews may be ancillary and even indispensable to this ultimate goal, but it can just as easily be—as is often the case when Jews get together to watch a movie, eat dinner, or play tennis—a pleasant way to pass time.**

2. **Jews need one another, and therefore congregations, to do primary religious acts that they should not, and probably cannot, do alone. Doing primary religious acts is the only way we have of growing as Jews. Consequently, it is also the only justification for the existence of a congregation. Everything else congregations do, Jews can always do cheaper, easier, and better somewhere else.**

3. Jewish religious growth requires other Jews, teachers, and a community. But it does not necessarily require a rabbi or a congregation. There have always been differing venues for Jewish religious growth—chavurot, independent minyanim, camps, institutes, Hillels, community centers, and federations; now there are even more.

4. **There are three ancient kinds of primary Jewish acts: communal prayer, holy study, and good deeds (or in the classical language of *Pirkei Avot: avodah,* Torah, and *g'milut chasadim*). This is not a capricious categorization. Prayer (*avodah*) is emotional: song, candles, dance, meditation, and silence— a matter of the heart. Study (Torah) is intellectual reading, questioning, discussion, and rigorous logic and argument—a**

matter of the head. And good deeds (*g'milut chasadim*) are public acts: helping, repairing, matching, fighting, and doing—matters of the hand. Only rare individuals are able to do all three with equal fervor and skill. And so our membership in a congregation and association with a broad spectrum of Jews will compensate for our personal deficiencies.

5. We can broaden the description of primary Jewish acts to include all mitzvot. Specifically, I (Noa Kushner) want to emphasize a religious connection to Israel as well as interpersonal ethics (*l'shon hara*, etc.).

6. One of the biggest challenges today, so common that it often goes unmentioned, is that there are a vast number of people who have never experienced the practice of mitzvot altogether. They have never had a powerful Shabbat. They have never been to a transformational seder or wedding. In the work of building Jews, there is no substitution for the firsthand experience. Mitzvot cannot be regarded from behind a screen or held at a polite distance.

7. The practice of primary Jewish acts is a nonnegotiable tool for building a Jewish life. Therefore, Jewish religious communities must first be living environments where people can practice mitzvot. This practice cannot be for display only, and it cannot be solely for educational purposes. It needs to be because we believe that Jewish religious experiences can transform: they can change lives, make meaning, and invest people in the world.

8. As well, while Lawrence Kushner was right that these mitzvot often require community, today we organize things differently. At The Kitchen, part of our vision is that our porous community is a part of a larger ecosystem that includes many overlapping communities, each with a different focus, that are designed to work together (e.g., Limmud, Hazon, Bend the Arc). We don't think of "Kitchen-ites" as "ours." Instead, our goal is to make them part of this larger ecosystem.

9. In order to maintain their congregations, Jews must do many other things that are not inherently Jewish. These secondary acts include maintaining a building, raising money, and perhaps forming a board of directors. (It should be here noted, however, that in the long history of our people there have been healthy, vibrant, and solvent congregations that had none of the above.)

10. Congregations, unfortunately, often get so caught up in doing secondary acts that they actually begin to think that maintaining the building, raising money, or the board of directors is the reason for the existence of the congregation. Their members are busy at work, but because they have forgotten why they are at work, their efforts are hollow and come to naught.

11. We tend to think of owning a building as a given, an obvious and inevitable good (and there is no fun or glory in renting, that's for sure). But how many communities would actually be better off if they allowed themselves to sell? What percentage of a congregation's budget, for instance, is devoted to paying off the mortgage or maintaining the physical plant? How many communities cannot effectively change or update the way they practice because they are "trapped" in their buildings? Given that communal norms have changed, could those monies be more effectively spent in other ways that grow Jews?

12. It's so easy for everything attached to a Jewish organization (websites! dues!) to become sacrosanct. But supportive facets of Jewish communal life (what Lawrence Kushner calls the secondary acts) are ripe for experimental approaches precisely due to the fact that they are *not* inherently holy. In other words, because the stakes are relatively low, we can afford to swing and miss.

"Irreverent Reverence": Purposeful Disruption and Experimentation

13. Precisely because they *are* inherently holy, we must also experiment with our approaches to Torah, *avodah*, and *g'milut chasadim*. At The Kitchen, we use "storahtelling" to translate all our Torah readings. We bring in members of the community who are improvisational actors to make it come alive. Yes, it's risky, but so is perpetuating a Torah service where no one is learning any Torah. Here, because the stakes are high, we can't afford to ignore possibilities. We've got to go beyond what's expected and accept that our leadership roles require us to take risks and be susceptible to new criticisms.

14. A goal of all institutions is stability and longevity. But, our question is: At what points do stability and longevity compromise the business of nourishing and enlivening Jews and Jewish experiences?

15. Forty years ago, Dr. Eugene Borowitz wryly proposed the creation of biodegradable congregations—communities that had predetermined life spans. (This may now be happening in many communities even though it was not part of the original plan.) To be sure, some synagogues will continue successfully on their current trajectories. But for many, it may now be time to consider "disruptive business models." Kodak, for example, lost sight of its primary mission of "capturing moments" and became fixated instead on its own technology. Our own "technology," too, is only relevant so long as it builds Jews and those ready to practice Jewish life.

16. At the same time, to be sure, an innovative idea is not inherently successful by virtue of its novelty alone. There is only one test: Does the idea build Jews?

17. Just because it works for one generation does not mean it will work for the next. In fact, we might even say that if it worked for one generation, that is a good indication that it will not work for the next.

18. I (Noa Kushner) was struck one evening when, as an in-joke, our Kitchen musicians started playing a *nigun* based on the theme song of The Breakfast Club (a popular movie from the 1980s). The place erupted. At that moment I realized that it wasn't hearing something secular that was surprising to the group—after all, how many times had we heard some Jewish twist on baby boomer favorites such as the Beatles or Joni Mitchell—what was surprising was that it was our secular music. The strong reaction was related to our surprise at the new feeling of having ownership over that cultural/religious moment.

Notes for Rabbis

19. **Rabbis should treat Jews more like rabbis. Jews should treat rabbis more like Jews.**

20. **Rabbis and congregants have it in their mutual best interests to encourage the rabbi to develop his or her own spiritual life and to discourage the rabbi from serving as a communal surrogate for religiosity or as a skilled but hollow performer. The leader of the prayers, in other words, must also pray.**

21. Every rabbi needs to create his or her own mission statement— not the fluff that customarily goes into resumes, but a mission

(a *sh'lichut*)—the reason you do the work; what you'd be willing to lose your job over.

22. The principal task of teachers and rabbis is not imparting Jewish knowledge but helping Jews and those engaging with Jewish life learn how to edit and to filter the ocean of now readily available information. This would naturally include helping those interested find other rabbis, teachers, and experiences.

23. It's time to quit asking: "Who is a Jew?" and, instead, ask: "Who wants to *do Jewish*?" Enough with being gatekeepers; it's time to invite in the people who might well want to connect with Judaism but don't know that they are welcome.

No Substitute for Content

24. **There is no evidence whatsoever to support the notion that people who are drawn into the congregation for an innocuous nonreligious event, such as gourmet cooking, move onto activities of more primary religious worth any sooner than if they had been left alone to discover their own inevitable and personal religious agendas and timetables. Indeed, there is substantial data to suggest that congregations that run many "basement" activities in hopes of getting people from there onto upper floors, only wind up adding on to the basement.**

25. At the same time, much of religious practice is also deeply social. Creating substantive, culturally resonant, social Jewish experiences (the Shabbat table comes readily to mind) will do for many what twenty classes or services cannot. If we don't see Jewish life modeled in real time by peers or teachers, we cannot imagine doing it ourselves.

Money and the Marketplace

26. **The way a congregation gets its money may be finally more important than how much it gets. Consider the religious impact, for instance, between congregations getting, say, half their operating budgets from (a) bingo, (b) a few wealthy members, or (c) dues. There is a widespread misconception that because the congregation is nonprofit and tax-exempt, it is therefore a charity. Actually, even though the analogy makes us uncomfortable, a congregation is (with the possible**

exception of offering membership to anyone with a financial hardship) precisely like a country club. And like all such clubs, you get what you pay for.

27. Today, in fact, most start-up communities do function like non-profits, especially those that serve younger audiences or participants that don't have the means to pay.

28. Asking participants to take financial responsibility for their community serves two critical functions: (1) This accepted responsibility can create ownership of a transformational experience. As the therapists say, "The payment is part of the cure." (2) The organization is less financially vulnerable and less dependent on foundational grants. Foundation money can help good ideas get started but will not carry them forever. As our Kitchen treasurer is fond of reminding us, "The foundation money is like heroin. Don't get addicted."

29. Membership dues are not inherently bad if the people paying for them are passionate about building the community. However, if the community is not valued, no dues structure (including making it free) can cover that up.

30. Rabbis and boards, fearing their congregations will get cheated by *schleppers* who merely want to use the community, have unfortunately responded by setting preconditions that preclude participation. But such preconditions limit everyone, even those with honest intentions. The reputation of Chabad, its responsiveness and institutional flexibility, is both a challenge and an inspiration to us. Should it really matter how long or if a person has been a member if he or she is ready to grow to another Jewish level?

31. In the contemporary marketplace, for-profit businesses are acting increasingly like nonprofits. For example, Lululemon is an athletic clothing company that, as part of their strategy, offers motivational materials and free communal yoga classes. Ben & Jerry's organizes groups around environmental awareness and activism. Jewish organizations must understand that we are now in direct competition with for-profits for our audience's time and attention, and act accordingly. Jews today will choose between Lululemon and shul. We know that our "product" is stronger than anything in the stores. But if we ignore issues of branding and strategy, we run the risk of our message going unheard in the marketplace.

Democratic Approach to New Ideas

32. The amount of creativity within a congregation stands in inverse ratio to the number of people, groups, or levels in the institutional hierarchy empowered to prohibit anything. With the exceptions of spending a congregation's money or using its name, the members of a congregation should not need anyone's permission to initiate anything—be it a letter in the bulletin or an alternate religious service.

33. The price of congregational vitality is the frequent appearance of confusion and even anarchy. The communal tolerance for such creative unpredictability is a learned skill. There can never be too many people trying too many things. If it's a good idea, people will keep coming. If it's not so good, no one will come. The committees, the board, and the rabbi ought not get into the business of approving or disapproving anything; they should only help whomever and whenever they can.

34. Social media makes it exceptionally easy for people to initiate their own Jewish communities or group experiences. If we see this groundswell as an opportunity, we can be instrumental in helping to build more Jews.

35. However, a caveat: the self organized events and ideas need to be in keeping with the mission. Ninety nine out of one hundred times they will be. But in the exceptional case, we don't direct resources or energy to things that people can find more easily elsewhere, and we don't try to be everything to everyone.

36. We have seen the commitment to a democratic style of leadership that results in handing over the reins to several enthusiastic but unqualified people. There is such a thing as over-sacrificing the needs of the many for the needs of the few.

Tent Pegs

37. Finally, the members of the congregation must nurture one another because they need one another; they simply cannot do it alone. Hermits and monasteries are noticeably absent from Jewish history; we are hopelessly communal people.

When the wilderness tabernacle is completed, near the end of the Book of Exodus, we are told, "And it came to pass that the tabernacle was 'one'" (Exod. 36:13). Commenting on this curious expression, Rabbi Mordecai Yosef Leiner of Izbica (d. 1854) observes:

> In the building of the tabernacle, all Israel were joined in their hearts; no one felt superior to his fellow. At first, each skilled individual did his own part of the construction, and it seemed to each one that his work was extraordinary. Afterwards, once they saw how their several contributions to the "service" of the tabernacle were integrated—all the boards, the sockets, the curtains and the loops fit together as if one person had done it all. Then they realized how each one of them had depended on the other. Then they understood how what all they had accomplished was not by virtue of their own skill alone but that the Holy One had guided the hands of everyone who had worked on the tabernacle. They had only later merely joined in completing its master building plan, so that "it came to pass that the tabernacle was one" (Exod. 36:13). Moreover, the one who made the Holy Ark itself was unable to feel superior to the one who had only made the courtyard tent pegs.[1]

Note

A slightly modified version of the original "The Tent Peg Business" was most recently published in Lawrence Kushner, *I'm God; You're Not: Observations on Organized Religion and Other Disguises of the Ego* (Woodstock, VT: Jewish Lights Publishing, 2010), 22–29.

1. Aharon Greenberg, ed., *Iturei Torah* (Tel Aviv: Yavneh, 1976), III.275.

Synagogue Work Will Drive You Crazy: Schizophrenogenic Inevitabilities in Congregational Practice

David A. Whiman

And Elijah approached all the people and said, "How long will you keep hopping between two opinions."

(I Kings 18:20)

Reb Nachman of Bratslav told the tale of the prime minister who came into the presence of the King and announced that the grain supply of the kingdom was poisoned. All who eat of the crop would go mad. The King ordered that the grain be destroyed."But your majesty," said the minister, "then all in your kingdom will starve." "Then let the people eat of the grain," said the King. "All save you and me. We will retain our sanity." "But your Majesty," replied the minister. "If all go mad save you and me then the people will think us mad and surely put us to death." "Then we too will eat of the grain," said the King, "but we will mark our foreheads with a sign so that when we see each other we will remember that we are crazy."

Our Sages teach that the highest in human behavior lies in the imitation of God's ways. "As God is called gracious be thou gracious; as God is called compassionate be thou compassionate; as God is called holy be thou holy."[1] Derived from the very nature of Divinity itself, these qualities are thought of as core religious values. These qualities, in turn, give rise to the "social virtues"[2] by which and through which a congregation is expected to function.

DAVID A. WHIMAN (C79) is rabbi emeritus of North Shore Synagogue and coauthor of *Learning While Leading: Increasing Your Effectiveness in Ministry* (The Alban Institute, 2000).

Accordingly, a synagogue is expected to be "compassionate and gracious, loving and true" (Exod. 34:6).

Social virtues generally fall within the category of *derech eretz* (the universally endorsed, socially acceptable, and honorable way to live one's life and interact with others). They are the premises that inform proper conduct within an organization. They frame the way people are expected to act with one another. Within a congregation, social virtues do not have the standing of mitzvah, but they operate with an equal if not higher authority.

Social virtues are easily recognized. They are the espoused ideals of a community. They are the articulated "what we do and do not do" in the synagogue. These often unrecorded folkways and social conventions have enormous hold and inform the expected and anticipated way of dealing with issues both important and mundane. Actions and decisions perceived to be contrary to the social virtues are often cited as compelling reasons to leave a congregation or religious community.

There are four generally accepted social virtues in the contemporary liberal synagogue. In the congregation, these virtues are usually paired and are identified as:

1. Care and support
2. Respect and sensitivity
3. Principle and fairness
4. Integrity and honor

The four social virtues are held up as cornerstones of synagogue life. They are laudable and consistent with Jewish values. They mirror attributes of the Divine. They are also said to apply to the corporate membership, the lay leadership, the clergy, and the professional staff. Imagine for the moment a congregation that embraced an antithetical set of social virtues and whose website described the synagogue as uncaring, unsupportive, unwelcoming, and hypocritical—an organization that sold out to expediency, failed to uphold its principles, and treated its members with impertinent disrespect. Who would join such a congregation?

While the four social virtues have meaning within Judaism, in contemporary American society they are also understood and defined in generally predictable ways.[3] The social virtues are laudable, but as defined they create conditions that make it increasingly difficult for synagogue professionals and lay leaders to function effectively.

In the secular world, help is broadly understood to mean offering approval and praise, all the while minimizing disapproval and blame. Thus in the contemporary liberal synagogue, care and support are increasingly understood as "giving me what I want, telling me what I want to hear, or accepting my priorities and reasoning with respect to the issue under consideration." Actions are deemed "helpful" to the extent that they meet this definition of the term. The anticipation and expectation is that a congregation, its clergy, and professional leadership will respond positively to requests and concerns. When people are given what they want, they deem the assistance and thus the individual providing it to be supportive and caring. Care in this case is categorically different from the traditionally understood notion of "pastoral care" (visiting the sick, comforting the bereaved, etc.).

Within the synagogue community, there is also an expectation that individuals will be treated with respect and sensitivity. Respect— again, as it is increasingly defined in the larger society—dictates that the reasoning process by which a person arrives at his or her conclusion or understanding of help should not be subject to another's question or examination. A congregant's reasoning process ought not be challenged. Thus, reasoning processes are off limits especially if they lead to a request for an exception or exemption from an applicable rule, requirement, or protocol. While basic fairness dictates that congregational rules, protocols, and requirements apply to the membership as a whole, a staff member who denies a request—which is thought reasonable and necessary, at least in the mind of the one who requests it—is subject to be labeled "unsympathetic or uncaring." The refusal is seen as a violation of the first social virtue. "I told them what I wanted but they wouldn't listen to me. They just don't care."

Just as another's reasoning process is off-limits, there is also an expectation that feelings must be validated. Should feelings and the reasoning that prompts them be questioned the inquiry is thought to be "insensitive." Sensitivity here means never asking the questions that would require another to check his or her reasoning, inferences, or assumptions for accuracy.

The following is an excerpt from a letter sent to the rabbis, executive director, and president of a large suburban congregation:

I am writing to bring to your attention the complete lack of sensitivity, respect and regard for my family as we approach our son's

Bar Mitzvah . . . I felt badly that no one at the Temple thought it necessary or appropriate to notify us that there had been a change in the clergy . . . It is not that we object to Rabbi X officiating as he has been warm and outgoing in all our encounters with him. What is objectionable is the complete lack of sensitivity that this information was not conveyed to us officially by the synagogue. A note or call would have been the polite, respectful and appropriate way to have conveyed this information to our family . . . If the Bar Mitzvah wasn't a few weeks away, we would leave the synagogue and go to a more organized, sensitive and welcoming place of worship. This is an instance where my family feels let down by our temple and the manner in which it is being administered.

While there could be any number of deeper reasons for this congregant's displeasure, note how the writer frames the complaint as a violation of the first two social virtues.

In addition to respect, care, and sensitivity, there is an expectation that the synagogue and its leadership will model the highest in ethical behavior. Congregations are called to be places of integrity and reliability. In short, synagogues should stand for something, and as such integrity is defined as faithful adherence to shared values and principles. To violate an articulated principle or protocol is not only unethical but hypocritical. Integrity is closely allied to strength understood not surprisingly as the capacity to hold to a principled position in the face of challenge, expediency, or another's advocacy to the contrary.

As long as all parties are in agreement, there is no problem in understanding the four social virtues as defined above. Congregational practice, however, becomes difficult—call it schizophrenogenic—in situations of conflict or disagreement because—as defined above—the four social virtues cannot be enacted at the same time. In cases of disagreement, synagogue professionals and lay leaders can be caring and helpful, supportive and considerate *or* they can demonstrate integrity and be strong, principled, and fair. But they cannot enact all four simultaneously. Because of the definitions ascribed to the social virtues—in situations of confrontation, embarrassment, or threat—the social virtues create conditions in which the congregation and its leadership cannot be faithful to at least one of the virtues that the synagogue espouses to embrace. In situations of stress or challenge, the synagogue will of logical necessity violate at least one of its core values precisely at the moment it will be expected to enact them all most passionately. In an attempt to uphold the sanctioned social virtues of the organization, synagogue professionals will either violate at least one or jump back and forth between contradictory propositions in the attempt to be faithful to the espoused values of the congregation.

The continuously fractious character of synagogue life coupled with a set of social virtues that often cannot be enacted simultaneously create conditions that are inherently and inevitably "crazy-making" for those who are tasked to model and live by them. The social virtues as defined inevitably will lead to charges of hypocrisy, face-saving strategies, paradoxical problem-solving, and a kind of designed blindness.

In a particularly telling example of this dynamic at work, the Dues and Review Committee of a large urban synagogue, operating on a fair-share system, determined after much consideration and discussion that a family was not paying its fair share. In conversation after conversation the family would not increase its contribution, and that stand was based not on financial hardship but what the family called principle. Their membership was "not worth" the expected amount of financial support. Further discussion ensued, but the family was adamant. Since the family did not have the right to set the level of its own contribution and there were no extenuating circumstances, the Dues and Review Committee and subsequently the Executive Committee of the congregation after long and extended discussion voted to terminate the membership of the family—on principle.

The family then complained to the clergy and to individual board members in a highly emotional and aggrieved manner, castigating the synagogue for acting in ways that were uncaring, disrespectful, unfeeling, and ultimately destructive to the Jewish identity of the family. Individual board members and people in the larger community challenged the decision, asking how a synagogue could possibly act in such an "uncaring way." Some board members, acting out of sense of "compassion and care" began to advocate for a reconsideration of the vote to terminate the family's membership. However, since the matter had now become public, other families of similar means accused the board of caving and threatened to decrease their contributions—on principle—out of a sense of equity and fairness.

The Executive Committee of the congregation was now in a bind. The committee could show strength, stick to the decision, and be principled, but only at the expense of violating the expectation that the synagogue was a supportive and caring organization. Some members of the board advocated for the first set of social virtues and some members for the second. Extended discussion at a board meeting brought no resolution to the matter. Caught in this double bind, the Executive Committee sent the problem back to the Dues and Review Committee.

After further discussion, a member of that committee was directed to talk with the family and signal how to present mitigating (but fictional) financial reasons for lower dues. Acceptance of the arrangement was contingent, however, on a promise of strict confidentiality on the part of the family. At the next meeting of the Dues and Review Committee, members spent considerable time disparaging the family that had prompted the predicament, labeling the family duplicitous, unprincipled, and unethical. The family was well aware of the financial protocols and practices of the congregation when joining, yet the family had "willfully failed to abide by them." The committee commended itself for making the contentious dilemma go away and for its wisdom in dealing with such an impossible situation.

This situation is a classic case of a double bind. For all the best intentions, synagogues often find themselves in them. When confronted with a double bind there is no way to make a right choice that satisfies all parties simultaneously since any and every choice will lead to a violation of basic principles. In such situations, an action that is necessary for success necessarily will lead to failure. The solution the committee utilized to address this predicament made the need for confidentiality an imperative, but since there are no secrets in a synagogue, the details of the deal soon leaked out and the committee was labeled hypocritical and unfair. Other families began to agitate for a reduction in their dues assessment. "Why should I pay if they aren't?" With the four social virtues in play, the problem would not go away.

Social virtues pose a problem for clergy as well. Since in times of disagreement it is not possible to enact all four simultaneously, clergy are often called on to behave in ways that violate at least one of the deeply held core values. Under the conditions set up by the social virtues as they are defined, rabbis, cantors, administrators, and educators are expected to be caring individuals of high principle who are asked to compromise their principles or disregard protocols when asked to make exceptions if that is what it takes to make a congregant feel cared for, happy, or supported. Such an action is usually framed as being flexible, showing compassion, or honoring a higher principle. "Rabbi, you know Judaism believes in family." However, a professional who subordinates the social virtue of integrity to that of support is then open to be labeled unfair, wishy-washy, or unprofessional by others. Should the clergy hold to principle at the expense of making a member feel supported then he or she can be characterized as uncaring, rigid, heartless, or destructive to the Judaism of the individual. The four social virtues *as they are defined and generally understood* are a trap. They inevitably create situations in which people can hold others to a schizophrenogenic set of standards. Thus, it is not uncommon for clergy and lay leadership to continually feel under attack for doing their job.

In the example cited above, also note that while the Dues and Review Committee labeled the family unethical and duplicitous, it commended itself for actions that were virtually identical. The family may have violated the fair-share dues policy of the synagogue but so did the committee. When the congregant did not play by the rules, the congregant was labeled as unprincipled and unethical. When the committee did not play by the rules and violated the fair-share policy creating a fiction for lower dues, it did not think of itself as similarly duplicitous, unfair, or unprincipled but rather applauded itself as clever and protective, all in the name of being realistic. In cases of a double bind/no-win predicament, cloaking rationalizations and defensive routines must of necessity come into play to avoid embarrassment.[4]

Defensive routines are policies, strategies, or actions that inhibit or eliminate the experience of threat or embarrassment but simultaneously prevent the identification, reduction, or elimination of the threat or embarrassment. Such routines are employed to avoid upsetting others or opening a can of worms.[5] Most people can identify the defensive routines used in their organizations, but, as in the case of the Dues and Review Committee, these same people are usually unaware when they are using the routines themselves. Acting in accordance with organizational defensive routines is done skillfully in the sense that the behavior is tacit and automatic. Organizational defensive routines are learned behaviors. They must be because psychologically different people come into an organization and use them in the same way. Additionally, they are triggered out of a desire to show concern or be realistic.

Individual and organizational defensive routines tend to cluster around important conflicts or issues. They are formidable impediments to learning. In fact, defensive routines ensure that an organization will not be self-reflective or open to error detection at precisely the moment when these two qualities are needed the most. The inconsistent application of the social virtues activates defensive routines that serve to camouflage or cover up the inconsistency itself.

Defensive routines are employed when people or groups believe that they are necessary for the organization to cope or maintain its own sense of positive self-regard. But here self-regard comes at a high cost. Since defensive routines are used to cover up errors that need to be corrected if the organization or group is to function effectively, covering up is a de facto commitment to continued ineffectiveness. If that is the case, covering up violates the most basic principle of sound leadership and responsible stewardship. Thus it is necessary to overlook the cover-up. At that point, the error, the cover-up, and the cover-up of the cover-up are now undiscussable and cannot be brought up. Synagogue professionals and lay leaders operating in such an environment often cannot act as they themselves might wish to act. If someone does surface the paradox or the cover-up, that person is subject to criticism or censure—the "whistle-blower syndrome."

There are four steps that predictably result in dealing with the internally inconsistent nature of the social virtues. These rules are derived from an internal logic that exerts a powerful impact on a congregation and the people in it.[6]

1. Embrace two mutually inconsistent propositions.
2. Act as if the two propositions were not inconsistent.
3. Make the inconsistency and the belief that there is no inconsistency undiscussable.
4. Make the undiscussability undiscussable.

Congregations and synagogue professionals are skillful at producing mixed messages and do so all the time, but—as seen in the example below—ironically the skillful production of such contradictory directives leads to a range of unintended and counterproductive consequences. Organizations, synagogues included, are theoretically designed and managed in such a way as to make management less difficult and yet the people in them often act in ways that make management more difficult. They embrace or produce inconsistent propositions and then attempt to deny or disguise the fact that they are doing so. They embrace the very paradoxical propositions that make the task of running their synagogues harder and signal that they expect everyone to play along with the contradiction.

By way of example, the president of a large urban synagogue had a meeting with the senior rabbi of the congregation. He advised the rabbi to get more people involved. The president explained that involvement was critical for the long-term success of the institution, and involvement was best accomplished by getting people to work on committees. "The way to get people to feel good about the congregation is to get them involved, get them working for the organization." The rabbi shared with the president that he agreed. In theory, involvement was an effective strategy to increase long-term retention. The congregation could certainly use additional volunteer workers. The problem, the rabbi explained, was that in the past, many of the people who had staffed congregational committees reported feeling devalued, manipulated, unappreciated, marginalized, and not at all involved in the final decision. In many cases, their efforts had been overruled at a higher level of organizational structure. Others felt that they had been expected to participate in a charade of decision-making because the final outcome was preordained. The president responded. "Rabbi, it's very important for the right people to keep control. And all the past presidents and board members agree with me. Trust me on this."

Here the president was signaling the need for meaningful involvement *and* coercive or manipulative control. Thus, the rabbi was counseled to get people involved in work that had every probability of distancing them from the very congregation that espoused their meaningful involvement. "Trust me" signaled the matter was not open to discussion. When professionals are managed in such a way, there is no way for them to succeed. Because they are in a no-win situation, they will act or be expected to act in a way that honors the undiscussability that strengthens the double bind even further. They are expected to play along with the situation even though they would like to change it. They then make their collusion covert and undiscussable.[7]

Contradictory propositions and the defensive routines they create take on a life of their own. They do not make a problem go away. They simply push the problem under the table, eventually to resurface in other and sometimes more destructive forms. Because synagogues operate with mutually contradictory definitions of the social virtues and because these virtues will inevitably generate double bind situations for those who try to manage them, many of the problems of the organization can never be resolved in a simple, straightforward way. The policies and procedures developed to address a conflict or controversy will inevitably double back to violate one of the valued social virtues of the organization. That in turn will cause new conflict or controversy requiring another set of problem-solving strategies, but because these strategies, too, will not solve the issue in the long run, synagogue leadership will be forced to generate an ever-growing body of rules and procedures. But since paradoxical propositions cannot be reconciled in practice, situations will continue to arise no matter the number of rules. Moreover since the rules act only to further cloak the contradiction, the rules will continually be questioned, skirted, or ignored. They can also generate a festering resentment in those on whom the rules are imposed.

Double binds are not only demoralizing for those who work within their context, but they necessitate that the defensive routines be protected and reinforced by the very people who would most like to see them gone. The protection, however, is usually covert and undiscussable, which makes the defensive routine appear self-protecting and self-perpetuating and becomes in turn self-proliferating. Additionally, the self-proliferating features of defensive routines are triggered whenever anyone tries to engage the double bind directly. Once individuals in an organization realize this, they tend to shy away from engagement in the name of being realistic: "It is what it is." In situations of double bind, defensive routines flourish and spread in a way that they cannot be managed.

Lay leaders and synagogue professionals will often confess that the very idea of removing defensive routines is unrealistic, futile, or foolishly idealistic. In this way, defensive routines become self-fulfilling and self-sealing. They are self-fulfilling because they create the conditions that make it naïve or dangerous to try to remove them, and they are self-sealing because they also create the conditions under which the self-fulfilling dynamic will never be challenged.[8]

Double binds are born of paradox and in turn create situations that prompt continued paradoxical reasoning.[9] The four social virtues as defined are a set up. Espousing them, lay leaders, members, and professionals alike often find themselves discouraged, frustrated, and upset, all of which in turn presents rich opportunity for the production of additional defensive routines. Synagogue work can be crazy-making because—to apply a line from Emily Dickinson—our congregations seem to dwell continuously in paradoxical possibility. While a paradoxical maxim— "everything is known and free will is given"—may be perfectly workable in theology, it is schizophrenogenic for those who must manage an organization in which they proliferate. We create organizational worlds that are contrary to our stated intentions and then spend a great deal of time on the defensive routines that distance us further from those intentions.

The situation described above is hardly unique to the synagogue. In a recent letter to the author, a physician described a similar dynamic at work in his profession this way: The so-called "Georgetown" principles of patient autonomy, non-malfeasance, benevolence, and justice are often in opposition as patients, families, and caregivers try to make decisions; and reflecting on his work in organizational development, Chris Argyris of the Harvard Business School wrote of corporate and educational institutions:

> We say we value openness, honesty, integrity, respect and caring. But we act in ways that undercut these values—not just once in a while, on very rare occasions, but regularly and routinely— whenever we face threatening or otherwise difficult situations. We then deny we are doing this and cover up our denial, thus trapping ourselves.[10]

The situation described above may seem depressing, even hopeless. The truth is because synagogues are human institutions, all synagogues are dysfunctional to a degree. But there is a decided advantage to knowing that such double bind functioning is predictable within the congregational setting. To use a military metaphor, synagogue work at times is like walking and working in a minefield. In such a circumstance, it is, first of all, critically important to know that you are entering one. In this case, ignorance is not bliss. An awareness of what predictably lies ahead may very well spell the difference between survival, dismissal, and long-term success. The best form of protection begins with knowledge and an awareness of what to expect. Knowing the crazy-making potential of the social virtues can be a kind of organizational mine detector, and while skirting the danger buried beneath the surface is a start, the better strategy in the long run is to surface the "explosive" consequences of the trap.

Understanding the four social virtues as they operate in the synagogue setting may be only a start, but it is a great advance nonetheless. The idea here is that it is the first step and a major step in making the unmanageable manageable. To state the case in a more technical way, mapping the causes of ineffectiveness and examining the manner in which they become self-sealing is in itself a positive contribution to diminishing the stress of congregational work and increasing the effectiveness of synagogue practice. The very act of mapping the causes of organizational defensive practice is a rare event in the congregational setting. Creating the rare event, then, is itself a sign of progress.[11]

A board, staff, or planning group introduced to the trap inherent in the four social virtues has a shared evaluative frame. The social virtues suddenly become not only pitfalls but diagnostic tools to be used in a shared evaluative process. The social virtues are easily recognizable when they are described in the shorthand categorization used here. Synagogue professionals and lay leaders now have a nontechnical language with which to speak about factors and dynamics they may well have intuited but could not be named or addressed. To develop a shared vocabulary it is helpful to learn this material as a group. Then naming a trap in a public setting is a way of calling a "time out" to group process.

By way of example, the membership committee of a synagogue that had been introduced to the social virtues was asked to contact a family that left the congregation shortly before the anticipated bar mitzvah of their oldest child. The family indicated by letter that the child's tutor was mean-spirited and uncaring and the rabbi who oversaw the program was cold, unresponsive, and completely lacking in sensitivity. It was hard enough to help their children build a positive Jewish identity without the synagogue working so hard to tear it down. The family was "forced to make other plans for the celebration" and made the point that they had shared with all their friends how badly they had been treated.

The committee requested a meeting with the rabbi to discuss this situation. He shared with the group that this student in particular had missed months of tutoring, was making no progress, and had failed to meet the timetable for completing the requirements of the program as established by the congregation. The child simply was not studying and had indicated no interest in the event beyond the party. The staff had tried without success to improve the situation. The parents had been contacted any number of times. Nothing seemed acceptable to the parents who offered any number of excuses but who had been unresponsive to any of the strategies suggested to move toward a more positive resolution.

The membership committee was very concerned. The chair reminded the rabbi that the good name of the synagogue was at stake, that finances were shaky, and that in a climate of declining affiliation every family was important. Flexibility and caring was the name of the game. But other committee members—who also served on the religious school committee—raised the need to protect the "integrity" of the synagogue's bar/bat mitzvah program. How could they mandate requirements and then let students slide around them? Fairness dictated that all students meet the same reasonable standards.

When the rabbi left the meeting, conversation shifted to a discussion of how the rabbi was using his time and if he was giving sufficient priority to building relationships with students in the religious school. One committee member raised questions about the rabbi's inability to prioritize. Another member of the committee then quipped, "OK. Now we're getting somewhere. The religious school committee tells our rabbi to uphold the standards we set for the bar/bat mitzvah program but Membership is now telling him to be so flexible that he will ignore them. And now we're going to take on the task of managing his calendar?" There was a short period of silence and then everyone began to laugh. Another committee member added, "OK. OK. Let's see if we can get ourselves out of the double bind business. Since bar/bat mitzvah is the reason most of our new families affiliate, maybe we should try to figure out a way to address the question of how we go about setting requirements with a population that does not necessarily share our priorities. Who do we need to get on board with this? Then we can figure out how to communicate the standards from the very start of affiliation and whose responsibility it is to uphold and enforce them."

At creation, Adam was given the ability to name the animals and creatures (Gen. 2:19). To name is to exert a measure of control over the thing named. In a fairy tale, conversely, to name the beast is often to rob the creature of its power. Knowing and naming the social virtues and their propensity to create no-win situations can be the source of a newfound leverage for problem-solving. Acknowledging that schizophrenogenic problem-solving is ubiquitous and surfaces in instances of embarrassment, threat, or disagreement is both a warning and prompt to avoid the trap. At the very least, learning the social virtues and how they operate in the synagogue setting is an invitation "to mark our foreheads"—a way to remain ever mindful of the predictably reoccurring paradoxical reasoning and ineffective behaviors that operate within a congregation. The goal is to take corrective action when they do. The old adage still applies: To be forewarned is to be forearmed.

Notes

1. *Sifrei, Eikev* 49.
2. The term "social virtue" was first used by Chris Argyris, professor at the Harvard Business School, in his work on Action Science.
3. Based on his research and work in organizational consulting, Argyris identified (1) caring, help, and support; (2) respect for others; (3) honesty; (4) strength; and (5) integrity as near universally accepted social virtues. He further defined the meaning of these virtues as they are understood in contemporary American society. See Chris Argyris, *Overcoming Organizational Defenses* (Upper Saddle River, NJ: Prentice Hall, 1990), 19–21.
4. Chris Argyris, *On Organizational Learning* (Oxford: Blackwell, 1992), 141–43. For a full discussion of double binds see Gregory Bateson, *Steps to an Ecology of Mind* (New York: Ballantine, 1972).
5. Ibid., 188.
6. Ibid., 58–59.
7. Chris Argyris, *Flawed Advice and the Management Trap* (Oxford: Oxford University Press, 2000), 68.
8. Ibid., 69–71.
9. Ibid., 159.
10. Chris Argyris, *Organizational Traps* (New York: Oxford University Press, 2010), 11.
11. Argyris, *Overcoming Organizational Defenses*, xv.

Yom HaAtzma-ut as a Religious Holiday: A Note Regarding the CCAR and the *American Jewish Year Book*

Joel B. Wolowelsky

The Six-Day War in 1967 precipitated a major reorientation of self-perception among world Jewry, stimulating Jewish self-pride, galvanizing Soviet Jewry, and reassessing the reliability of support from the Christian world. The pervasive fear of immediate national annihilation some two decades after the Holocaust dramatically and unexpectedly relieved by what seemed to be a modern-day miracle called for a religious response by many. For example, Milton Himmelfarb, then coeditor of the *American Jewish Year Book*, ended his personal column in *Commentary* on the lessons learned from the Six-Day War as follows:

> In this last third of the 20th century we may be beginning to believe again that the history of the Jews points to some kind of providential order, which—for reasons having to do not with our merits, but at most with the merits of the Fathers—has a special place for it.

> . . .

> When the Psalmist says, "I," the pronoun is singular and plural, individual and collective, personal and referring to the children of Israel—as in that other verse from the last of the Hallel psalms: "I thank Thee, for Thou hast answered me, and art become my salvation."[1]

JOEL B. WOLOWELSKY, Ph.D. is dean of the faculty at the Yeshivah of Flatbush in Brooklyn, New York. His most recent book is *To Mourn a Child: Jewish Responses to Neonatal and Childhood Death* (New York: OU Press, 2013).

The Religious Zionist/Modern Orthodox community responded liturgically regarding the newly established holiday of Yom Y'rushalayim (Jerusalem Day) as it had for Yom HaAtzma-ut (Israel Independence Day). It added various holiday Psalms and the recitation of *Hallel* to the service.[2] In 1969, Yavneh, the Religious Jewish [University] Students Association,[3] was preparing under my editorship the publication of *Veheveti*,[4] a booklet describing for its members —primarily Religious Zionists and Modern Orthodox students—the prayer service for Yom Y'rushalayim and Yom HaAtzma-ut. As stated in the Introduction, "Yavneh present[ed] *Veheveti* in appreciation of the religious dimension in the establishment of *Medinat Yisrael* [the State of Israel]." At that time, I noticed that Yom HaAtzma-ut was not included in the calendar of the *American Jewish Year Book*—a calendar that, as Jonathan D. Sarna and Jonathan J. Golden would later characterize it, had become "the 'official' calendar of the American Jewish community."[5] I wrote to the editors asking about the omission.

The *American Jewish Year Book* was sponsored by the American Jewish Committee (AJC). The AJC had long resisted a formal Zionist identity. In 1942, a group of Reform rabbis, reaffirming the classical position within Reform Judaism opposing Zionism, withdrew from the Central Conference of American Rabbis to form the American Council for Judaism (ACJ). A good number of people who were or had been associated with AJC were to be found among the membership and leadership of the ACJ, the only national Jewish organization ever founded specifically to oppose the idea of a Jewish state.[6]

> Despite incremental changes in its views since the founding of the State of Israel in 1948, the AJC still was, at the beginning of June 1967, the major national Jewish body that was most self-consciously American, most reluctant to acknowledge links to other Jewish communities beyond those of religion and philanthropy . . . Still an explicitly non-Zionist and self-consciously "American" organization, it lacked a vision of Jewish peoplehood and a visceral feeling of common destiny with the Jewish state.[7]

The Six-Day War changed that orientation.

The threat had been so grave and the victory so complete that the religiously minded could easily see the Six-Day War as a case of divine providence and a possible harbinger of the messianic era. Indeed, to Israelis and Jews around the world, the victory, following the traumatic weeks of worry, appeared as a miraculous deliverance. And no less so to the leaders of the AJC.[8]

The annual meeting [of the AJC in 1968] marked Israel's twentieth anniversary with a resolution reflecting sentiments that would have been anathema before 1967: "The overwhelming and spontaneous response of American Jewry when Israel was threatened last year has made manifest to all the deep personal attachment and the profound sense of a shared history and destiny that organically connect American Jews to Israel."[9]

However, this changed attitude was not reflected in the response of November 28, 1969, to my query by Martha Jelenko, then associate editor of the *Year Book*: "The editors of the AMERICAN JEWISH YEAR BOOK feel that Yom Ha-Atzmaut and Yom Yerushalayim are Israeli national, not religious holidays, and therefore are not to be included in our calendar."[10]

Perhaps this actually reflected the attitude of the editors (Himmelfarb's sensitivities quoted above notwithstanding) or a debate going on among the staff and lay leaders regarding the new pro-Zionist orientation of the AJC.[11] In any event, the conclusions to be drawn from the Six-Day War were not lost on the Reform Movement. At its eightieth anniversary convention, held in Houston, Texas, in June 1969, the CCAR adopted a resolution "to institute Israel Independence Day as a permanent festival to be observed annually on the fifth day of Iyar as part of our spiritual history and religious life."[12] This was reaffirmed in a resolution adopted by the CCAR at the ninety-ninth annual convention of the CCAR in Israel in March 1988, wherein it noted that at its 1970 convention on Mount Scopus in Jerusalem the CCAR had proclaimed Israel Independence Day a permanent religious holiday.

Remembering this some years later, I brought Jelenko's response to the attention of Rabbi Joseph B. Glaser, then executive vice president of the CCAR. He wrote to Bert Gold, then executive vice president of the AJC, reminding him: "The Reform Movement has indeed recognized Yom Ha-atzmaut as a religious holiday, and I believe the [Orthodox] Rabbinical Council of America and the [Conservative] Rabbinical Assembly have done the same." A few days later, Himmelfarb wrote to Glaser: "Mr. Gold has shown us your letter of November 13 [1975]. We have decided to include Yom ha^czma³ut in future calendars."

However, changed attitudes apparently take a while to take hold, and in 1984, I noticed that Yom HaAtzma-ut was no longer listed in the *Year Book*'s liturgical calendar. I called this to Glaser's attention on September 26, 1984, and reminded him of our previous exchange. He took the matter up with David Gordis, then executive vice president of the AJC. Himmelfarb responded on October 3, 1984:

> In 1977 and 1978 we listed *Yom ha^czma³ut* and *Yom ha-Sho³a wehagevurah* as well. Since 1979 we have called them Israel Independence Day and Holocaust Memorial Day. Mr. Wolowelsky will find both on page 345 of the current YEAR BOOK.
>
> The reason for the change was our suspicion, perhaps unworthy, that some of the people consulting the YEAR BOOK might not be Hebraist enough to understand those agglomerations of consonants, vowels, and diacritical marks.
>
> I am sorry you had to waste your time on something like this.

When Glaser shared this response with me, I pointed out that the matter was really not feared confusion over "those agglomerations of consonants, vowels, and diacritical marks" in the annual calendar of the *Year Book*. The fact was that the editors had decided to drop the reference to the holiday in the *Year Book*'s liturgical calendar of Festivals and Fasts. Realizing this, Glaser sent the following hand-written note to Himmelfarb on October 19, 1984:

> The problem with Yom Hashoa and Yom Haatzmaut is not in the annual calendar but in the monthly one. People will be using that—otherwise why would you publish it. It is conceivable that someone would thus miss them altogether or draw the conclusion that they were not liturgical—which they have been so declared by the Rabbinic groups. It's not a "waste of time"—it is an important principle. We deliberated long and hard on whether these should be declared religious holidays. What's the big deal? All you have to do is add two lines. If you're worried about the Satmar picketing you, we'll take care of them.

Three days later Himmelfarb responded with his own hand-written note: "This will be done in vol. 86. Vol. 85 calendars have already been set."

It is not clear what fueled this continued reluctance to recognize Yom HaAtzma-ut as a religious holiday. Recently, Lawrence Grossman, now director of publications at the AJC and formerly editor of the *American Jewish Year Book*, wrote to me: "I would guess that the reluctance to list the days as religious holidays had to do with the fact that there were still influential older lay people around who would have reacted negatively. I'm sure that Milton Himmelfarb and Bert Gold had no personal objections."[13] In any event, Glaser in the end helped the *Year Book* editors overcome their resistance.

Notes

1. Milton Himmelfarb, "In the Light of Israel's Victory," *Commentary* (October 1967): 61.

2. So too the Conservative siddur adds *Hallel* for both holidays. Regarding Yom HaAtzma-ut, the Religious Kibbutz Movement and Conservative Judaism had each added a form of *Al HaNisim* in the *Amidah*, mirroring the liturgical additions for Purim and Chanukah. I have contrasted these two versions of *Al HaNisim* in my book *The Mind of the Mourner: Individual and Community in Jewish Mourning* (New York: OU Press, 2010), 114–18. A newer version of *Al HaNisim* in the Conservative siddur *Sim Shalom* is closer in spirit to that of the Religious Kibbutz Movement. Regarding the Six-Day War, see, e.g., Shear Yashuv Cohen et al., "The Religious Meaning of the Six-Day War: A Symposium," *Tradition* 10, no. 1 (Summer 1968): 5–20; and David Berger et al., "Reflections on the Six-Day War after a Quarter Century," *Tradition* 26, no. 4 (Summer 1992): 6–25. (Note the remarks of David Singer, then editor of the *American Jewish Year Book*.) On Satmar's anti-Zionist philosophy, see Norman Lamm, "The Ideology of the Neturei Karta According to the Satmar Version," *Tradition* 12, no. 2 (Fall 1971): 38–53.

3. The history of Yavneh was recently presented in Benny Kraut, *The Greening of American Orthodox Judaism: Yavneh in the 1960s* (Cincinnati: Hebrew Union College Press, 2011).

4. Joel B. Wolowelsky, ed., *Veheveti: The Prayer Service for Yom HaAtzmaut and Yom Yerushalayim, Including Additional Rituals for the Passover Seder and the Emended Text for the Nachem Paragraph of the 9 Av Amida* (New York: Yavneh, The Religious Jewish Students Association, 1970).

5. Jonathan D. Sarna and Jonathan J. Golden, "The Twentieth Century through American Jewish Eyes: A History of the American Jewish Yearbook, 1899-1999," in *American Jewish Year Book 2000*, ed. David Singer and Lawrence Grossman (New York: American Jewish Committee, 2000), 5.

6. Marianne R. Sanua, *Let Us Prove Strong: The American Jewish Committee, 1945–2006* (Waltham, MA: Brandeis University Press, 2007), 19–20.

7. Lawrence Grossman, "Transformation through Crisis: The American Jewish Committee and the Six-Day War," *American Jewish History* 86, no. 1 (March 1998): 28, 42.

8. Sanua, *Let Us Prove Strong*, 141.

9. Grossman, "Transformation through Crisis," 53.

10. Copies of the personal correspondence quoted in this article have been deposited with the American Jewish Archives.

11. For example, Sanua explains that the silence of the *Year Book* on the issue of the Vietnam War reflected an intense struggle going on behind the scenes as staff, lay leaders, and the membership debated on whether the AJC should take a public stand on the War and what the wording of such a statement might be. Sanua, *Let Us Prove Strong*, 229.

12. *Year Book of the Central Conference of American Rabbis* 79 (New York: CCAR, 1970), 143.

13. Lawrence Grossman, e-mail to author, November 13, 2012.

Understanding the Two Creation Narratives in Genesis: Just How Many Beginnings Were There?

הבנת שני סיפורי הבריאה בספר בראשית:
כמה ראשיות היו באמת?

Daniel M. Berry

1. Introduction

The first word in the Hebrew Genesis 1:1, as traditionally vocalized and pronounced, means literally "In a beginning." Regardless, tradition apparently has it meaning and translated as "In the beginning." The literal meaning is considered as contradicting what was believed to be reality, one creation from nothing (i.e., ex nihilo) by God. Consequently, Rashi, the noted medieval commentator, suggested a syntactic solution, based on mimicking the sentence structure of the second creation narrative in the second part of Genesis 2:4, which appears to imply one beginning, *the* beginning. This syntactic solution, however, requires a change from the traditional vocalization and pronunciation of the second word of Genesis. Upon close examination, the second creation narrative and Rashi's syntactic solution are shown to imply multiple creations as does the literal first creation narrative. This article argues that we should accept the traditional, Masoretic vocalizations along with their literal meanings. It then mentions some biblical consequences of those literal meanings. The article concludes with explorations

DANIEL BERRY is professor of Computer Science and Software Engineering, University of Waterloo, Waterloo, Ontario, Canada, dberry@uwaterloo.ca. The author thanks Rabbi Lori Cohen and an anonymous reviewer of this article for their comments on previous drafts.

of the relation of the literal meanings and modern cosmological science and of the implications of this relation on Judaism.

2. Problems with the First Sentence of the Bible

The first sentence of the Bible, Genesis 1:1:

בראשית ברא אלהים את השמים ואת הארץ:

is traditionally vocalized as:

בְּרֵאשִׁית בָּרָא אֱלֹהִים אֵת הַשָּׁמַיִם וְאֵת הָאָרֶץ:

The Bible, as written, has no vowel signs and punctuation marks. So we depend on a Masoretic tradition that has recorded vowels and punctuation and has preserved the pronunciation and pauses for centuries.[1] This and other Jewish traditions concerning the Bible are very strong and resist change. These traditions, as *apparently* reported by the Hertz *The Pentateuch and Haftorahs* (HPH)[2] has the first sentence translated as and meaning:

In the beginning, God created the heaven and the earth.

with בְּרֵאשִׁית translated as and meaning "In the beginning."

If the meaning of the בְּרֵאשִׁית were, in fact, "In *the* beginning," בראשית would have been vocalized as בָּרֵאשִׁית, with a definite article, the ָ, *kamatz* (קמץ), underneath the ב that means "in." What is there in Genesis 1:1, בְּרֵאשִׁית, without a definite article and with an implicit indefinite article, the ְ, *sh'va* (שׁוא), under the ב, means "In *a* beginning." Succinctly said, what is *not* in Genesis 1:1,

בָּרֵאשִׁית בָּרָא אֱלֹהִים אֵת הַשָּׁמַיִם וְאֵת הָאָרֶץ:

means

In the beginning, God created the heaven and the earth.,

and what *is* in Genesis 1:1,

בְּרֵאשִׁית בָּרָא אֱלֹהִים אֵת הַשָּׁמַיִם וְאֵת הָאָרֶץ:

means

In a beginning, God created the heaven and the earth.

When a sampling of native speakers of Hebrew, known to the author in Israel, were asked for the meaning of the word בְּרֵאשִׁית, they all said that the word means "in the beginning," perhaps from the influence of the familiar English translations. When the author reminded them that the word really means "in a beginning," they were initially surprised, but after thinking about it a second or two, they agreed with the author. The misunderstanding of בְּרֵאשִׁית extends to the Even-Shoshan dictionary of the Hebrew language,[3] which says that בְּרֵאשִׁית means בַּתְּחִלָּה or בָּרִאשׁוֹנָה, both with definite articles.

Also in English, there are phrases that do not mean literally what people understand them to mean. For example, the phrase "head over heels," meaning "flipping," should be "heels over head." The head is normally over the heels, and flipping causes the heels to be over the head.

3. The Septuagint and Onkelos's Targum

There is historical literary evidence that בְּרֵאשִׁית was originally understood as saying "In a beginning." The Septuagint, the translation of the Bible into Greek, written circa 270 B.C.E., provides as the translation of בְּרֵאשִׁית, εν αρχη (en arkhé).[4] There is *no* definite article. If there were, the translation of בְּרֵאשִׁית would have been written εν η αρχη (en hé arkhé). This Greek translation was based on a copy of the Hebrew Bible that predates the Masoretic text that we use today. This fact is evidence that at *no* time did the first word of Genesis 1:1 have a definite article.

Onkelos translated Genesis 1:1,

בראשית ברא אלהים את השמים ואת הארץ:

to Aramaic, in what is known as the *Targum*, as

בקדמין ברא אדוני ית שמיא וית ארעא:[5]

He did not translate

בראשית ברא אלהים את השמים ואת הארץ:

as

בקדמינא ברא אדוני ית שמיא וית ארעא:

That is, he did not introduce any definite article to בקדמין. On-kelos's translation of Genesis 1:1 is yet more evidence that at *no* time did the first word of Genesis 1:1 have a definite article.

Given the evidence that the original Hebrew Genesis 1:1 was always understood as meaning

In a beginning, God created the heaven and the earth.,

from where does the current seemingly traditional understanding of Genesis 1:1 as meaning

In the beginning, God created the heaven and the earth.

come?

4. Rashi's Construction

Rashi (Rabbi Shlomo ben Yitzchak), in the eleventh century, under-stood God's creation of our universe as a true miracle, as creating everything ex nihilo. Since before this creation, there was nothing, not even time, the creation must have happened at *the* beginning.[6] Rashi was evidently aware of the literal reading of Genesis 1:1, but tried to explain in his commentary on Genesis how Genesis 1:1 could be understood as saying "In the beginning" by use of grammatical gymnastics.[7] Taking advantage of the Bible's lack of vowels and punctuation, he took the first two sentences as one, by treating Genesis 1:1 as a relative clause modifying Genesis 1:2:

בְּרֵאשִׁית בְּרֹא אֱלֹהִים אֵת הַשָּׁמַיִם וְאֵת הָאָרֶץ,
וְהָאָרֶץ הָיְתָה תֹהוּ וָבֹהוּ וְחֹשֶׁךְ עַל־פְּנֵי תְהוֹם וְרוּחַ אֱלֹהִים מְרַחֶפֶת
עַל־פְּנֵי הַמָּיִם:

The merged sentence can be translated[8] to English as:

In the beginning of God's creating the heaven and the earth,
the earth was unformed and void, and darkness was on the face
of the deep, God's wind flew over the face of the waters.

Before explaining what prompted Rashi to form the merged sen-tence, consider the grammar rules about *construct* forms in Hebrew.

The first three words of the merged sentence, בְּרֵאשִׁית בָּרָא אֱלֹהִים, is a construct. In a construct, all words but the last are in the construct form, and any definite article is put in the last word, a noun that is not in the construct form, for example, as in:

משרד ראש הממשלה

The Prime Minister's Office.

However, if the last word of the construct is a proper noun (e.g., אלהים), which cannot take a definite article, the *understood* definite article is lost, for example:

משרד ראש ממשלת מדינת ישראל

The State of Israel's Prime Minister's Office.

To arrive at the merged sentence, Rashi argued in his commentary that ראשית is purely a construct form that cannot appear as a stand-alone noun. It must always be followed by at least another noun X. Thus, X ראשית really means "beginning of X" for some X. Rashi's conclusion was that in בראשית ברא, X is ברא, and, therefore, ברא must be a noun (i.e., בְּרָא), and not a verb (i.e., בָּרָא).

There is disagreement about some of the details of Rashi's construction. For example, the Ramban (Rabbi Moshe ben Nachman), in the twelfth century, observed that ראשית appears several times in the Torah as a stand-alone noun (e.g., in Leviticus 2:12 and Deuteronomy 33:21).[9] Where ראשית appears as a construct form (e.g., in Exodus 23:19, Numbers 15:20, and Deuteronomy 18:4), it means "first fruit" (e.g., of a harvest). When ראשית appears as a stand-alone noun, it is used in this sense of first fruit. So what would be the first fruit of a created universe? Its beginning, its big bang!

The first commentary in בראשית רבה[10] takes the word בראשית as meaning "with wisdom" or "with Torah," so that

בְּרֵאשִׁית בָּרָא אֱלֹהִים אֵת הַשָּׁמַיִם וְאֵת הָאָרֶץ:

can be read as

With wisdom, God created the heaven and the earth.

or as

With Torah, God created the heaven and the earth.

While this commentary goes in a direction different from that of this article, it does use ראשית as a stand-alone noun and ב as the preposition "With." In Hebrew, as in English, "wisdom" is a general collective noun, and no definite article is needed to get its general sense.

Getting back to Rashi's grammatical argument, Rashi argued that merging Genesis 1:1 and 1:2 makes the resulting sentence about the creation structured like the so-called second creation narrative that begins in the clause that is in the second part of Genesis 2:4, hereinafter called "Genesis 2:4b":

ביום עשות יהוה אלהים ארץ ושמים:

The traditional understanding[11] of this second creation narrative can be expressed as:

on the day of *YHVH* God's making earth and heaven.

Genesis 2:4b begins with a three-word construct, the first of which is a prepositioned noun in construct form naming a time duration, the second of which is a noun in construct form naming an action, and the third of which is a name of God, just like Rashi's merged Genesis 1:1–2 begins.[12] (There is more on this sentence in Section 6.)

While Rashi's construction is grammatically correct, it, nevertheless, requires changing the vocalization of בָּרָא ,ברא, to בְּרֹא. The tradition is quite strict against such changes. Also, who is to say that this change of the second word's vocalization is better than changing the vocalization of בראשית from בְּרֵאשִׁית to בָּרֵאשִׁית? In summary, Rashi offered a syntactic change to Genesis 1:1–2 in order to obtain the "In the beginning" understanding of בְּרֵאשִׁית.

The main source for the production of the King James (KJ) English translation of the Bible[13] was the Septuagint.[14] If indeed the Septuagint translates בְּרֵאשִׁית as meaning "In a beginning," then how did the KJ version end up with בְּרֵאשִׁית translated as "In the beginning"? There is evidence that the authors of the KJ translation consulted sources that were influenced by Rashi's commentary.[15] Apparently, KJ's translators liked the idea of creation ex nihilo and felt that "In the beginning" was more in line with that idea than "In a beginning." The KJ translation ended up influencing the producers of Jewish–English translations, including that of HPH[16] to the extent of imitating the KJ translation's use of "And" to begin narrative sentences that begin with ו in the original; its use of "thou," "thee," and "thy";[17] and clearly, its rendition of Genesis 1:1.

Ephraim Speiser's recent conversational English translation of Genesis 1:1, adopted by the Jewish Publication Society,[18] is

When God began to create heaven and earth, . . . ,
sidestepping the issue entirely.

Rashi's construction was, in the last analysis, unnecessary. One can still understand creation as being ex nihilo for any "a creation," even if the creation being described is not the only "the creation." So there is no loss in miraculousness in understanding Genesis 1:1 as it is written. Also, while ex nihilo means "from nothing," it is clear, at least in the context of creation by God, "from nothing" means "from no thing" and not "from entirely nothing." Our universe was created by God from God's six days of work and possibly from God's wisdom.

Finally, observe that Rashi's understanding of Genesis 1:1–2:

In the beginning of God's creating the heaven and the earth,
the earth was unformed and void, and darkness was on the face
of the deep, God's wind flew over the face of the waters.

does not force that there is only one beginning and does not preclude that there are multiple beginnings. All it says is that in the beginning of God's creation of the heaven and the earth, namely our heaven and our earth, such and such happened. It leaves open the possibility that there were other creations, although not of *our* heaven and earth, and it says nothing about what might have happened at any other creations. It appears that even though Rashi may have been trying to say that there was only *one* beginning by putting in an understood definite article, he did not succeed. His construction is just as indefinite about the number of creations as is the original understanding:

In a beginning, God created the heaven and the earth.

All told, the evidence suggests that the traditional vocalization of Genesis 1:1,

בְּרֵאשִׁית בָּרָא אֱלֹהִים אֵת הַשָּׁמַיִם וְאֵת הָאָרֶץ:

is what was intended and that Genesis 1:1 means

In a beginning, God created the heaven and the earth.

This meaning implies the existence of multiple creations. For some implications of this conclusion on the reading of the rest of Genesis, please consult the section titled "A Semantic Solution" in the author's earlier paper on this subject.[19]

5. Related Work

Other modern authors have noted this problem with the traditional translation of Genesis 1:1. For example, Nancy Abrams and Joel Primack, in writing about quantum cosmology and Kabbalah, observe that "The opening words of Genesis might be better interpreted, 'In A beginning.'"[20] Also, Daniel Matt, in writing about God and the Big Bang, offers that "perhaps we should translate the opening words of Genesis not as 'In *the* beginning . . .' but 'In *a* beginning, God created . . .' In fact, this represents a more literal rendering of the original Hebrew: *Be-Reshit*, 'In a beginning.'"[21]

Works that comment on the problem with Genesis 1:1 but side with Rashi include (1) "The Plain Meaning of Genesis 1:1–3" by Harry Orlinsky,[22] (2) *The Book of Genesis: Chapters 1–17* by Victor Hamilton,[23] and (3) "The First Six Days" by Morris Engelson,[24] the author of *The Heavenly Time Machine: Essays on Science and Torah*.[25] Curiously, none of these even mention the possibility of understanding בְּרֵאשִׁית as "In a beginning."

Works that comment on the same problem and come to the conclusions that indeed בְּרֵאשִׁית means "In a beginning" and that there might be multiple beginnings include (1) "The Restrictive Syntax of Genesis i 1" by Robert Holmstedt[26] and (2) "In the Beginning?" by Karljürgen Feuerherm.[27] Holmstedt gives a good summary of the arguments for and against understanding בְּרֵאשִׁית in Genesis 1:1 as meaning "In the beginning." In the end, he concludes that this understanding is untenable. While arguing for yet another grammatical structure for understanding Genesis 1:1, he concludes that "there are potentially multiple ראשִׁית periods or stages to God's creative work."[28]

Feuerherm summarizes various arguments for interpreting
בְּרֵאשִׁית as "In a beginning." He agrees that there is no definite article in בְּרֵאשִׁית, but argues that this lack does not imply
the existence of an indefinite article. For example, the lack of a
definite article in front of a plural noun P does not imply that
there is an indefinite article in front of P, because "a" in front
of a plural noun does not make sense. Thus, he is unprepared
to accept that the lack of a definite article in בְּרֵאשִׁית implies
multiple beginnings. While certainly a plural noun P with no
definite article in front cannot be understood as "a P," it *can* be
understood as "some P," and "some P" does imply that there
are multiple and other P.

6. Rashi Revisited

The strongest reason for not accepting Rashi's construction is that
in a very fundamental way, the beginning of Rashi's merged Genesis 1:1–2:

$$בְּרֵאשִׁית בָּרָא אֱלֹהִים אֵת הַשָּׁמַיִם וְאֵת הָאָרֶץ,$$

is *not* structured like Genesis 2:4b:

$$ביום עשות יהוה אלהים ארץ ושמים:$$

The first has אֵת ה־ in front of each direct object—the two nouns
naming what God created—and the second does not, and this
structural difference gives rise to a *big* semantic difference!

If there were definite articles in the direct objects of Genesis 2:4b,
as there is in the KJ translation,

in the day that the LORD God made the earth and the heavens,

the clause would be

$$ביום עשות יהוה אלהים את הארץ ואת השמים:$$

as in Genesis 1:1, albeit in reverse order.[29]

What is this אֵת that appears twice in Genesis 1:1 and twice in the
modified Genesis 2:4b? It is a preposition that announces a definite
direct object. Consider the three related sentences:

I saw the bear.	רָאִיתִי אֶת הַדּוֹב.
I saw a bear.	רָאִיתִי דּוֹב.
I saw Dov.	רָאִיתִי אֶת דּוֹב.

The direct object, "the bear" (הַדּוֹב), in the first sentence is definite because of the "the" (ה) at the beginning of הַדּוֹב, and the direct object, "Dov" (דּוֹב), in the third sentence is definite because the direct object is a proper noun. The direct object, "a bear" (דּוֹב), in the second sentence is indefinite. Notice how אֵת disambiguates between seeing a bear and seeing someone whose name is the word "Dov."

This אֵת is essential to be able to read II Samuel 12:1,

וַיִּשְׁלַח יְהוָה אֶת־נָתָן אֶל־דָּוִד:

as saying that God sent Nathan to David and not as saying that God sent a gift to David, even though in the ironic sense, God did send a painful gift to David, someone who clearly pointed out David's moral failing in connection with Batsheva. The lack of this אֵת is what prevents Genesis 1:1,

בְּרֵאשִׁית בָּרָא אֱלֹהִים אֵת הַשָּׁמַיִם וְאֵת הָאָרֶץ:

from being read as about someone or something named "B'reishit," saying that

B'reishit created God, the heaven, and the earth.,

which would be written in Hebrew as

בְּרֵאשִׁית בָּרָא אֵת אֱלֹהִים אֵת הַשָּׁמַיִם וְאֵת הָאָרֶץ:

So, getting back to Genesis 2:4b, the clause

בְּיוֹם עֲשׂוֹת יְהוָה אֱלֹהִים אֶרֶץ וְשָׁמָיִם:

with no definite direct objects cannot be saying

in the day of *YHVH* God's making the earth and the heaven.,

similar to its KJ translation. The clause

in the day of *YHVH* God's making the earth and the heaven.

would be in Hebrew

ביום עשות יהוה אלהים את הארץ ואת השמים:

which is not what is there in Genesis 2:4b. The clause

ביום עשות יהוה אלהים ארץ ושמים:

cannot even be saying

in the day of *YHVH* God's making Earth and Heaven.,

with Earth and Heaven as proper nouns similar to the way it is translated in the HPH.[30] The clause

in the day of *YHVH* God's making Earth and Heaven.,

with "Earth" and "Heaven" as proper nouns would be in Hebrew

ביום עשות יהוה אלהים את ארץ ואת שמים:

which is not what is there in Genesis 2:4b. The clause

ביום עשות יהוה אלהים ארץ ושמים:

must, therefore, be saying

on the day of *YHVH* God's making *an* earth and *a* heaven.,

referring to *one* earth of many and *one* heaven of many, namely *our* earth and *our* heaven, which were created on *the* day of the creation of *our* universe. This correct understanding of Genesis 2:4b is consistent with the correct understanding of Genesis 1:1:

In a beginning, God created the heaven and the earth.,

the heaven and the earth *in which we live*, this beginning being but one of many. The correct understandings are consistent, because each implies the existence of multiple creations. (There is more on multiple creations in Section 8.)

Rashi and we would like Genesis to say,

In a specific beginning, ours, a specific earth-and-heaven, ours, was created.,

but Genesis does not ever say what we would like. When Genesis pins down one, the day or the earth-and-heaven, the other is only one of many possible. Shades of relativity and the uncertainty principle![31] Genesis 1:1 pins down the earth-and-heaven to ours, but it was created in one of many possible beginnings. Genesis 2:4b pins down the beginning to ours, on Tishrei 1, but in that beginning one of many possible earth-and-heaven combinations was created.

One might argue that the author or the transcriber of Genesis made a mistake in Genesis 1:1, leaving out the definite article. If there is a mistake in Genesis 1:1, then this same mistake, the leaving out of the definite article, is made also in Genesis 2:4b, that is, in both creation narratives. This repetition of one specific kind of omission error in two separated sentences describing the same event is too much of a coincidence.

While the omission of the definite article in Genesis 1:1 is apparent only in the traditional vocalization of the text and is invisible in the visible letters, the omission of the definite articles in Genesis 2:4b is clear in the visible letters. Therefore, there is very little doubt about what Genesis 2:4b says.

It seems clear that the author of Genesis is talking about multiple creations. (See Section 8 for a discussion about what these multiple creations might be.)

7. Rashi Painted Himself into a Corner

Interestingly, Rashi painted himself into a corner over the number of creations. After arguing so fiercely that there was only one creation in the face of Genesis 1:1's literal statement to the contrary, he needed some additional finessing to account for two creations.

Chumash: The Gutnick Edition—The Book of Genesis has a commentary on Genesis 1:1:

RASHI: The word *Breishis* is crying out for a Midrashic interpretation: *Breishis* means "two beginnings" (ראשית ב'), suggesting that God created the world for the sake of the Torah which is called "the beginning of His way" (Prov. 8:2) and for the sake of the Jewish people who are called "the first of His grain" (Jer. 2:3).[32]

Rashi had the solution under his nose and did not have to go through double contradicting doses of linguistic gymnastics to get this two-beginning interpretation.

8. Some Cosmology

This article rises to the challenge posed by Philip Cohen and Hava Tirosh-Samuelson in their "Editors' Introduction: Why Science Matters to Judaism" in the Judaism and Science symposium issue of this journal[33] by trying to show a connection between the new understandings of Genesis 1 and 2 and current cosmological science.[34]

Many of the articles in the Science Issue (e.g., Norbert Samuelson's,[35] Victoria Ziva Frappollo's,[36] Peter Ochs's,[37] Bradley Shavit Artson's,[38] and Toba Spitzer's[39]) seem to assume that there is no reconciliation between:

1. scientific truth about the creation of our universe and its history before morally aware men[40] appeared on Earth and
2. the description of the same in the Bible.

Still others have commented on the difficulties reconciling science with the Bible.[41]

Perhaps, there is no reconciliation if one takes *translations* of the Bible as literal. On the other hand, if one takes the Bible in its original Hebrew wording, there is sufficient imprecision that the book of Genesis can be read as consistent with science as we know it today. This observation seems to be underlying Laurie Green's article "The Case for Science Education in Our Religious Schools"[42] in the Judaism and Science Issue.

Some Jews believe that the Torah is the word of God:

וזאת התורה אשר שם משה לפני בני ישראל, על פי אדוני ביד משה.

This is the Torah that Moshe put before the Children of Israel, *according to the word of God*, by the hand of Moshe.

On the assumption that God wrote Genesis, then what is God trying to say with the understanding described in this article of Genesis's description of the creation of our universe?

The Ramban somehow determined that our universe started off as an infinitesimally small ball containing *all* the matter that is now in our universe (i.e., what we now know as the Big Bang). Professor Gerald Schroeder, MIT physicist, cosmologist, and molecular biologist turned biblical scholar, says in *Genesis and the Big Bang*, "Nahmanides's account of the first seconds of the universe reads something like this: At the briefest instant following creation all the matter of the universe was concentrated in a very small place, no larger than a grain of mustard."[43] Bernard Chavel's English translation in *Ramban, Commentary: Genesis* says, "Now with this creation, which was like a very small point having no substance, everything in the heavens and on the earth was created."[44] The Ramban lived in the thirteenth century, some 200 years before Christopher Columbus, and some 250 years before Galileo Galilei got into trouble with the Catholic Church for claiming that the earth orbited around the sun and not vice versa. In spite of how little the science of his time understood even the solar system, he managed to understand essentially the Big Bang. Incredible! He must have been thought by the scientists of the day a total crackpot, but since he was a rabbi, he could be forgiven for not understanding science. From where did the Ramban get his understanding of the creation?

The Ramban was a kabbalist. His commentaries on the Torah were based on his knowledge of Kabbalah. While it is hard to see how Genesis 1 and 2 can be read as describing the Big Bang, the description of the beginning of our universe in Kabbalah can be read as describing the Big Bang. The Kabbalah is at least as old as the written Torah and some consider it to be part of the Oral Torah given by God at Sinai, along with the Written Torah. Abrams and Primack say that Kabbalah says that at the beginning of our universe, חכמה (wisdom) was "a single creative sparkpoint—an almost vanishingly small capsule of eternal creativity,"[45] and from that point, at the size of a thought, it expanded to the universe that we see now. Richard Friedman, in his book about the divine mystery of the disappearance of God, in a section titled "Big Bang and Kabbalah," summarizes Kabbalah as saying that the creation of our universe takes place within God: "[P]rior to the creation the deity became concentrated into a *point* . . . At a particular moment, for reasons unknown to anyone, this point burst out, forming a group of 10 emanations . . . The emanations from the point, which are called the *Sefirot*, contain all the matter that became the stars, planets, stones, and living things of the universe. The universe expands out from the point and becomes differentiated into all these things."[46]

One of the ways that Kabbalah describes the expansion of our universe is as the result of the wind from a powerful blast of God's wind.[47] This blast of God's wind might come from reading, as Schroeder suggests, Genesis 1:2 as saying

> The earth was unformed and void, and darkness was on the face of the deep. God's wind flew over the face of the waters.

Perhaps, God, the author of Genesis, has written something that was digestible to scientifically naive mankind and that nevertheless gave clues of what really happened that could be understood with both very careful reading and sufficiently advanced scientific knowledge.

More recently, Gerald Schroeder has read Genesis 1 as describing 15.75 billion years of our time as being equivalent to almost six days of God's time.[48] Science tells us that our universe is about 14 billion years old, give or take 4 billion years. Note that about 14 billion minus 5773, the current year on the Hebrew calendar, is still about 14 billion.

To understand Schroeder's argument, it is necessary to understand basic time dilation from relativity. Consider someone sending a marble to you every second. Pretend that there is no friction to slow the marble down; the marble is rolling on a perfectly smooth floor. How much time is there between the arrivals to you of successive marble? The answer, you say, is "one second," and you are correct. Suppose you start moving away from the person sending you the marbles. How much time is there now between the arrivals of successive marbles? The answer, you say, is "I don't know exactly, but certainly *more* than one second," and again you are correct.

Schroeder asks us to imagine God sending a light flash every second since the Big Bang. Since the Big Bang, our universe has been expanding, initially at an extremely and unimaginably fast rate and then slowing down gradually. The flashes arrive not every second, but spaced much *longer* apart. Using the known rates of our universe's expansion, as is shown below, we can calculate that 6 days of seconds as counted by God equals 15.75 billion of our years plus or minus, well within the range of what science believes is the age of our universe.

To answer the question "Why does the Bible use God's days through to the end of day 6?" Schroeder posits that because man did not exist until near the end of day 6, there were no people to establish *our* frame of reference for counting days. From near the end of day 6 onward, the Bible uses people days. Using the known rates of the expansion of our universe God-day-by-God-day, Schroeder determines that:

- the end of God's Day 1 = 8 billion of our years,
- the end of God's Day 2 = 4 billion more of our years,
- the end of God's Day 3 = 2 billion more of our years,
- the end of God's Day 4 = 1 billion more of our years,
- the end of God's Day 5 = .5 billion more of our years, and
- the end of God's Day 6 = .25 billion more of our years,

for a total of 15.75 billion of our years. Schroeder observes that what the Bible says happens on any God-day corresponds remarkably well with what science says happened in the corresponding people-year epoch. According to Schroeder, "They match up close enough to send chills up your spine."[49]

When Genesis says that our universe was created in *a* beginning, what is God trying to tell us? For sure, God is trying to tell us that there were or are multiple creations. Where and when are they? How are they happening? There are at least two possibilities:

1. serially (i.e., one after the other)
2. concurrently (i.e., at overlapping times)

A third possibility is a combination of these two.

Whether multiple creations are happening serially depends on the resolution of a debate over future histories of our universe.[50] To understand this debate, it is necessary to understand that cosmology has determined that our universe has been expanding since the Big Bang at an incredibly fast rate that is now much slower than initially. That is, while the matter within each galaxy is not expanding, the space in which the galaxies sit is expanding. The rate of the slowdown of the expansion is critical in determining the future history of our universe.

Two possible future histories of our universe are as follows:

1. There is enough matter in our universe that gravitational attraction among the matter in our universe will cause the

expansion of our universe to slow down, stop, and begin to contract, leading to what has been called the "Big
Crunch," a singularity like that just before the Big Bang. If
the Big Crunch were to duplicate the singularity that led to
the Big Bang, the Big Crunch could lead to yet another big
bang. Perhaps there is an unending stream of big bangs,
expansions, contractions, and big crunches, that is, serial
multiple creations.

2. There is not enough matter in our universe to lead to a Big
Crunch. While there is enough matter within a galaxy and
within a cluster of galaxies to keep them from expanding,
there is not enough matter in the whole universe to stop and
reverse the expansion that is taking place in the so-called
empty space between clusters of galaxies. Instead, the expansion will slow down, but never stop completely.

If the expansion of our universe continues forever, its stars
will burn out, one at a time. Our entire universe would eventually cool down, in hundreds of billions of years, to its room
temperature, fairly close to absolute zero ($-273.15°C$), to a
state called the "Big Whimper."

Perhaps, in Genesis 1, God is trying to tell us that the first
history is the correct one. Science says that the deciding factor is the amount of matter in our universe: whether there is
enough matter that gravitational attraction between the matter
eventually wins out over the expansion started at the Big Bang.
It appears that the debate is being resolved towards the Big
Whimper, because, using the brains God gave us, we are learning that that there is just not enough matter in our universe to
stop and reverse the expansion.

As this debate is being resolved, cosmology has discovered,
using quantum theory applied to the instant of a big bang, that
there may be concurrent multiple universes. Our universe is just
one of countlessly many universes that have been, are being, and
will be born, each in its own big bang and each with its own laws
of physics that possibly differ from those of ours. Some of these
other universes might end up in a big crunch. Perhaps, this sense
of multiple universes is what God means by our universe being
created in *a* creation and being one of the universes created on the
day it was created.

9. Judaism and Cosmology

The relationship between (1) the first creation narrative and (2) what science knows about the creation of our universe is analogous to the relationship between (1) what parents describe to their young children about from where they came and (2) the full details about sex.

When a child asks his or her parents "Where did I come from?" most parents leave out the messy details of the sex act and explain that "Your mother and father loved each other so much that we wanted to make a baby with whom we could share our love. So your father planted a seed in your mother's egg in her tummy and that began to grow to become you." Note the emphasis on the good of the act and the love. Note also the possible reordering of events to suggest that the making of the baby was a planned event preceded by a decision to have the baby. Some parents tell this love-based description from their embarrassment to describe the details of the sex act and a desire not to reveal that the pregnancy was unplanned, accidental, or even contrary to intentions.

Other parents, such as this author, suffer no embarrassment when describing the details of the sex act. Yet, they too have learned, perhaps the hard way, to tell the love-based description. Most little children are just not ready to even imagine, let alone understand, the details of the sex act. Thus, in any case, the love-based description seems to be at about the right level of detail for little children's understanding. The description's foci are on the making of the child who asked the question "Where did I come from?" and on the idea that the child's birth was *full of love and good.*

In the same way, God's description of the creation of our universe in Genesis 1 is at the right level for people that existed at the time Genesis 1 was written, people with very primitive scientific knowledge. This description focuses (1) on the good that God did in creating the heaven, the earth, and all that are in them and (2) on the creation of the people who were able to ask "Where did I come from?" At the end of each day, God saw that what he had done during the day that just ended was good, and God's final creation was the human. Just as young children are not ready to understand the details of the sex act, early humans were not intellectually ready to understand the Big Bang, modern cosmology, and evolution. So,

God had to give a goodness-based description that leads to the creation of humans, such as what appears in Genesis 1. As humans, using the brains that God gave them, have learned enough about our universe to understand the Big Bang and the current understanding of cosmology, it has become possible to reread Genesis 1 and the Kabbalah and to see that with suitable interpretations of the original Hebrew, Genesis 1 and the Kabbalah may have been describing the Big Bang and modern cosmology after all.[51]

All this science calls to question Judaism's centrality of Earth and man in God's creation. Even if, contrary to our past belief, Earth and man are not central to God's creation, Judaism is for human life on Earth for as long as humans will be around, and it is up to we humans to help ensure, by our behavior, as commanded by the Bible, that Earth remains a hospitable home for humans. As observed by Rabbi Lori Cohen, on reading an earlier draft of this paragraph, just as God saw the work of each day and declared it to be טוב, because we humans are made in God's image, we need to daily evaluate the work of our hands and the words of our mouths, to see if we too can declare them to be good.

We may not be God's only creation. Nevertheless, we are with no less love from God than we thought we had when we thought we were central. Just as a parent loves all of his or her children fully and equally no matter how many he or she has, God loves fully all morally aware creatures no matter how many earths and heavens God has created.

This article is based on and is a significant extension of the author's article titled "Understanding the Beginning of Genesis: Just How Many Beginnings Were There?" in *Jewish Bible Quarterly* 31, no. 2 (2003): 90–93. This article is available for download from http://jbq.jewishbible.org/assets/Uploads/312/312_berry.pdf.

Notes

1. *JPS Hebrew–English Tanakh* תנ״ך (New York: Jewish Publication Society, 1999); J. M. Hoffman, *In the Beginning: A Short History of the Hebrew Language* (New York: NYU Press, 2006).

2. J. H. Hertz, *The Pentateuch and Haftorahs: Hebrew Text English Translation and Commentary* (Brooklyn, NY: Soncino, 1960). Many English translations provided in this article are the author's own. On the other hand, when a translation is claimed to be Jewish traditional, it is coming from the HPH.

3. A. Even-Shoshan, *The New Dictionary: Complete Treasury of the Hebrew Language* (Jerusalem: Kiryat Sefer, 1983), in Hebrew (אברהם אבן־שושן, המלון החדש: אוצר שלם של הלשון העברית, קרית ספר, ירושלים).

4. BlueLetterBible.org, http://www.blueletterbible.org/Bible.cfm?b=Gen&c=1&t=LXX#top (accessed June 1, 2012).

5. Mechon-Mamre.org, "Targum Onkelos M'nukad," in Hebrew (תרגום אונקלוס מנוקד), http://www.mechon-mamre.org/i/t/u/u0101.htm (accessed June 1, 2012).

6. בראשית רבה 1:10 points out that Rabbi Yona said in the name of Rabbi Levi, "Why was the world created with a ב (the first letter of בראשית)? The ב is closed at the sides but is open in front (in the Hebrew writing direction), so you are not permitted to investigate what is above, below, and behind, in particular you are not allowed to know what was before the creation." H. Freedman, "Genesis, Chapter I, Bereshith," in *Midrash Rabbah Genesis*, 3rd ed. (London: Soncino Press, 1983), 1–15; J. Neusner, *Genesis Rabbah: The Judaic Commentary to the Book of Genesis, A New American Translation*, vol. 1 (Atlanta: Scholars Press, 1985).

7. Chabad.org, "The Complete Jewish Bible, With Rashi Commentary, Torah—The Pentateuch Bereishit—Genesis—Chapter 1," http://www.chabad.org/library/bible_cdo/aid/8165/showrashi/true (accessed August 1, 2012); H. M. Orlinsky, "The Plain Meaning of Genesis 1:1–3," *Biblical Archaeologist* 46, no. 4 (1983): 207–9.

8. This translation is the author's, not Rashi's; after all, Rashi did not speak English! As a matter of fact, Richard Elliott Friedman translates Genesis 1:1–3 as "In the beginning of God's creating the skies and the earth—when the earth had been shapeless and formless, and darkness was on the face of the deep, and God's spirit was hovering on the face of the water—God said, 'Let there be light.'" thus combining Genesis 1:1, 2, and 3 into one sentence. R. E. Friedman, *The Bible with Sources Revealed: A New View Into the Five Books of Moses* (San Francisco: HarperOne, 2003); R. Loewe and E. Fox, "Bible, Torah Translations by Jews," in *Encyclopedia Judaica*, 2nd ed., ed. F. Skolnik and M. Berenbaum (Farmington Hills, MI: Thomson Gale, 2007), vol. 3, 624.

9. ראשית appears as a stand-alone noun elsewhere in the Bible (e.g., in Isa. 46:10).

10. Freedman, "Genesis, Chapter I, Bereshith"; Neusner, *Genesis Rabbah*.

11. The HPH translation is "in the day that the Lord God made earth and heaven," and the King James (KJ) translation is "in the day that the LORD God made the earth and the heavens." Each uses "Lord" or "LORD" in place of the Tetragrammaton for God's name that the author's translation shows literally. In addition, the author prefers to translate ביום עשות as "on the day of . . .'s

making," with a possessive preceding the gerund "making" instead of the past tense verb "made," to capture the original's use of the construct form noun עֲשׂוֹת. See Section 6 for a discussion arising from the two "the"s in the KJ translation.

12. The follow-on to this observation of structural similarity deals with the shift from אלהים to יהוה אלהים as the name of God and a shift from impersonal and purely divine justice to human-centric divine justice combined with mercy or compassion. As noted by Friedman, Genesis 1 calls God only אלהים. Friedman, *The Bible with Sources Revealed*. Most of the rest of the Torah calls God only יהוה. Genesis 2 and 3 call God יהוה אלהים, as sort of a transition between the two ways of calling God. See also note 29.

13. See BlueLetterBible.org.

14. *JPS Hebrew–English Tanakh*; R. Loewe and E. Fox, "Bible, Anglo-Jewish Versions," in *Encyclopedia Judaica*, vol. 3, 614.

15. *JPS Hebrew–English Tanakh*.

16. Loewe and Fox, "Bible, Anglo-Jewish Versions."

17. A. T. Levenson, "Ambivalences: Jews and the King James Version," www.bibleinterp.com, *The Bible and Interpretation: In My View Articles*, http://www.bibleinterp.com/opeds/lev358025.shtml (accessed August 1, 2012).

18. *JPS Hebrew–English Tanakh*.

19. D. M. Berry, "Understanding the Beginning of Genesis: Just How Many Beginnings Were There?" *Jewish Bible Quarterly* 31, no. 2 (2003): 90–93, http://jbq.jewishbible.org/assets/Uploads/312/312_berry.pdf.

20. N. E. Abrams and J. R. Primack, "'In a Beginning . . .': Quantum Cosmology and Kabbalah," *Tikkun* 10, no. 1 (January–February 1995): 70.

21. D. C. Matt, *God and the Big Bang: Discovering Harmony between Science and Spirituality* (Woodstock, VT: Jewish Lights Publishing, 1996), 26.

22. Orlinsky, "The Plain Meaning of Genesis 1:1–3." This article contains the clearest translation of Rashi's commentary on Genesis 1:1 that this author has seen.

23. V. Hamilton, *The Book of Genesis: Chapters 1–17* (Grand Rapids, MI: William B. Eerdmans Publishing Co., 1990).

24. M. Engelson, "The First Six Days," *Further Essays from the Author of The Heavenly Time Machine*, http://www.pcez.com/~jmsc/heavenly_tm_essy_6day.html (accessed August 1, 2012).

25. M. Engelson, *The Heavenly Time Machine: Essays on Science and Torah* (Portland, OR: Joint Management Strategy, 2001).

26. R. D. Holmstedt, "The Restrictive Syntax of Genesis i 1," *Vetus Testamentum* 58, no. 4 (2008): 56–67.

27. K. G. Feuerherm, "In the Beginning?" *Combined Religion Program, Canadian Corporation for Studies in Religion* (2009), http://www.new. ccsr.ca/wp-content/uploads/2013/01/combinedprogram2009.pdf.

28. Holmstedt, "The Restrictive Syntax of Genesis i 1," 56.

29. The reversal in order reflects a difference in viewpoints in the two creation narratives. The first creation narrative takes God's viewpoint, is heaven centered, and consequently, "heaven" comes first. The second creation narrative takes Man's viewpoint, is human centered, and consequently, "earth" comes first. Friedman, *The Bible with Sources Revealed*. See also note 12.

30. Hertz, *The Pentateuch and Haftorahs*.

31. T. Ferris, *The Whole Shebang* (New York: Simon & Schuster, 1997); S. W. Hawking, *The Illustrated Theory of Everything: The Origin and Fate of the Universe* (Beverly Hills, CA: Phoenix Books, 2003).

32. C. Miller, *Chumash: The Gutnick Edition—The Book of Genesis* (Brooklyn, NY: Kol Menachem, 2005), 3.

33. P. Cohen and H. Tirosh-Samuelson, "Editors' Introduction: Why Science Matters to Judaism," *CCAR Journal* (Winter 2012): 3–11.

34. The author had written Sections 2–7 and part of Section 9 of this article and was prepared to submit it to this journal when the Winter 2012 issue appeared. He knew that he had to add more to this article to place it into the context established by the articles of the Winter 2012 issue. The result is Section 8.

35. N. M. Samuelson, "The Challenges of the Modern Sciences for Jewish Faith," *CCAR Journal* (Winter 2012): 12–27.

36. V. Z. Frappollo, "Searching for the Quantum God: On Judaism and Modern Science," ibid., 28–49.

37. P. Ochs, "Judaism and Physics," ibid., 58–71.

38. B.S. Artson, "Revisiting Creation, Natural Events, and Their Emergent Patterns," ibid., 72–83.

39. T. Spitzer, "Why We Need Process Theology," ibid., 84–95.

40. A. S. Maller, "A Jewish View of the Evolution of Religion," ibid., 96–110.

41. Matt, *God and the Big Bang*; G. L. Schroeder, *Genesis and the Big Bang* (New York: Bantam Books, 1990).

42. L. Green, "The Case for Science Education in Our Religious Schools," *CCAR Journal* (Winter 2012): 186–93.

43. Schroeder, *Genesis and the Big Bang*, 65.

44. C. B. Chavel, *Ramban, Commentary: Genesis* (New York, NY: Shiloh Publishing House, 1971), 25.

45. Abrams and Primack, "'In a Beginning . . .': Quantum Cosmology and Kabbalah," 70–71.

46. R. E. Friedman, *The Disappearance of God: A Divine Mystery* (Boston: Little, Brown, and Company, 1995), 228–29.

47. Matt, *God and the Big Bang.*

48. Morris Engelson gives yet other calculations that yield various estimates, including 14.23, 15.3, and 16.4 billion years, all in the same neighborhood of what science believes to be the correct age of 13.7 billion years. Engelson, *The Heavenly Time Machine.*

49. G. L. Schroeder, "The Age of the Universe," http://www.aish.com/ci/sam/48951136.html (accessed August 1, 2012). On the other hand, Friedman criticizes Gerald Schroeder for not being sufficiently trained in biblical Hebrew grammar and having thought that two Hebrew words that happen to begin with the same two letters share a root. Friedman, *The Disappearance of God.* This mistake has nothing to do with Schroeder's arguments about God's time and the mapping of God's first six days to billions of people years. In any case, the discrepancies between the biblical and scientific accounts can be chalked up to the former's use of an abstraction designed to be absorbed by early humans and which is slightly fudged to emphasize the goodness of the events, as is discussed in Section 9 of this article.

50. Ferris, *The Whole Shebang*; S. W. Hawking, *A Brief History of Time,* 10th anniversary ed. (Toronto: Bantam Books, 1998); Hawking, *The Illustrated Theory of Everything*; S. W. Hawking and L. Mlodinow, *The Grand Design* (New York: Bantam Books, 2010).

51. In an attempt to answer why the cosmological Big Bang and Kabbalah agree so much, Friedman says, "God is not pictured in [Kabbalah] as creating a world on a table before him the way a carpenter makes a chair. The creation is a process that occurs within God." Friedman, *The Disappearance of God,* 228. Friedman adds, "Kabbalah conceives of . . . a God who inheres in the universe . . . In the Kabbalistic conception, God is in the universe (and the universe is in God)." Ibid., 242. Friedman suggests a possible explanation of the similarity between Kabbalah's and modern science's conceptions of the origins of our universe is that "*given* that humans are part and parcel of the cosmos, the way in which the universe formed is part of our own composition and experience... To the extent that the universe still reverberates with the Big Bang, it reverberates in all beings; and those beings with the furthest developed state of consciousness—which on this planet includes humans—may be capable of being in touch with that part of our formation: through tools of the intellect if they are cosmologists . . . through tools of mysticism if they are Kabbalists." Ibid., 245.

On the other hand, it could be that God, through direct authorship or inspiring human authors, was planting clues about the truth of how our universe was made in the Written and Oral Torah, in the Bible and in Kabbalah, that would be finally understood for what it really means when our human knowledge and understanding had advanced enough to figure the truth out.

The Garden of Eden: Peeling Back the Layers to Reveal the Simplicity of the Story

Michael D. Oblath

"A myth has never happened, but it happens every day"
—Gaius Sallustius Crispus

The Garden of Eden story of Genesis 2:4–3:24 is a biblical narrative with which many are familiar. The story has been examined and discussed innumerable times; the literature is vast. There are many Genesis commentaries filled with discussions about the meaning of "knowledge" in its various permutations. Many comment about the "temptations" of the snake and the weakness of Adam and Eve, or perhaps, in a better order, Eve and Adam. In fact, this story has been investigated, evaluated, interpreted, and taught in sectarian and secular settings. And, in many ways, it remains a perplexing dilemma. When I was working on my doctorate at UC Berkeley, my Sumerian professor made a comment along the lines of, "Why do you want to work in Hebrew Bible; everything has already been done there." Not necessarily. The Garden of Eden has always tempted me to continue pursuing this text. I have always striven to try and analyze the story at a very "basic" level, if possible.

Yes, the Garden story is very familiar to us. Our familiarity is, however, influenced and prejudiced by our various religious traditions. Seldom are we able to separate the snake from canonical preconceptions of trickery, evil, and cunning. We are conditioned to understand the Tree of the Knowledge of Good and Evil as simply the Tree of Knowledge. This alters our own knowledge of the meaning of the Hebrew text and the story itself. Frequently,

MICHAEL D. OBLATH (C78) is adjunct professor of Hebrew Bible at Alaska Pacific University and rabbi of Congregation Beth Sholom, Anchorage, Alaska. He received his Ph.D. in Ancient Near Eastern Religions from the University of California and Graduate Theological Union, in Berkeley, California, in 2001.

we comprehend God's role in the story as that of an omnipotent and omniscient deity, when the story itself limits that perception. Moreover, and perhaps with the greatest negative influence, we teach the story as one that explains the origin of inescapable sin in the world, with blame and responsibility falling firmly on the female of our species.[1]

What I am suggesting is support of one particular analysis that has been pushed, sometimes perhaps mockingly, into the background. We too quickly cast aside the primary mythological presentation of the carnal imagery and power of the Tree of the Knowledge of Good and Evil.[2]

Nevertheless, a careful reading of the Hebrew text, by itself or in comparison with ancient Near Eastern literature, reveals a beautiful mythological story of origins and human development. We enter the mind, history, and culture of ancient Israel and comprehend how they viewed several essentials of human life and growth from three thousand years ago.

So, to a quick review of the story: *YHVH* plants a garden in Eden, creates a man from the dust of the earth, and puts him in the garden. The man is to till the soil and cause the vegetation to grow. An interesting aside: The Hebrew used to describe the tilling of the soil, לעבד את־האדמה, is the same used to describe what the man does when expelled from the Garden. The only difference seems to be that in the consequences that *YHVH* lists in "cursing" the man, he will sweat more when he is doing the same thing he did inside the Garden. It does not seem to be all that much of a punishment. Anyway, *YHVH* has also planted two, fully grown trees in the Garden: the Tree of Life and the Tree of the Knowledge of Good and Evil. The powers of these mythical trees are not evident to us until later in the story.

Now, *YHVH* commands the man not to eat of the Tree of the Knowledge of Good and Evil, for if he does eat of it, he will die. "Dying" is not explained at this point. We do not know if this is immediate, drop-down-dead dying or postponed-to-a-later-time dying. Interestingly, *YHVH* hides this information until the end of the story.

Meanwhile, *YHVH* does notice that the man needs a companion. He creates all the animals, bringing them to the man so that he may name them. Their presence, however, does not bring companionship to the man, so *YHVH* creates another human from the man's side (or rib).

At some time later, the woman encounters a snake at the Tree of the Knowledge of Good and Evil. Within their dialogue, the snake convinces her that she will not die if she eats the fruit. As with *YHVH*, the snake does not explain the type of death involved. He does, however, explain more than *YHVH* had, noting that they will become like gods, knowing good and evil.

So, she eats and gives the fruit to the man to eat; their eyes are opened and they realize they are naked. Being then bashful, they hide when they hear *YHVH* walking in the garden. *YHVH*, in one of the best double-takes in theater, reasons it out that they have eaten from the Tree of the Knowledge of Good and Evil and lists the consequences for their actions, dealing with the snake first, then the woman, and then the man. He then evicts them from the Garden of Eden, for they have indeed become like the gods. Nevertheless, instead of preventing their further access to this particular tree, the text notes specifically that *YHVH* sets up a permanent guard against access to the Tree of Life. Thus, the humans are prevented from maintaining their immortality, revealing the purpose to us of that particular tree.

Within this story there are several features that reveal the author's meaning(s). This intent may be determined through the investigation of three issues:

1. The reason for the eviction.
2. The result of eating from the tree.
3. What it means to be equal to God.

The Eviction

A simple reading of the story, in 3:22–23, clearly states the reason for the eviction: "And *YHVH Elohim* said, 'Now that the man has become like one of us, knowing good and evil, what if he should stretch out his hand and take also from the Tree of Life and eat, and live forever?' So, *YHVH Elohim* banished him from the Garden of Eden." The reason? The humans had become like the gods. The snake was, therefore, correct.

The Eating

But, what is it that happens when they eat from the tree? They are supposed to die. A careful look at the language and text of the story is revealing. In 2:17 *YHVH* tells the man that he will die if he eats the fruit of the Tree of the Knowledge of Good and Evil. He apparently accepts this, but we do not at all have any sense as to the exact meaning of *YHVH*'s words, nor do we have any sense at all if the man has an awareness of what *YHVH* is telling him. As mentioned before, will the man drop dead immediately or will he eventually die sometime later in his life? We do not know at this time.

But, at the same time, *YHVH*'s vague consequence serves to highlight the drama to come in the conversation between the woman and the snake. For, the snake presents the argument that they will not die. As readers, we think that both *YHVH* and the snake are correct, but as they are both not revealing the entirety of truth, they are both, perhaps intentionally, being deceptive. That deception helps build the tension leading to the eviction.

As well, one may ask a speculative question or two: Is the snake being deceptive? After all, he lives in the Garden; he knows the two humans are immortal. What would make him think that death, therefore, has anything to do with the eating of this "forbidden fruit"? He does not know that *YHVH* must maintain the distinction between the gods and humans. In other words, eating this fruit requires they must leave the Garden.

As a relevant aside, in 2:19–20 the man is given a rather interesting and revealing task. Within the context of the ancient Near Eastern world, these verses take on a new meaning. He is told to name the animals. *YHVH* would bring an animal to the man. First, he would consider it, and then give it a name. In keeping with ancient Near Eastern traditions, in order to do this, the man, thus, had to be able to recognize the inner essence of the animal, to know its core being. This, in turn, implies a certain level of wisdom on the man's part.[3] And further, this awareness, on our part, challenges the generally accepted interpretations of the Tree of the Knowledge of Good and Evil as a source of human wisdom.

The man even continues his naming process after *YHVH* creates the woman from his side/rib. The text reads, in verses 22–23:

ויבן יהוה אלהים את הצלע אשר־לקח מן־האדם לאשה ויבאה
אל־האדם: ויאמר האדם זאת הפעם עצם מעצמי ובשר מבשרי לזאת
יקרא אשה כי מאיש לקחה־זאת

And *YHVH Elohim* built the rib/side, which He had taken from the man, into a woman. Then He brought her to the man. And the man said, "This, now, is bone of my bone and flesh of my flesh. This will be called woman for from a man was this one taken."

Having been presented this final animal to name, the man responds with a positive recognition that at last, he has met his "help meet." His comment is, essentially, "This is the female of the species. I am the male (אִישׁ) and this is the female (אִשָּׁה)." In other words, "This is the feminine human and I am the masculine human." Then there follows the parenthetical statement (from the author) that humans get married in a particular way. It is not a reference to the man and woman engaging in sexual intercourse.

Here, the text presents us with the mythological origin of human marriage. As a mythological tale, the story is one of origins and natural events. This is clear from the "punishments" brought to bear against the man, woman, and snake. It is also clear from the presence of other aspects of mythology: the presence of magical trees in this garden, the source of the world's four great rivers, and it contains an animal and a deity that can walk and talk with humans.[4]

Nevertheless, following the creation and identification of the female, the text does note that they were naked and not bashful or shy, in verse 25:

ויהיו שניהם ערומים האדם ואשתו ולא יתבששו

And the two of them were naked, the man and his female, and they were not bashful.

This is critical, as the story immediately follows with the phrase, in 3:1:

והנחש היה ערום מכל חית השדה אשר עשה יהוה אלהים

And the snake was more *arum* than any creature of the field that *YHVH Elohim* had made.

This immediate repetition of the word *arum* is a word play on the state of *arum* in which the male and female existed. This word, in reference to the snake, is usually translated as "subtle," "cunning," or perhaps even "conniving." Nevertheless, regardless of the later religious interpretations of this entire story, there seems to be no justification for that understanding. Even given the other occurrences of *arum* that are translated as meaning "subtle" or "cunning," it is likely that these translations are based solely on the canonical interpretations of the Eden story. All uses of *arum* in the Hebrew Bible are easily understood within the semantic field of "naked."[5]

As difficult as this passage might be, we must start with the clear play on the preceding reference to the male and female. They were naked and not embarrassed. Thus, the snake must initially be viewed as "naked among the other animals" or "the most naked of the animals." But it is clear that these translations do not seem to make a great deal of sense.

Nevertheless, within the semantic field of "naked" we may suggest any number of possibilities, the least of which, if at all, should be "cunning" or "subtle." I would suggest, however, translations along the lines of "exposed," "open," "up-front," "revealed," or, more probably, "honest." It is within that context that we must understand the introduction of the snake in the story.

The snake's honesty is made clear in a correct reading of the conversation with the female. His comment to her, in 3:1, is:

ויאמר אל־האשה אף כי־אמר אלהים לא תאכלו מכל עץ הגן

and is usually translated as a question:

> And he said to the woman, "Has God indeed said that you shall not eat from every tree in the garden?"

With this question from the snake, it has been understood that he is trying to throw the female off balance and trick her into answering incorrectly. But it is essential to understand the two key elements in this statement. The first is אף כי, usually translated as a leading indicator of a question in this verse. It occurs twenty-four times in the Hebrew Bible and never introduces a question, except, supposedly, here.[6] The other occurrences carry the meaning "even so" or "thus," the exact translation depending on context.

The second key word is מכל. In its usage in the Hebrew Bible the most common meaning is "from all" or "from any."[7] Therefore, the snake speaks to the female, saying:

> Thus has God said, "you cannot eat from every (of every) tree in the Garden."

This is, in keeping with the label of *arum* as "honest," a true statement. The snake's point is not to trick her/them into eating, but rather to convince her/them that God has not told them the entire truth. She responds truthfully, but with an additional comment (3:3):

> The female said to the snake . . . God said, "You shall not eat of the fruit . . . nor shall you touch it, or you shall die."

On Becoming Equal

The snake's point is then made (verse 4):

> You will not die; for God knows that when you eat of it your eyes will be opened, and you will be like the gods (or God), knowing good and evil.

Again, the snake (like *YHVH*) is perhaps not as revealing of Truth's totality. But his point is to clarify *YHVH*'s concern that the humans not be like God. The snake knows that eating of the Tree of the Knowledge of Good and Evil will render them like the gods. As stated previously, he also knows that eating from the Tree of Life renders them immortal, hence, "You will not die."

It has long been taught that what is occurring here is a separation of humanity from God, perhaps even a spiritual separation. This story is not concerned with this, or with the later religious intention of reducing this separation and returning to the Garden. It is, rather, a story of *YHVH* insisting that humans and gods remain distinct from each other. They can be friends, but not equal friends. Even in the Garden, this distinction is absolutely clear.

So, what does happen when they eat from the tree? The only thing that occurs, the immediate effect of eating the tree's fruit is stated in verse 7:

ותפקחנה עיני שניהם וידעו כי עירמם הם

> Then the eyes of both were opened, and they knew that they were naked.

All else that follows after this statement is only a consequence of knowing they were naked. Embarrassment, shame, and hiding are not direct results of eating the fruit. The **only** effect of the tree was to make them aware they were naked.

So, what is this tree? The text calls it the Tree of the Knowledge of Good and Evil. We tend, throughout our religious traditions, historically, and even today, to refer to this tree as the Tree of Knowledge, period. Thus we ascribe to it all varieties of knowledge: morality, ethics, divine knowledge, science, wisdom, etc. And it is easy to see why we can reach these conclusions, for "knowledge" is a broad subject, including all of those wonderful things that we, as humans, might comprehend and thus label as "knowledge."[8]

Nevertheless, the tree's meaning is much more narrowly defined in the story. It is never referred to as, simply, the Tree of Knowledge. It is only called the Tree of the Knowledge of Good and Evil. Why? Because the grammar of the name does not allow any other reading. The Hebrew name עץ הדעת טוב ורע being in construct form, cannot be split into individual parts.

But, what does the "knowledge of good and evil" (דעת טוב ורע) actually mean? Obviously, this tree gives the "knowledge of good and evil," but what is that? The phrase, "knowing good and evil" appears to be idiomatic. It occurs only a few times in the biblical text: in Deuteronomy 1:39, II Samuel 19:35–36, and here in Genesis. Even so, the meaning is clear from the context of all three passages:

Deuteronomy: And as for your little ones . . . your small children, who today do not *know good and evil* . . .

II Samuel: But Barzilai said to the king, "How many years have I still to live, that I should go up with the king to Jerusalem. Today I am eighty years old; can I *know good and evil*? Can your servant taste what he eats or what he drinks? Can I still listen to the voice of singing men and women?"

Genesis: ". . . when you eat of it . . . you will be like the gods, *knowing good and evil* . . . Then the eyes of both were opened, and they knew that they were naked . . ." [my italics]

So, what is it that little children do not yet have, that Barzilai has lost, and that the two humans acquired by knowing they were naked? The knowledge that the male and female acquire from the tree is carnal knowledge, the awareness of their nakedness, the awareness of their sexuality. The tree, plain and simple, gives them the ability to create, and they thus, in *YHVH*'s own words, become equal to the gods. They are able, for the first time, to create.

Prior to eating from the tree, they were naked and not bashful. After eating, they need to dress, for they are embarrassed by their nakedness. The stage in life, through which one passes, which is described by that Garden of Eden event, is puberty. The Tree of the Knowledge of Good and Evil represents puberty, pure and simple.

And *YHVH*'s response? In the eyes of the biblical Israelite that wrote the story, they are punished for doing what they did. In actuality, the list of "punishments" reads more like a list of "these are the consequences for doing what you have done." At no time in the story do we read that they have committed a sin. As with mythological tales that explain origins and natural events, the consequences of eating the fruit of the Tree of the Knowledge of Good and Evil are first, the humans are able to create descendants, introducing childbirth and responsibilities of family. As humans, they have become (but yet, they cannot be) equal to the gods. Thus, *YHVH* must take away access to the Tree of Life. They then become mortal. Therefore, they will eventually die.

As indicated above, once humans eat from the Tree of the Knowledge of Good and Evil, we move ourselves out of the Garden. Given this, we also understand why Adam and Eve are prohibited access to the Tree of Life. Once one has passed through puberty, one cannot return to the other side. Because the boy and the girl ate from the Tree of the Knowledge of Good and Evil, so do we. We eat of its fruit because they did. It is a mythological tale and in a certain, intriguing sense, if they had not eaten the fruit, we would not be here. In the author's context and mind, we **are** here, so therefore it was necessary for them to eat from that tree.

In addition, perhaps one of the most perplexing religious concepts has been the subjugation of women to the unenviable position of the one that introduced sin into the world. She does not do this. She eats first because the ancient Israelites recognized a common, easily observed, physiological pattern and inserted it into the story. Girls, in general, enter puberty before boys. They eat from the tree first.

Sin has nothing to do with this story; not unless puberty is considered a sin. In the author's view, if *YHVH* had not created humanity to populate the world, He would not have planted that particular tree in the Garden. In a sense, His will was for the male and female to leave the Garden of Eden. He wanted the world populated. For the world to be populated, the male and female had to leave the Garden. They were only doing what God wanted in the first place. Where is there sin in doing God's will?

Finally, I would like to suggest an interesting theological speculation. It is worth considering the roles played by *YHVH* and the snake in this story, especially pertaining to the topic of death.

Let us evaluate the snake's perspective first. We might be able to surmise that, since the snake knows what the Tree of the Knowledge of Good and Evil is all about, he also knows what the Tree of Life is all about. He therefore knows that these two humans are immortal. So, without an awareness of *YHVH*'s reaction and imposed consequences, his statement to the female is absolutely true. They will not die, but merely acquire the ability to create and thus become equal with God. The snake is, within the context he knows, absolutely honest, and correct.

God, on the other hand, knows that they can also eat from the Tree of Life, knows as well that if they eat from the Tree of the Knowledge of Good and Evil they will become equal with God. Why put the tree there in the first place, if not to have them eat from it? Or, as perhaps with Job, God is really the one doing the tempting. And anyway, with all that, He still tells them that they will die. He reveals neither the entire truth nor the immediate consequences; what's an eight-year-old to know? God thus appears to be much more manipulative and much less honest than the snake.

Nevertheless, this is an ancient story, written within the context of many other ancient Near Eastern creation myths and tales. It is a particular Israelite perspective. And, it has been covered over the centuries with layer upon layer of religious interpretations that have hindered and muddied our ability to see its beauty and depth. And, no, it never happened, and yet our lives bear witness to the realization that it happens every day.

This paper was originally delivered at the Society of Biblical Literature International Meeting, July 1, 2009, in Rome, Italy.

Notes

1. J. Eckstein, "The Fall and Rise of Man," *Journal for the Scientific Study of Religion* 5, no. 1 (1965): 71–72. W. E. Phipps, *Genesis and Gender* (New York: Praeger, 1989), 26–35. For a very thorough explanation and review of the vast amount of literature regarding the Garden story (even as long ago as 1987), please refer to

C. Westermann, *Genesis 1–11: A Commentary* (Minneapolis, MN: Augsberg Publishing House, 1987): 178–278. Also, refer to A. J. Bledstein, "Are Women Cursed in Genesis 3.16," in *A Feminist Companion to Genesis,* ed. A. Brenner (FCB 2; Sheffield: Sheffield Academic Press, 1993); A. Brenner, *The Intercourse of Knowledge: On Gendering Desire and "Sexuality" in the Hebrew Bible* (Biblical Interpretations Series 26; Leiden: Brill, 1997); J. N. Lohr, "Sexual Desire? Eve, Genesis 3:16, and תשוקה," *Journal of Biblical Literature* 130 (2011): 227–46.

2. Westermann, *Genesis,* 243.

3. Ezek. 28:12–13. Although possibly deriving from a different Eden tradition, this passage would indicate recognition that humanity was wise in the Garden.

4. While given the many writings that have been offered regarding the subject of mythology, I would strongly recommend the reader refer to the well-presented text by Frankfort: H. and H. A. Frankfort, *The Intellectual Adventure of Ancient Man* (Chicago: The University of Chicago Press, 1946).

5. Gen. 3:1; I Sam. 19:24; 23:22; Isa. 20:2–4; 58:7; Ezek. 16:7, 22; Amos 2:16; Job 5:12; 15:5; 22:6; 24:7, 10; 26:6; Prov. 12:16, 23; 13:16; 14:8; 22:3; 27:12; Eccl. 5:14.

6. Deut. 31:27; I Sam. 14:30; 21:6; 23:3; II Sam. 4:11; 16:11; I Kings 8:27; II Kings 5:13; Ezek. 14:21; 15:5; 23:40; Hab. 2:5; Prov. 11:31; 15:11; 17:7; 19:7; 21:27; Job 9:14; 15:16; 25:6; 35:14; Neh. 9:18; II Chron. 6:18; 32:15.

7. Two clear examples are Gen. 6:19–20 and Gen. 31:37.

8. Another earlier positive interpretation of this story was offered by Eckstein, "Fall and Rise." He proposed that the "fall of man" was actually a "rise of man." The eating of the fruit from the Tree of the Knowledge of Good and Evil was a mythological representation of the *very* much earlier evolution of an upright stance in humans. It is a fascinating psychological argument, yet to me lacks a discussion and analysis of what "they knew they were naked" actually means in the text. When considered in relation to the end of Genesis 2, it is clear that there is an obvious juxtaposition of the two states of physical nakedness. Therefore, the awareness that they gain of this nakedness must have primary meaning to this story. Westermann, *Genesis,* 242–48. H. Gunkel, *Genesis* (Macon, GA: Mercer University Press, 1997): 10–31. Although Gunkel comes close to identifying puberty as the function of the tree (p. 29), he avoids the sexual indication. Rather, he prefers to see "judgment" as the knowledge gained. D. Rudman, "A Little Knowledge is a Dangerous Thing—Crossing Forbidden Boundaries in Gen 3–4," in *Studies in the Book of Genesis,* ed. A. Wénin (Leuven: Leuven University Press, 2001), 461–66.

The Binding of Isaac (A Different Version)

Mordecai Roshwald

Before reading the following text the reader is advised to carefully peruse Genesis 18:17–33 and 22:1–19.

Preface

One day—on the eve of a freezing evening, to be exact—I found on my desk the story of the Binding of Isaac (*Akeidat Yitzhaq*) (Gen. 22:1–19), actually a different version of the story, which is reproduced here in English translation.

How the few pages reached my desk and where they came from I do not know. Perhaps I have forgotten this detail, or maybe I have suppressed such details for reasons that the psychologists eagerly try to uncover. As far as I am concerned, it is the new story itself that matters, while its sojourn for many generations— or even a couple of millennia—in a hidden place does not interest me at all. Such circumstantial details are but a protective shell hiding a new meaning—indeed, a new revelation—which is the essence of the tale.

This new version of the famous story, which has probably been a part of the daily morning prayer for centuries, exceeds the confines of place and time, as it ascends into the sphere of absolute truths, the truths of religion, ethics, philosophy, or their combination.

Truths of this kind—whether hidden in the Dead Sea Scrolls or hibernating in the Cairo *genizah*, whether pronounced in Jerusalem or heard in Athens, whether dormant in an ancient scroll or awakening in the mind of an anonymous writer in our times—invite the reader to ponder and reflect, and to pass his or her own judgment.

MORDECAI ROSHWALD is professor emeritus at the University of Minnesota in Minneapolis. He has also taught in universities in Israel, the United Kingdom, Canada, and Taiwan. He has an M.A. (1942) and Ph.D. (1947) in Philosophy from the Hebrew University in Jerusalem, where he was a student of Martin Buber and Leon Roth.

The New Version of the Binding of Isaac

And it happened after these things, that God tested Abraham and said unto him, Abraham! And he said, Here I am.

And He said: Take thy son, thine only son, whom thou lovest, and get thee into the land of Moriah, and there raise him for a burnt offering on one of the mountains that I will tell thee.

And Abraham heard the word of God, but believed not in what his ears perceived. He stood dumb and opened not his mouth for a moment that could not be measured, for it became crowded with thoughts chasing each other with the speed of lightning.

Finally he opened his mouth and cried in a voice of vigor: O God, my God! Is it Thou that callest me? Dost Thou not remember that when Thou hast told me of Thy resolve to destroy Sodom and Gomorrah in order to punish the evil people there, it occurred to me that perhaps there were fifty righteous men in the city and I said: That be far from Thee to do after this manner, to slay the righteous with the wicked, and that the righteous should be as the wicked (cf. Gen. 18:25).

I was afraid that Thou mayest kill me, for I am but dust and ashes, and Thou livest for ever. Yet I reminded Thee: Shall not the Judge of all the earth do the right judgment? (ibid.).

For Thine is the might and Thou pursuest justice, and the way for my progeny on earth is to walk in Thy ways and learn to distinguish between righteousness and iniquity, between good and evil.

And, indeed, Thou hast not killed even one righteous man in Sodom, and Lot and his wife and their daughters were taken out of the city in time.

But now Thou hast changed Thy countenance. Thou tellest me to take my son, who hath not sinned and hath not done evil, and make him an offering to Thee. An innocent will be slaughtered and his father will be the slayer. An act of horror on divine order! Did Satan incite Thee? Hast Thou forsaken the path of righteousness and chosen the way of evil?

Didst Thou not tell Cain, who had killed his brother Abel, "cursed art thou by the earth, which opened its mouth to soak thy brother's blood" (Gen. 4:11). Hast Thou not proclaimed for ages to come, "Whosoever sheddeth man's blood, by man his blood shall be shed"? (Gen. 9:6). But now, He who said all that decideth that I have to murder my own son.

Indeed, on my way from Ur Casdim to the land of Canaan, and when I walked along its length and breadth, I saw the people of the land pass their sons and daughters through fire, human sacrifices to gods of wood and stone, deeds that my soul abhorred. But now Thou demandest that I follow in the ways of the peoples that know Thee not and call not out to Thee?

No, my God, I will not follow Thy command. Maybe Thou art another god, not the God I had known. For a god who commandeth to kill the innocents is a god of evil!

I will not obey Thee. I will watch over my son, Isaac, whom I love with all my heart and all my soul and all my might. I will protect him from Thee and from whoever threatenth him.

And Abraham concluded his speech, while standing before God, waiting for His word or for His punishment, but firm in his resolve to protect Isaac.

God's answer sounded promptly. Blessed art thou, Abraham, for thou speakest words of truth. When I asked thee to sacrifice Isaac on one of the mounts, I asked not for his life and I would not have allowed thee to sacrifice him. I wished only to test thee and see whether thou art the Abraham who worrieth about the righteous in Sodom and Gomorrah, the Abraham who loveth his fellow humans and ardently pursueth justice. I was afraid you might have grown old and were no more faithful to your own self and to me.

Hadst thou tried to fulfill My request, I would have removed thee from My heart's concerns and would not have kept My covenant with thee to make thy progeny a chosen people and a holy nation.

Yet, Abraham, thou hast passed the test. Thy vitality hath not vanished and thy spirit hath not collapsed. Thou hast not changed and thy spirit did not stumble. Just as thou hadst cared for the well-being of the righteous, who were not found in Sodom, thou showest concern for thy son, Isaac, without fear and tremor before God who pretendeth to be an evil and cruel being.

A covenant binds us and will continue as long as thy descendants obey My guidance and keep My ways, to do justice and judgment (Gen. 18:19). Be blessed thou and thy children, and by thy seed may all the nations of the earth be blessed (Gen. 22:18).

Throwaway Women: Ruth as Response

David J. Zucker

Introduction

Too often in the biblical period women were treated as "throwaway" characters. Male voices far outnumber those of women's, and men are about ten times more likely to be named in the Bible than are women.[1] In that sense the Book of Ruth is exceptional, for it places women in a very prominent position. Nonetheless, on the face of it, Naomi and Ruth have limited status within the community. With good reason Naomi says, "Call me Mara . . . for [God] has made my lot very bitter" (Ruth 1:20). Even earlier she had said that the hand of God had struck out against her. Naomi and Ruth are dependent upon societal mores to eke out their living. As vulnerable widows they need to take advantage of the Deuteronomic legislation that allows them to glean in the fields following the harvest (Ruth 2:2; Deut. 24:17–22).

We cannot *know* what were the intentions of the author of Ruth; consequently this analysis may be a kind of modern midrash, projecting twenty-first-century sensibilities on the ancient text. Yet, this article suggests how the author of the Book of Ruth apparently consciously connects and contrasts its narrative, and in particular its conclusion, to two early episodes in the Bible where women are treated as dispensable characters,[2] even though in its present form, the "tale of Ruth is purged of the many unseemly elements of the two previous"[3] narratives. These incidents found in Genesis are the stories of Judah and Tamar (Genesis 38) and Lot and his daughters (Genesis 19). "Such intertextual links are not mere niceties"[4] but a deliberate

DAVID J. ZUCKER, Ph.D. (C70) recently retired as rabbi/chaplain at Shalom Park, a senior continuum of care center, Aurora, Colorado. His latest books will be published this year: *The Bible's PROPHETS: An Introduction for Christians and Jews,* as well as *The Bible's WRITINGS: An Introduction for Christians and Jews* (Wipf and Stock, 2013). He publishes in a variety of areas. See his website, www.DavidJZucker.org. He wishes to thank Moshe Reiss, Julie W. Dahl, Jolain R. Graf, Martin S. Cohen, and the unnamed reviewer for reading this manuscript in an earlier form and offering wise suggestions.

decision to link together the three stories. In each of those cases the father (father-in-law) regards his daughters (daughter-in-law) as expendable. These are tales of crass and immoral behavior in their own right, and additionally each leads to incest. The Book of Ruth suggests a response, that men in authority should protect the vulnerable and look after their welfare. In the way that the Book of Ruth is crafted, by virtue of their union, Boaz not only rescues Ruth from widowhood and provides her with an heir, he also redeems the history of their two families, his own and that of Ruth. He offers redress for past improprieties. Through this device the book's author rewrites wrongs.

The book probably was written late in the biblical corpus.[5] While this is a matter of some debate between scholars, whether or not Ruth is Exilic or post-Exilic is less an issue than that the author knew of the stories of Lot and his daughters and Judah and Tamar.

Lot and Judah

In the concluding verses of Genesis 19, Lot with his two virgin daughters is dwelling in a cave in the hill country. The girls, believing that the three of them are the only living beings on earth, get their father sufficiently inebriated so that each in her turn lays with him in order to get pregnant. Although abhorrent as an act of incest, their goal was to see that humanity would not cease to exist. For this act of incest they are roundly condemned. What is often neglected is the fact that prior to this, while still in Sodom, Lot was more than willing to betray his parental responsibility to protect the honor, and perhaps the very lives, of his own innocent daughters. He willingly offered them as playthings, as sexual objects to the depraved citizens of Sodom in place of Lot's visitors. "Look, I have two daughters who have not known a man. Let me bring them out to you, and you may do to them as you please; but do not do anything to these men" (Gen. 19:8). Lot treats his daughters as throwaway characters. They are dispensable commodities, free to discard in order to preserve his own sense of personal honor. These women are so marginalized that (unlike Tamar in chapter 38) there is no reference to their actual names. Nahum Sarna writes that while there is no explicit condemnation for the actions of the two girls in the biblical text, "their anonymity implies censure."[6] Being so belittled by their father, and having no mother present to offer perspective or counsel, in their lack of self-regard, they are both willing to pervert society's mores for the very purpose of furthering Lot's seed. The chapter concludes with the incestuous birth of Moab, the eponymous ancestor of the Moabites, and Ben-ammi, the eponymous ancestor of the Ammonites. The reference to these children is meant as a slur on Israel's nearby tribal cousins: They each are the product of an incestuous union. Years later another child will be born, for Ruth is a Moabite.

Genesis 38 centers on Judah and his family. Judah marries a local Canaanite woman, Bat Shua. In time they have three sons, Er, Onan, and Shelah. Judah takes a wife for his firstborn, Tamar. Er however, is wicked in God's sight and so God put him to death. Then Onan, Er's next younger brother refuses to properly perform the role of *levir/ yibom* (brother-in-law), for he withdraws early during intercourse spilling his seed. Onan wishes to protect his own inheritance rights. This is displeasing to God, who then puts Onan to death. Judah then tells Tamar to return to her father's house, to await the time when the third son, Shelah, will be of age to marry her. Judah, however, has no intention of letting this come about. He turns his back on her and ignores Tamar's "unmarried and un-marriageable" state of affairs. He procrastinates and does nothing to resolve the issue in a forthright manner. Instead of perhaps returning Tamar's dowry, he leaves his daughter-in-law both literally and figuratively in a no-man's land. Technically she is betrothed to Shelah. She is virtually without options open to her. Similar to Lot's attitude towards his daughters, for Judah, Tamar is likewise a throwaway character. He feels no need to do anything to resolve her—and by extension his—problem. Tamar then acts on her own to find a solution to her dilemma. When it is reported to Judah that she is pregnant, and obviously not by Shelah, Judah is delighted. He imagined that this unresolved, and in his thinking, irresolvable problem would now go away. Judah's response is immediate: "Bring her out and let her be burned." Yet this is not to be, for Tamar proves who the father is. To his credit, Judah does have the decency to say, "She is more in the right than I." Nonetheless, the result is the incestuous birth of Perez and Zerah, and Perez is Boaz's ancestor.

Ruth, Genesis 38, and Genesis 19: Parallels

In order for people to understand that Boaz's marrying Ruth wiped out the stain of their respective families, the author of the

Book of Ruth may have clearly and consciously connected this book with the earlier episodes in Genesis.[7] Consequently there are many themes that appear in Ruth, which were found previously in Genesis 38 and Genesis 19. To cite but one example, which shall be elaborated upon below, in all three stories, a "father or father-figure becomes responsible for the perpetuation of the family, although the initiative in all three narratives is taken by the widow/daughter herself who secretly or by guile offers herself to the 'father.'"[8] The ancient hearers and readers of Ruth were meant to make these connections.

Broad Outline: Leaving Home; No Spouse; Locale; Need to Become Pregnant

In broad outline, in both Ruth and Genesis 38 and 19, a particular family moves away from kin and establishes a new home elsewhere. Elimelech, Naomi, and their sons leave Judah for Moab (a not too subtle reference to both of those ancestors). Judah leaves his kin behind and moves to Adullam. Lot and his daughters leave Sodom for the hill country. At this new locale, two sons (Chilion and Mahlon, and in the case of Judah, Er and Onan), marry local women (woman), but then those sons die, leaving behind widow(s). Lot's daughters, too, are without living spouses; they are in net effect, widowed.

In these narratives, all or a significant part of the action takes place away from the traditional land holdings of Israel.

A central theme, one that connects the characters of Ruth, Tamar, and Lot's daughters, is that a woman seeks a way to become pregnant to ensure protection for herself and to carry on the family line. She achieves this goal using an unconventional method. Ruth (at Naomi's urging) goes down to the threshing floor and offers herself to Boaz; Tamar successfully disguises herself as a ritual prostitute (k'deishah) in order to lay with her father-in-law; and Lot's daughters, believing themselves to be the last humans on earth, get their father drunk and then lay with him.

Spousal Death; Lack of a Viable Spouse

In each case, in the Book of Ruth, as earlier in Genesis 38 and 19, a central character's longtime spouse dies: Naomi's husband, Elimelech; Judah's wife, Bat Shua; and Lot's unnamed wife. Although the details differ, in all three narratives, it is the lack of a viable spouse that serves as the catalyst for action.

Symbolic Names

The Book of Ruth is filled with symbolic names. Naomi means pleasant, Mahlon and Chilion convey respectively the sense of illness and devastation, Elimelech and Boaz are interpreted in the Rabbinic literature as having a figurative meaning.[9] Bethlehem, the home city of Elimelech and Naomi is literally House of Bread. Ironically, at the beginning of the narrative there is no bread; a famine forces the family to leave to seek respite in nearby Moab. Ruth and Boaz's son's name, Obed, may have symbolic value.[10]

In Genesis 38, Judah settles for a time in a place named Chezib, which derives from the word meaning failure. It was at Chezib that Bat Shua gave birth to their third son, Shelah, and according to Rabbinic tradition (*Midrash B'reishit Rabbah* 85:4), she *failed* to give birth to any more children. The first two sons are named Er and Onan. The word Er is spelled *ayin reish*, which, when reversed spells out the word *ra* (evil). Onan might derive from the word meaning sorrow (see Gen. 35:18), or from the word for nothing (*ayin/ein*). The name of Judah's third son, Shelah, when vocalized differently,[11] can mean hers.[12] Here, his name would prefigure his proposed future role in terms of levirate marriage as *yavam*, Tamar's future brother-in-law/husband. In Genesis 19, the text itself puns on the names of Moab and Ammon (Gen. 19:37–38).[13] The name Lot is connected to the Hebrew word *lat* meaning secrecy. In the secrecy of their cave, Lot's daughters lay with their father.

In a number of cases, these symbolic names in Genesis connect to the plot of Ruth. Chezib is connected to the word for failure, and more specifically the failure to have more children. Naomi comments that she will fail to have more sons. Er is a symbolic name, according to Rabbinic tradition, for Er was destroyed (*hu-arah*) from the world, and both of Naomi's sons die, as does her husband. The Rabbis (*Midrash B'reishit Rabbah* 85:4) connect the name Onan to the word for grief (*animah*), and the death of Naomi's husband and sons brings grief to her family. The name Lot is connected to the Hebrew word meaning enwrap (*lut*) as with a cloth (see I Sam. 21:10) or as a covering as in a sign of mourning (*lot*) (see Isa. 25:7). Ruth asks Boaz to spread his robe over her, to enwrap/cover her.

Enterprising Women

There are many women in the Bible who are strong, powerful, and determined characters. Although hardly an exhaustive list, they include Eve, Sarah, Rebekah, Leah, Rachel, Madam Potiphar, Miriam, Rahab, Deborah, Yael, Abigail, Bathsheba, and Esther. As Susan Niditch has remarked, these "women . . . are markers and creators of transition and transformation . . . The women succeed in behind-the-scenes ways . . . and their power is in the private rather than in the public realm."[14] To this list also belong Naomi, Ruth, Tamar, and Lot's daughters.

But Women Are Marginalized

In all three narratives, the women are marginalized. Ruth has voluntarily left home; she is a stranger, an "Other," in Bethlehem. She self-identifies as a foreigner (*nochriya*) (Ruth 2:10).[15] Tamar is sent away from her husband's home by her father-in-law Judah to await a young man she comes to believe will never arrive. Through their very anonymity, Lot's daughters are relegated to a secondary position. "A corollary of being marginalized is that one can no longer use the normal channels of society to gain one's rights. When women cannot acquire the necessary son by pursuing the law and demanding their right, they must resort to trickery, which is closely linked to their sexuality."[16]

Seeking a Redeemer; Doing So "in the Dark"/Unconventionally

Ruth, at Naomi's suggestion, seeks out the help of Boaz at night, after he has eaten and drunk, away from the sight of others, specifically at the threshing floor. Taking matters into her own hands, she effectively offers herself to Boaz. She uncovers his "feet," a term, which many scholars suggest, is a euphemism for his sexual organs.[17]

Tamar, guided by her own inner resources, and on her own volition, seeks out her father-in-law. Figuratively speaking, Judah is in the dark as to her real identity. Lot's daughters, the older as the younger, who are living in the darkness of a cave (Gen. 19:30), get their father inebriated to the point where he is figuratively, and perhaps literally, in the dark. He unwittingly becomes the father/grandfather of their children.

In the case of Naomi/Ruth, as in the case of Lot's daughters, an older woman (and we have no way of knowing how close in age were Lot's daughters) instructs her younger companion what to do, and how to do it, as a mother might do for a daughter.[18]

Older Men/Younger Women

In all three narratives, the chief male character is an older man, and the woman a person young enough to be his daughter, and in the case of Lot, they are his daughters, and Tamar is Judah's daughter-in-law.

Paying a Payment

In Ruth, following their night spent together, Boaz sends Ruth forward not only with a verbal promise to intervene on her behalf, but also with a gift of six measures of barley. Judah, whose act seems more on-the-spur-of-the-moment, offers his staff and his seal in pledge for payment. There is no equivalent payment with Lot's daughters, although one might argue that the fact that the daughters are pregnant—which was their goal—is a kind of payment.

Naming the Children

Despite the extraordinary circumstances that result in the birth of the respective children, in each case, the resulting offspring are not anonymous. Ruth/Boaz's son is Obed, Tamar/Judah's children are Perez and Zerah, and the respective sons of Lot's daughters are labeled as the eponymous ancestors of the Moabites and the Ammonites. Earlier, in Genesis, the text gave details about the birth of Perez, the son of Tamar/Judah. This contrasts with the case of Lot/Lot's daughters' offspring, who are castigated as the children of incest. That the Tamar/Judah conjugation is also incestuous effectively is ignored, if not unmentioned; it certainly is not condemned.

Mother/Grandmother/Father/Grandfather

In each of these biblical narratives, important characters take on multiple roles. The text labels Boaz as Naomi's redeemer (Ruth 4:14). Then Naomi is termed the child's *omenet*, which often means the one who nurses the child, but in this context it means that she took care of Obed or even adopted him (Ruth 4:16). As noted by J. Cheryl Exum, the story conflates Naomi with Ruth as the seducer of Boaz, and in addition Naomi represents a wife/husband/mother to Ruth as well as a wife to Boaz and father and mother to

Obed.[19] Both Naomi and Boaz refer to Ruth as my daughter (Ruth 1:11–12; 2:8; 3:1, 18). In Genesis, Judah serves as father/grandfather for his sons, as did Lot earlier in Genesis.

Only One Sexual Encounter

According to Jewish tradition, Boaz only lay with Ruth the one time. The same is true for Judah and Tamar (Gen. 38:26) and Lot and his daughters.

Boaz as Righteous Man

The three central male figures in these narratives are Lot, Judah, and Boaz. Each in his turn both acts and also speaks, which then forms the basis for an evaluation of his behavior. Lot's deeds are repugnant, and his words are self-condemnatory. He mocks his role as a parent by betraying his innocent children. As noted above, "Look, I have two daughters who have not known a man. Let me bring them out to you, and you may do to them as you please; but do not do anything to these men." Judah turns his back on Tamar, rejecting his role of in loco parentis, and he would have her languish in a state of perpetual and irredeemable widowhood. At the dénouement of the chapter, Judah states clearly that Tamar is not only righteous, but also *more* righteous than he is himself (Gen. 38:26). In admitting that Tamar "is *more* in the right" than he is (*tzadkah mimeini*) he condemns himself. Judah concedes that what she did was the correct thing, but he refuses to admit his multiple wrongful acts. Judah does not say that he was wrong and she was right. He says she was *more* righteous than I. He refuses to take responsibility for his betrayal of a sacred trust, that of the powerful male figure in a patriarchal society who should protect those in his care. Only Boaz through deed and word does what is moral and righteous in the situation he faces. Boaz's deeds stand out because without a compelling personal need, he does the right thing.[20] He is even more praiseworthy because, unlike Lot and Judah, he is neither parentis nor in loco parentis, rather he is only a related party.

Boaz's actions stand out because they are largely done in the public arena. The author of Ruth also makes a claim that the community approves of what he has done. It is the community that proudly claims Obed and celebrates his birth. It is Naomi's women neighbors that actually name Obed.

Conclusion

Ruth stands on its own merits; when read through the lenses of Genesis 38 and 19, it has even greater meaning. In the Book of Ruth, the author achieves an important goal. This goal seeks to counter the taint of two episodes in Genesis where men betrayed their sacred trust towards women in their care, treating them as throwaway characters to be dispensed without remorse. By having Boaz intervening on Ruth's behalf, and then by actually marrying her, Boaz resolves her immediate problem, but on an even deeper level the author of Ruth shows that men can do what is just and right. Boaz's actions are in startling contrast to both Judah's indifference to Tamar's plight and the earlier callous attitude of Lot toward the welfare of his innocent daughters. At the conclusion of Ruth, Naomi's women neighbors name the child, suggesting a communal acceptance of the *go-eil/ yavam* (redeemer) position of Boaz. Through his deeds additionally he redeems/redresses the past. As Boaz says to Ruth, so may it be said of him: "Your latest deed of loyalty is greater than the first."

Notes

1. Carol L. Meyers, "Every Day Life: Women in the Period of the Hebrew Bible," in *The Women's Bible Commentary*, ed. Carol A. Newsom and Sharon H. Ringe (Louisville: John Knox Press, 1998), 252.

   Namelessness often is equated with someone being a throwaway character. Lot's daughters are unnamed, as is the nearer relative in Ruth 4, and all are throwaway characters. Yet namelessness/throwaway character is not a hard-and-fast rule. Tamar who initially is treated as a throwaway character, is named, but this may be because she becomes the principal matriarch for the line of Judah's descendants.

2. Tamara Cohn Eskenazi discusses "Ruth's Relationship to Other Biblical Books" in the Introduction that she authored in the *JPS-Ruth* commentary. While there are relationships with other books as well, she explains, "Ruth evokes Genesis in a number of ways. First, the book explicitly mentions some of the ancestors in Genesis by name . . . Judah, Tamar, and Perez . . . [T]here are some parallels and allusions . . . Ruth's Moabite origin brings to mind the story of Lot's daughters and the birth of Moab (Gen. 19:30–37)." Tamara Cohn Eskenazi and Tikva Frymer-Kensky, *The JPS Bible Commentary—Ruth* (Philadelphia: Jewish Publication Society, 2011), xxi.

   Ruth has been analyzed from a variety of perspectives. It is of particular interest in terms of women's studies; for example,

Judith A. Kates and Gail Twersky Reimer, eds., *Reading Ruth: Contemporary Women Reclaim a Sacred Story* (New York: Ballantine, 1994). See also Edward E. Campbell, *Ruth* (AB 7; Garden City, NY: Doubleday, 1975); Robert L. Hubbard, Jr., *The Book of Ruth* (New International Commentary on the Old Testament) (Grand Rapids, MI: William B. Eerdmans, 1988); Jack M. Sasson, *Ruth: A New Translation with a Philological Commentary and Formalist-Folklorist Interpretation*, 2nd ed. (Sheffield: JSOT, 1989), Frederic W. Bush, *Ruth/Esther* (WBC 9; Waco, TX: Word Books, 1996); Kirsten Nielsen, *Ruth: A Commentary* (Old Testament Library) (Louisville, KY: Westminster John Knox, 1997); Todd Linafelt, *Ruth*, and Timothy K. Beal, *Esther* (Berit Olam) (Collegeville, MN: Michael Glazier/Liturgical Press, 1999); and the aforementioned Eskenazi and Frymer-Kensky volume.

The book is freighted with many different undercurrents, but the focus in this article is on at least one major reason why Boaz marries Ruth. "Boaz has no obligation to offer marriage since levirate marriage is a matter for brothers who live together, and there is no good reason to suppose that Boaz is a brother either of Elimelech or Mahlon." Danna Nolan Fewell and David Miller Gunn, *Compromising Redemption: Relating Characters in the Book of Ruth* (Louisville, KY: Westminster/John Knox, 1990), 89. Current scholarship now challenges the notion that "Ruth's marriage to Boaz represents a levirate marriage." Eskenazi and Frymer-Kensky, *Ruth*, xxxv. See discussion of this point, xxxv–xxxviii.

3. Nehama Aschkenasy, "Language as Female Empowerment in Ruth," in Kates and Reimer, *Reading Ruth*, 121.

4. Eskenazi and Frymer-Kensky, *Ruth*, xxii. In the Introduction, Eskenazi refers to Fisch's exploration of this issue: Harold Fisch, "Ruth and the Structure of Covenant History," *Vetus Testamentum* 32, no. 4 (October 1982): 425–37. Nielsen has written, "Ruth belongs within an intertextuality of women's stories that deal with infertility and the triumph over it. The most obvious examples of women who do their utmost to get a son [include] . . . Lot's daughters . . . and Tamar." Nielsen, *Ruth*, 13.

5. Ziony Zevit, "Dating Ruth: Legal, Linguistic and Historical Observations," *Zeitschrift für die Alttestamentliche Wissenschaft* 117, no. 4 (Jan. 24, 2006): 574–600. See also Eskenazi and Frymer-Kensky, *Ruth*, xvi–xix.

6. Nahum N. Sarna, *The JPS Commentary—Genesis* (Philadelphia: Jewish Publication Society, 1989), comment to Genesis 19:32. Sarna also writes: "There is no way of knowing if [Lot's daughters'] intent was the renewal of the entire human race, as [Midrash] Genesis Rabba 51:10 sees it, or just the perpetuation of their father's name as Radak [Rabbi David Kimhi, twelfth/thirteenth century] believes."

7. Ruth and Boaz are the great-grandparents of King David, which is acknowledged in the last sentence of the book. It could be that Boaz's redress/redemption also removes possible slurs about the Judah-Moab ancestry of David.

8. Fisch, "Ruth," 429. Adding examples from Genesis 13, Fisch offers a table with eight categories that link Ruth with Genesis [13,] 19, and 38. Fisch, "Ruth," 430–31.

9. *Midrash Ruth Rabbah* 2:5; 6:4. See also Leila Leah Bronner, "The Regime of Modesty: Ruth and the Rabbinic Construction of the Feminine Ideal," *From Eve to Esther: Rabbinic Reconstructions of Biblical Women* (Louisville, KY: Westminster John Knox, 1994), 67–71. Boaz in Hebrew indicates power. C. J. Labuschagne, "The Crux in Ruth 4:11," *Zeitschrift für die Alttestamentliche Wissenschaft* 79 (1967): 366–67. In her analysis of the Ruth story, Bal points out that "Boaz's name means the powerful/potent." Mieke Bal, *Lethal Love: Feminist Literary Readings of Biblical Love Stories* (Bloomington and Indianapolis: Indiana University Press, 1987), 75.

10. The name Obed in Hebrew is traditionally translated to mean work but the form *avodah* means religious service as in sacrifice or liturgy; thus his name can mean the servant who honors God in the correct manner, or may obliquely refer to David, who certainly is depicted in Chronicles as being very devout. Thanks to Moshe Reiss for this insight.

11. According to Rabbi Bahya ben Asher (Spain, d. 1320) in his *Commentary on the Torah*, "The scroll of the Torah is [written] without vowels, in order to enable [a person] to interpret it however [one] wishes . . . without vowels [one] may interpret it [extrapolating from it] several [different] things, many marvelous and sublime." S. Parpola, "The Assyrian Tree of Life: Tracing the Origins of Jewish Monotheism and Greek Philosophy," *Journal of Near Eastern Studies* 52 (1993), 206.

12. David Silber, lecture on Ruth and Genesis 38 (Limmud Colorado, May 28, 2011).

13. The word Moab is a "popular etymology based on Hebrew *me-'avi*, 'from [my] father.'" Sarna, *Genesis,* comment on 19:37.

14. Susan Niditch, "Genesis," *The Women's Bible Commentary,* ed. Carol A. Newsom and Sharon H. Ringe (London: SPCK; Louisville, KY: Westminster/John Knox, 1992), 25. Niditch's frame of reference is the women in Genesis; her description fits many other biblical women as well.

15. See Francis Brown, S. R. Driver, and C. A. Briggs, *Hebrew and English Lexicon of the Old Testament* (Oxford: Clarendon Press, 1962), 649, which explains that in some cases *nochriya* is even used as a synonym for harlot (see Prov. 3:16).

16. Nielsen, *Ruth,* 16–17.

17. Campbell, *Ruth*, 121; see Bal, *Lethal Love*, 70. Nielsen suggests that Ruth uncovered her own genitals, *Ruth*, 69–70.

18. There also are contrasts between the narratives. While Ruth openly identifies herself to Boaz, actively seeking his help to resolve her dilemma, Tamar and Lot's daughters conceal their relationships to achieve their goals.

19. J. Cheryl Exum, "Is This Naomi," in *The Practice of Cultural Analysis*, ed. Mieke Bal (Stanford: Stanford University Press, 1999), 200–202. This role and gender blurring are also discussed in Fewell and Gunn, 81–82 and Ilana Pardes, *Countertraditions in the Bible: A Feminist Approach* (Cambridge: Harvard University Press, 1992), 102–12. Thanks to Moshe Reiss for pointing out this article.

20. Boaz "marries Ruth not because he has to but because he wants to, because her acts of *hesed* and her virtues as 'a fine woman' ('*eshet hayil*, in 3:11) have captivated him. These inspire him to act likewise." Eskenazi and Frymer-Kensky, *Ruth*, xxxviii.

Maayanot (Primary Sources)

The Laws of *M'sirah* in *Shulchan Aruch, Choshen Mishpat*, Chapter 388: Introduction, Translation, and Afterword

Stephen M. Passamaneck

"Am I my brother's keeper?"

(Gen. 4:10)

Introduction

1. The sections of the *Shulchan Aruch* usually have precise and clearly understood titles that indicate the content of the section. Indeed the title of chapter (and section) 388 of *Choshen Mishpat* is painfully to the point. Chapter 388 concerns only one offense, that of "informing," or, as it is rendered here, "unlawful delivery." The reason for this departure from the customary terminology will be explained shortly. This offense mirrors the profound tragedy and terror of medieval Jewish life, in which one Jew, out of fear or out of hope for personal gain or out of desire to curry favor or for some other unknown reason, aids and abets "violent persons"—often identical with non-Jewish authorities—to seize the property or the person of a fellow Jew. The informer—the "unlawful deliverer"—was execrated and reviled for that act, and he or she faced the most severe punishments that the Jewish community had the power to impose. Even the threat to inform against (or unlawfully deliver) a fellow Jew met with grave punishment—including in some cases death. This offense had the potential to expose an entire community to depredations (after all, if one Jew were a likely target for

STEPHEN M. PASSAMANECK (C60) is professor emeritus of Rabbinic Literature HUC-JIR/Los Angeles. Prof. Passamaneck went into full retirement in July 2013, after having completed fifty years on the faculty of the College-Institute.

such depredations, what might the community as a whole yield?); Jews might be forced to take sides against each other, thus destroying the internal cohesion of the community.

2. The informer in Hebrew is the *moser* and the unlawful act he or she performs is *m'sirah*, both from the verbal root *msr* (to hand over, to deliver). The root also is the origin of the Hebrew word for tradition, something that is handed over from one generation to the next generation. The word is also quite close to the meaning of the Latin word *traditio*, which is the etymological ancestor of the English word "treason." Indeed I have suggested elsewhere that *m'sirah* (informing) is as close as one gets in ancient and medieval Hebrew legal terminology to the offense of treason. The concept of *m'sirah* does indeed involve the giving of information, but it implies much more than the retailing of information as the sense of the root indicates. The verb bears the meaning of physically "handing over" a person or property (or both) to "violent persons," who will harm that fellow Jew as a consequence of the information given or the delivery effected. Although "informing" is not a biblical offense that carried a capital penalty, the Rabbis of the Talmud had no hesitation about attaching a capital penalty, under certain circumstances, to *m'sirah*.

Therefore I have chosen to render the various terms derived from the root *msr* as "unlawful delivery" or "unlawful deliverer" and not as the customary "informing" or "informer." This translation appears to be closer to the meaning of the Hebrew root. Admittedly, the element "unlawful" is certainly not explicit in the root, but it is obviously necessary to the meaning of the root in the context of these rules, and in any event the root does not in its basic sense mean "to inform." The informer may indeed proffer information, but Jewish law speaks of him or her in the language of delivery (*msr*) as one who "hands over" something or someone to someone else. The phrases "unlawful delivery" and "unlawful deliverer" thus appear to convey the sense of the Hebrew more accurately. (On the matter of a capital punishment see BT *B'rachot* 58a.)

3. The unlawful deliverer should not be confused with the modern whistleblower, who exposes wrongdoing in business or in government or in other institutions that affect the public welfare by making hitherto private information public thus exposing wrongdoing

to the public benefit. The public thus becomes aware of crimes that have been allowed to continue in secrecy. The whistleblower undertakes a very risky enterprise by going public with information he or she possesses; he or she may face serious retaliation, but the whistleblower ultimately is hailed as a public benefactor and hero. Not so the informer in Jewish law; no miscreant stood lower in the eyes of the Rabbis or in the eyes of the community than the informer (the unlawful deliverer).

4. Every effort has been made to present a clear rendition of the text, but the cadences of medieval Hebrew do not always harmonize with the cadences of twenty-first-century English. The language of the Hebrew text in fact reflects Mishnaic usage, Talmudic usage, and both early and late medieval rabbinic styles. Therefore occasional liberties with the phrasing of the text that do not alter the meaning of the material have become necessary to achieve clarity of expression. Bracketed material represents a fuller statement of the necessary halachic context. Parenthetical material represents the author's attempts to supply greater clarity for the English reader. I am most grateful to Rabbi Neal Scheindlin, who read my manuscript and offered valuable observations and corrections.

5. If we may consider the responsa literature as a series of "snapshots" of Jewish life and practice at a certain time and a certain place, how might one characterize the Codes, or, more accurately, the Restatements? The term "code" often suggests a work that supersedes what has gone before. The word "restatement" does not bear this connotation, and surely the halachic "codes" could not and did not supersede previous works. As a result, they could never be quick "snapshots"; they are rather akin to detailed "landscapes." A section of a restatement presents the features of an entire area of the halachah describing its principal elements and a good deal of significant detail. We see before us a total "landscape." Not everything may be visible in detail but the panorama is clear. Thus if we wish to know how Jewish tradition has shaped this or that area of Jewish practice, the Restatements will be the best source. Albeit practice has changed radically over the centuries, the broad directions, the landscape, emerges clearly. Moreover, if we read the Restatements carefully and search between the lines, we shall also become aware of the ideals and beliefs that have animated Jewish

practice over the long centuries. This characterization appears particularly apt with respect to Chapter 388.

This translation is, of course, a portion of Joseph Caro's (Ottoman Empire, 1488–1575) monumental restatement of the halachah, *Shulchan Aruch*. He based his restatement on three previous works, the epitome of the halachah by Alfas, *Maimonides's Mishneh Torah,* and the halachot of Rabbi Asher ben Yehiel; and where he felt it necessary, he relied on the works of a number of other major authorities. The glosses, which have been duly labeled as such here, came from the pen of R. Moses Isserles, Caro's Polish contemporary (1520–1572), who drew upon both Ashkenazic and Sephardic authorities to provide a fuller scope to Caro's brief statements. (This is particularly notable in matters where Ashkenazic ritual practice differed from Sephardic ritual practice.)

All of the Isserles glosses appear here in italics. Other material in italics is occasionally interspersed in the Caro text; these elements also come from the pen of Isserles, but are not introduced as glosses. All the italicized text has customarily appeared in the "Rashi" typeface, which was often used as we would use italics today. These italicized portions first appeared in the earliest editions containing Isserles's contributions (Cracow, 1574–1594, 1580 and ed. Cracow 1580. The former edition appeared over a twenty-year span; the latter edition appeared in a single year. The timing is established by the notation on the respective title pages of the names of the Polish kings during whose reigns the two works were published). The first edition of Caro's restatement had appeared in Venice in 1564. The italicized elements also note the sources of Isserles's remarks; these source references have not been translated here. To do so would have overstepped the clamant limitations of space, and anyone interested in such sources need only consult any modern edition of the *Shulchan Aruch.*

6. In the almost five hundred years since the appearance of the *Shulchan Aruch* (Venice 1564–1565) it has grown from a handy guide for students to a massive multivolume structure of text complemented with learned rabbinic commentary by some of the greatest rabbinic authorities of the seventeenth and eighteenth centuries. Although modern Jewish life in the main hardly reflects the prescriptions and instructions of the *Shulchan Aruch,* the work

still projects the broad outlines, and the multitudinous detail, of traditional Jewish life and practice. It should not be dismissed as an antiquated relic of a world that has long passed away. We should not choose to dismiss the foundational principles and practices that have given Jewish life its vibrancy and depth even while Emancipation in the late eighteenth and nineteenth centuries refocused much of the interest and energy of large segments of Jewry away from the four ells of the halachah. The work instructs us of a world that has passed to be sure, but it also speaks to us of the principles, practices, and ideals that endure.

Translation

Shulchan Aruch, Choshen Mishpat

The Laws Concerning One Who Personally Destroys the Property of His Fellow and the One Who Unlawfully Delivers His Fellow to Violent Persons and Who Calumniates Him

388   The Party Who Has Incurred Damage to His Property Swears an Oath and Takes [Restitution from the Person Who Caused the Damage].

388:1   A person damages his fellow's property but does not know the value of the property he damaged [or destroyed]. The person suffering the loss swears an oath [as to the value of the property in question] and takes restitution from the one who caused the damage. How does this work? A takes B's wallet and throws it into a body of water or into a fire, or he hands it to a violent person who destroys it. The owner of the wallet declares that it was full of gold pieces. The person who caused the damage asserts he does not know what was in the wallet; perhaps it was dust or straw. The person who suffered the loss then swears an oath, while holding a holy object and takes [what he claims as it value. This is the case] provided that he shall claim something [of a nature and value] that he may reasonably be considered to possess, or that he is esteemed [to be a person with whom others are likely] to deposit [such a sum or item]. [Further,] it is the practice of the people of that place to put [such an amount or item] into a wallet like the one taken. *A money bag in a sack on a Sabbath or Festival, [when handling money is forbidden] is deemed [proper] practice in this situation.* If, however, it is not their practice to put [such an object or amount of money] into this container the injured party has acted negligently [and endamaged himself]. *The injuring party is free from liability.* How [may this occur in practice]? A person snatches a goatskin water bottle or a fully covered basket and throws it into the sea or burns it. The injured party claims it contained pearls. He is not believed [if he makes such an assertion]. There is an opinion that holds this last provision to be the rule even if there were witnesses that [the valuable items] were in the bag or basket; the injurer is not liable because [the injured party] acted negligently as has been explained. If [the injured party] seized [some recompense from the injuring party,] the court will not hear a suit for the return of what he seized. He shall swear an oath that the container held (e.g.) pearls, and he takes [his damages] from whatever [the injuring party may] have with him. And thus in any similar case. If the injuring party knew that there were gold pieces in the wallet, but he did not know how many: if the injured party says [there were] a thousand, then he takes a thousand [from the injurer] without taking an oath [thereon] provided that he is deemed [a person likely to posses such a sum]. [This is] because the injuring party is [properly] obligated to swear an oath, but he is not able to do so [since he does not know the exact member of gold pieces involved]. *There are those who hold the opinion that the injured party swears an oath and takes [what he claims;] such is the essence of the matter.*

388:2   One unlawfully delivers property (i.e., not belonging to him) to a violent and terrorizing person whether Jewish or non-Jewish. [That unlawful deliverer] is liable for the loss [to the rightful possessors] of whatever the terrorizer has taken [and is to make good the loss] from the best of his property, even though [such deliverer] did not physically handle the goods but was only the facilitator [of the loss].

If the one [who unlawfully delivered the property] dies, (the injured party) collects (damages) from his heirs as (is the case) with all causers (of pecuniary) injury.

There is an opinion that holds that (this last provision about col-
lection from heirs) applies when the injured party had instituted
proceedings [against the deceased unlawful deliverer]; but if no
lawsuit had been instituted, the heirs are not liable to make good
the loss. A woman has unlawfully delivered [another's property].
We place her under a temporary excommunication. If she owns
property independently of her husband, she makes her victim
whole again. If she has melug *property [specified in her wedding*
contract] her husband enjoys the use of it as long as he lives. [If
she] predeceases her husband, [he] is liable to make the [victim
of the unlawful delivery] whole; and so with any other victim of
hers. The husband in this matter [stands] only as an heir who is
liable for restitution.

[All this] applies when the unlawful deliverer acts of his
[or her] own accord. If non-Jews, or violent Jews, forced
him [or her] to show [the property to be confiscated] and
he [or she] did so, such a one is free from liability. [If they
forced him or her] to show (i.e., lead them to) his [or her]
[property for confiscation] and he [or she] showed his [or
her] property and someone else's property, he [or she] is
liable in damages.

If [the unlawful deliverer] physically handled [the goods]
even though he was under duress, he is liable in damages
because the person who saves himself at the expense of
another's property is held liable in [damages]. How [does
one imagine the circumstances of this last provision]? The
terrorizer decrees that he be brought enough wine or straw,
or what have you. A [Jewish] unlawful deliverer stands
and declares, "Such and such a person has a warehouse of
wine, or straw, in such and such a place." [Henchmen] go
and fetch [the goods]. The [Jew] is liable in damages.

GLOSS: Even if they chastised him [(i.e., threatened and brow-
beat him) without telling him why they were doing that] and he
showed [his tormentors] someone else's property (to induce them
to take it and stop terrorizing him), he is liable in damages. Du-
ress is strictly defined as beating and [physical] punishment; [the
definition does] not [include depredations against his] property.

A person sees that he is in danger of harm. It is permissible
for him to save himself even though [thereby] harm may

come to someone else [provided of course that there is no unlawful delivery].

388:3   A king tortures [a potential unlawful deliverer] until he shows [the king or nobleman, etc.] the whereabouts of his fellow's property [that fellow having already fled from the royal presence]. He shows the property under duress. He is not liable in damages because if he does not show it [to the king, the king] would [continue to] have him beaten or [perhaps] put to death.

388:4   A [Jew] physically handled the property of another [Jew] and gave it to a violent terrorizer. He is liable in damages in any event, though the king (i.e., the terrorizer) forced him to bring [the goods]. *[Two partners jointly held a note of debt.] A nobleman forced one of them to forgive the debt. [That partner] is not liable in damages because [the forgiveness of debt] does not [meet the definition of physically giving].* When does this rule apply? If the violent person [king, nobleman, etc.] forced [the Jew] to bring [the goods] and he did bring them, the goods not having come under the control of the violent person [until the Jew delivered them].

If however the violent person terrorized the Jew until he showed him [the location of the goods], and the violent person stood by the property, [the property] has effectively come under his dominion and control. [That is, he can control it and move it.] [If] the violent person placed the Jew under duress forcing him to transport the goods to another location—even if the transporter is the [very] unlawful deliverer who showed [him the goods in the first place—albeit he was forced to do so], the Jew is not liable in damages. Once the violent person stood by the warehouse [where the goods were stored] everything in it [is deemed] lost as if it had been [completely] burned.

388:5   There were litigants who were quarreling over land, or moveable property, each one asserting it belonged to him. One of them unlawfully delivered [the property] to a violent person. We place him under a *nidui* excommunication (i.e., a short-term excommunication) until he shall have restored the matter to its original status, and remove the violent person from among them. [Then] they shall take the matter to a Jewish Court.

GLOSS: In any case, the person [who introduced the violent person into the matter] is not an unlawful deliverer even though he caused the other litigant great loss. The category of unlawful deliverer applies only to one who causes harm [to another] with the intent [to do so,] not to one who intends to vindicate [what he believes to be] his own [property.] There are those who disagree and hold the opinion that he is deemed an unlawful deliverer, and [such a one] is liable to make good all the damage he caused his fellow, if his fellow had not been reluctant [to go to a non-Jewish court]—and all the more so [is he liable] if he had been first warned that they should not go to a court of violent persons, but he transgressed [in this respect]. He falls under the law of the unlawful deliverer.

388:6 A person is seized [by violent non-Jews] for his fellow [Jew—i.e., a hostage]. The violent persons have taken valuable property from him because of his fellow. His fellow is not obligated to make [the hostage] whole. No one seized because of his fellow, for whom that fellow Jew bears liability [to make him whole], except for one seized for [the payment of] the fixed amount of tax which each man is required to pay every year, and the special gift which each man gives to the King when he, or his military entourage, visits. One is obligated thereon provided that [The Community] shall take [the money] from him with an explanation [of why he is obligated] with respect to such and such a person [and do so] in the presence of witnesses. This is explained in Chapter 128.

388:7 One has witnesses appearing against him [asserting] that he unlawfully delivered property [to violent persons]. For example, [they allege] that he himself showed [the goods to violent persons] or he was forced [in the matter] and he physically handled and gave the property [to the violent persons]. The witnesses do not know how much he caused [the victim of the unlawful delivery] to lose. The victim asserts, "He caused me such and such an amount of loss." The unlawful deliverer denies the [amount] of the claim. If the victim has [already] seized [property to that

amount], a Jewish court does not hear a case against him;
but he swears an oath [while] holding a holy object and
takes lawful possession of what he has seized. *[There is an
opinion that where there exists doubt in the case, the seizure is
invalid.]*

If the injured party has not seized property [of the unlawful deliverer,] we do not take [property] from the unlawful
deliverer unless there is clear proof [of the amount of his
liability. If the parties clearly knew the amount involved]
but it was necessary to strike a bargain with the nobleman
[no doubt the personage who forced the Jew to deliver another's property unlawfully] for such and such an amount
[perhaps somewhat less? See *Ba'er Heitev* ad loc.], the injured party swears an oath and takes [what recompense
is available]. There is an opinion that holds that if the unlawful deliverer says, "I do not know the amount you lost
because of me," the injured party swears an oath [as to his
loss] and takes [what he is able to take in recompense].

*GLOSS: All this concerns unlawful delivery of property. If how-
ever one unlawfully delivered the person of his fellow to violent
men, the victim swears an oath and takes (recompense for the loss
he suffered owing to his seizure). Thus if one caused the arrest
and seizure of another, he is tantamount to one who has physically injured him and must make him whole from all damages [he
suffered thereby]. One says to his fellow, "You have unlawfully
delivered me" [to a violent person and the other party denies it
entirely]: the deliverer shall swear an equitable oath [required in
cases where the accused denies the accusation completely]. There
is an opinion that this oath is to be taken in the presence of the
nobleman [to the effect that] he did not deliver [his fellow] to
that authority. It is not necessary to undertake this [oath of] innocence unless there is one witness who does testify that [the
accused] did [indeed] unlawfully deliver [that person to violent
persons]. Non-Jews are not trustworthy [witnesses] in this matter (i.e., that A did in fact deliver the person of B).*

*Two persons acting together unlawfully delivered [a third party
to a violent person]: each one shall make good half [the victim's
loss]. If they acted one after the other, the second party is ex-
empt [from liability]. As long as the victim was not released*

[from the first person's custody] in the unlawful delivery, the injury proceeds from the first party. And if a Jew did not deliver him [having seen what the Jew did], but a non-Jew or a violent person [also] saw what the Jew did so that they would tell the violent person (i.e., the nobleman), what the Jew saw or did is irrelevant [the Sefer Meirath Einayim commentary ad loc. omits the negative particle so that the reading is clearer: even if the Jew did turn in his fellow, non-Jews would also certainly inform the authorities so that the Jew can hardly be said to be the author of his fellow's misfortunes].

There are those who hold that a person who has been struck by his fellow Jew may take his complaint to a non-Jewish court even though this causes the person who hit him great harm.

388:8   We do not place an unlawful deliverer who, of his own accord, showed [violent persons the property of a fellow Jew] under an oath, neither a biblical oath nor a rabbinical oath, because he is an evil person. No one is more unfit to take an oath than he.

Even if one has not yet unlawfully delivered [a person to violent handling] but only [threatened to do so] saying, "I shall go and I shall turn you in . . .," if he says this publicly, he becomes unfit to give testimony in court. In this situation we do not invoke [the Talmudic concept] that one may boast yet not act. There are those who differ [on this point] unless that person regularly does so (i.e., threaten to turn people over to the non-Jewish authorities). Even if we do not know whether or not he customarily [boasts in this fashion], in any event the person opposing him (i.e., the injured party) is able to use non-Jewish aid to save himself [from the threat], even though [the threatener] may suffer damage [thereby].

However, the unlawful deliverer who has been forced to show [where another's goods are located] or to bring them [to his tormentors], and who has physically handled them [in doing so], even though [he] is liable to make restitution, he is not [deemed] a wicked person. He is only liable for restitution [but not opprobrium]. We may put him under oath, as we [may do] with other fit and proper persons.

GLOSS: Similarly, if he admitted to being an unlawful deliverer but there are no witnesses [to his act], even though he does not become unfit [to swear an oath or to give testimony] on the strength of his admission, in any event he is liable to make good [any loss he caused by unlawful delivery].

388:9 It is prohibited to deliver a Jew unlawfully into the power of a non-Jew, whether his person or his property [is delivered], even if he were a wicked and sinful man and even if he has caused [one] grief and vexation.

GLOSS: [This provision contemplates vexation caused by] speech alone. If however A has unlawfully delivered B's [property or person to violent men], A may retaliate [in kind] because it is lawful to kill [that unlawful deliverer] where one is apprehensive that [one's antagonist] may turn and unlawfully deliver him to violent persons—or it is impossible to save oneself by another means. If however it is possible to save [oneself from the depredations of the unlawful deliverer, the case becomes like that of] two persons who unlawfully deliver each other. Whoever has caused his fellow the greater amount of loss is obligated to make [him] whole by a full indemnity [i.e., the full indemnity for the amount beyond what loss each had caused the other that cancel each other out]. Anyone who unlawfully delivers [a fellow] Jew into the hands of [violent] non-Jews, whether in his person or his property, has no portion in the World to Come.

388:10 It has been deemed permissible to kill the unlawful deliverer in any place, even at the present time; and it is permissible to kill him before he should make such an unlawful delivery. When one has declared: "Lo! I shall deliver [unlawfully] A, [referring] to his person or his property [or both!]—even a small amount of property—he has exposed himself to [the possibility of] death. We warn him and tell him, "Do not unlawfully deliver!" If he arrogantly says, "No! I shall [unlawfully] deliver him!" it [then] becomes a religious obligation to kill him. Anyone who steps forward to kill him is meritorious.

GLOSS: If there is not [sufficient] time to warn him [before he acts], the warning is not necessary. There is an opinion that holds that one is not to kill the unlawful deliverer unless it is not possible to be saved from him by [destruction of] one of his limbs, e.g., by cutting out his tongue or blinding his eyes. He is no worse than any other pursuer [who may be deterred by inflicting a serious wound on him].

388:11 [Once] the unlawful deliverer has accomplished what he purposed to do; it is forbidden to kill him unless he is regarded [owing to his repeated threats to deliver others unlawfully], as a [genuine threat to the welfare of the Community]. [This one] shall be killed lest he shall unlawfully deliver others!

388:12 Anyone who unlawfully delivers [an entire] Community and causes it grief and suffering, may [in turn] be delivered to non-Jewish authority for flogging, scourging, and fining. It is forbidden [to hand him over] because of the suffering [of a] single [individual in the Community].

GLOSS: If one engages in counterfeiting, or the like, and [because of this] there is fear that he may cause harm to the many [i.e., the Community] we warn him that he should not do it! If he disregards the warning, it is permissible to deliver him [to non-Jewish authority], asserting that no one else [beside him] is engaged [in that offense]. If one wishes to flee, and not pay the non-Jewish authority what he is [lawfully] obligated [to pay in taxes, etc.], and some other person has made [this] known [to the non-Jewish authorities], this [latter] person is not held to be an unlawful deliverer, because he has only caused him to lose what he was required to pay. In any case, the person [who turned in the tax evader] has done wrong because he is like one who has returned lost property to a non-Jew. If he has caused [the tax evader] harm [by his act], he is obligated to make good [any loss] he caused him.

388:13 It is prohibited to destroy the property of an unlawful deliverer even though it is lawful to destroy his body. His property [goes to] his heirs. *[There is an opinion that holds that it is permissible to take his property for oneself, because the prohibition is against destroying it, not against seizing it.]*

388:14 We take testimony [against an accused] unlawful deliverer outside his presence.

GLOSS: It is not necessary that such testimony [against him or her] be entirely congruent [on all points—that is, the witnesses may present testimony that does differ in some details].

388:15 It has been well established that if a person has unlawfully delivered a Jew, in his person or his property [to non-Jewish authority] on three occasions, they [i.e., the Community] takes counsel and confers [on the way] to remove [this threat] from the world, (the sentence continues in the gloss:)

> GLOSS: by means of [some] cause, even though it is forbidden to kill [the person] directly [i.e., for a person simply to murder him "with hands"]. A person has spoken of possibly effecting an unlawful delivery before the Community in Council. The violent person (i.e., the non-Jewish authority), hears of this and [he] causes [the Community or some of its members] harm. Even though this person does not fall under the category of unlawful deliverer, in any event, they [i.e., the Community] punish him as the judges [there] see fit [to do]. A person has sent his agent to perform an unlawful delivery. If the agent is known to perform [such acts], having done so on other occasions, the person who sent him [to perform unlawful delivery] is culpable [in this unlawful delivery]. We do not invoke the rule that "There is no agent for an unlawful act" [and thus the principal would not be held to account; the agent is, in other matters, held to be an independent actor]. The agent here is a known performer of such acts. [This principal cannot hide behind the agent.] Similarly, if A handed B's paid-off note to a non-Jew and knew that the non-Jew would present it to a nobleman who would demand payment on it [a second time!] from the Jew B, A is obligated to make B whole.

388:16 [Regarding] expenses incurred to remove the unlawful deliverer [from the community]: all Jews resident in the city are obligated to contribute to them—even those persons who pay their taxes in another place.

Note: The best secondary source on the matter of the unlawful deliverer is the D.H.L. dissertation of Julius Kravetz, of blessed memory, *The Informer*.[1] This excellent work was never published, and scholarship is much the poorer for its absence in print.

Comment 388:15

The statement in the gloss that it is forbidden to kill the unlawful deliverer "with hands" (*b'yadayim*), that is, with a direct immediacy, suggests a time and place when Jews could not impose any sort of capital penalty. In the Babylonian Talmud, however, one who threatened such treachery was killed forthwith: Rabbi Shela had no compunction about killing the man who had exposed him to one government investigation and who was about to expose his questionable actions once again (BT *B'rachot* 58a). Overall, Jewish legal tradition has no difficulty in decreeing death for the unlawful deliverer.

Afterword

The laws defining the *corpora* and the penalties of *m'sirah* present an aspect of medieval Jewish life that we may find distasteful. We do not care to think of our ancestors capable of treachery against each other; or as currying favor with authority to someone else's hurt in order to gain some advantage; or as engaging in criminality; or as desperate victims of torture who would do anything to end their agony. All of this is most melancholy indeed, and we need not dwell upon it overmuch.

We should not however declare ourselves free to forget it. These rules may present us with cautionary tales for our own time. To dismiss them merely as an inglorious feature of our Jewish past is also unwise, because we cannot know the future.

One very clear idea emerges from the laws of *m'sirah*: one must not expose a fellow Jew (much less the Jewish community) to the depredations of the non-Jewish world. Granted that most Jews today live in societies in which they enjoy a large measure of personal freedom, equal citizenship with others, political rights, and much else, we should never forget that we are nonetheless a tiny minority despite political and social equality or any prominence, power, or wealth that individuals may enjoy. We are yet vulnerable to forces quite beyond our control. That vulnerability should not, of course, blunt our desire to affect the world for good nor make us mute in the face of injustice. To adopt such postures would be a craven abdication of our ideals. Yet we should be careful that our zeal does not fracture our community so that others may manipulate our divisions to our ultimate hurt.

We must never allow ourselves to expose our fellow Jews to opprobrium (or worse) unless their acts become a threat to the very welfare of us all. Only in such dire circumstances does our tradition allow us "to blow the whistle" on the acts of some of us.

This may also be an enduring lesson of the laws of *m'sirah* for the twenty-first century.

The laws against *m'sirah* were, at bottom, laws to protect both the individual and the unity of the community. Individuals were not to betray each other to outside forces for gain or glory. In our own world, though a far different one from the societies of the Talmudic era or the various societies of the medieval world, we are still bidden to keep the welfare of our brethren protected—unless they are criminals whose acts dishonor us all.

How this lesson of *m'sirah* might actually play out in our changing world of events cannot of course be predicted. Future events and future crises lie beyond our knowledge. The lesson of the laws of *m'sirah* however endures in the Talmudic dictum that all Jews are responsible one for the other (BT *Sh'vuot* 39a), which appears to be one Rabbinic answer to Cain's arrogant and immemorial question, "Am I my brother's keeper?"

Note: The prohibition against informing has surfaced recently in a most unpleasant matter. Some members of Chasidic sects invoke the rule against informing to dissuade people from giving the authorities information about child molesters in their midst, despite the clear provision that a community may inform against one of its members when that person has engaged in criminality that would embarrass the entire community and has refused to desist from the behavior. It is most unfortunate that rules designed to curb unlawful depredations against Jews have been twisted to shield criminals from lawful prosecution.[2]

Notes

1. Julius Kravetz, *The Informer* (unpublished D.H.L. dissertation, HUC-JIR, 1961).
2. See http://www.nytimes.com/2012/05/10/nyregion/ultra-orthodox-jews-shun-their-own-for-reporting-child-sexual-abuse.html. For an excellent and timely treatment of this matter, which inter alia involves the problem of *m'sirah*, see Steven H. Resnicoff, "Jewish Law and the Tragedy of Sexual Abuse of Children—The Dilemma within the Orthodox Jewish Community," *Rutgers Journal of Law and Religion* 13, no. 2 (Spring 2012): 281–362.

Response to the Winter 2013 Symposium Issue

Congratulations to Eve Ben-Ora and Vicki Reikes Fox for their fine guest editing of "Inspiration & Opportunity: The Arts and Jewish Life," the symposium issue of the *CCAR Journal* for Winter 2013. In explaining "the results of what happens when an artist looks at Torah," they taught us that even as we worry about the words needed to make us holy as Jews, we need to think about what makes us wholly Jewish as well. That includes being open to powerful visual images of *chidur* hidden within the text. I was especially pleased to know that the College–Institute is beginning to incorporate that truth in its curriculum. This is as it should be.

Our tradition reminds us that there is a special role for the senses in Jewish life. The taste of the Israelites' tears, the sight of the rainbow, the smell of the spices, the sound of the shofar, the touch of the Torah—all have a place in Jewish life and as such a place in the synagogue. However, the story of Bezalel and Oholiab teach that some among us possess the heightened senses found only in the heart and soul of the artist. The works of their hands—gifts from God—need celebration and recognition. But how do we do that practically?

Over twenty years ago, the American Guild of Judaic Art chose Shabbat Vayak'heil as National Jewish Art Shabbat. It still exists, as does the Guild and a growing number of Jewish artisans focusing primarily on *klei kodesh*. Our synagogues do celebrate Jewish music and Jewish books; but, surprisingly given Jewish support for the visual arts, we rarely do anything to celebrate them in our communities.

"Inspiration & Opportunity" shares models that have worked and organizations that exist, but the publication primarily focuses on larger Jewish communities and congregations having greater wherewithal. In contrast, National Jewish Art Shabbat can take annual roots in a synagogue setting with a simple display of

RABBI AVI MAGID (C75) recommended the creation of a National Jewish Art Shabbat in 1992 as keynote speaker at the annual meeting of the American Guild of Jewish Artists. He is now retired and writing books for children and is currently working on a history book for young adults entitled *Springfield Had No Shame: The 1908 Race Riot That Created the NAACP.*

chanukiyot belonging to temple members. Then with, say, a religious school project in the second year, perhaps a member of the American Guild of Judaic Art as an artist-in-residence in the next—and Jewish Art Shabbat becomes a "tradition." NATE provides curricular material. *Reform Judaism* devotes an annual issue to it. Add in visits to the spectacular Bezalel Academy for Art and Design on a synagogue tour of Israel and perhaps an artistically inclined student will take a college semester in residence there or even a full Fine Arts degree. As a result, art becomes another spiritual path bringing many others closer to their heritage.

When I was ordained in 1975, my parents gave me a silver *yad* created by Ludwig Alpert, the Bezalel of the twentieth century. Engraved upon it were the words *Achen yesh Adonai bamakom hazeh* (Truly *Adonai* is in this place). Learning about the power that resides within visual representations of our faith is an extraordinary gift that we can offer our congregants, a gift that will strengthen us as well.

Poetry

Rabbi Stripped Naked

Daniel Meltz

I
still think about him after all these years, the way he grabbed me
after class and pulled me
up to the roof, the way he cornered me
and smacked me,
the hairy arms in leather straps. I
still picture him under the locker room shower. I
can summon up my overnight with him and his beautiful wife. I
dream him. I
Google him. I
remember his fallopian squiggles on the blackboard. I
remember his Talmud lesson about a master and his slave. I
remember the rumors about his nervous breakdown. I
think I'll write a book about him. I
drove past his apartment in Teaneck. I
knew he couldn't possibly live there now. I
realized it was just a building in Teaneck. But I
thought of it as a perfect representation of him, a gorgeous fake
    castle he took me
to once. And it was there in his throne room that I
began to fall out of love with him as I
simultaneously fell for the student he'd so thoughtlessly invited
    along with me,
the son of another rabbi.

DANIEL MELTZ is a technical writer at Google who taught the deaf and blind as
a younger man. His poetry has been published in *Best New Poets 2012*, *American
Poetry Review*, *upstreet*, *Mudfish*, *Audio Zine*, *Assisi*, *Temenos*, *FortyOunceBachelors*,
and others.

Minchah

Steven Sher

Late afternoon
in the pantry
with the curtain
drawn, I daven

thirty thousand feet
above the Earth
somewhere between
the two coasts

while the plane
gently *shuckles*
and my eyes close,
engines humming.

STEVEN SHER's latest books are *Grazing on Stars: Selected Poems* (Presa Press, 2012) and *The House of Washing Hands,* forthcoming from Pecan Grove Press. He lives in Jerusalem. Find out more at stevensher.net.

Refer to Maker

Elias Lieberman

Her file lies open
on my desk.
I mine it for data as I
prepare her funeral service.

Hebrew name.
Date and place of birth.
Names of children.

Turning the page
I find a copy of
two returned checks
each bearing the bank's instruction
"Refer to Maker."

So we shall.

ELIAS LIEBERMAN (C84) has served as rabbi of the Falmouth Jewish Congregation on Cape Cod, Massachusetts, since 1990.

Death, Be My Teacher

Ben Kamin

It's not that I wish to leave
But knowing that you are, sooner or later, on your way
Has at last given me the calm that eluded
When I was more about being in the *New York Times*
Than being in the times of my friends.

So when they came to fire me,
I saw people whose lives I'd touched
And whose hearts had become wounds.

Now I know
That I confused youth with wisdom, status with knowledge.
I fell over myself plotting promotions and pining for jobs.
I lived with the myth that life
Is boundless
And that rivers don't run into the sea.

But what I know now has let my soul
Wash itself clean.
I confronted the flaws of self-interest ,
The hurried discourse that smothered the lingering moments of
    conversation,
The realization that someone's handwriting on a personal letter
Is the transcript of a human soul seeking a warm hand.

I lost the need to talk and found so much serenity in listening.
I was able, with your urging, Death, to laugh at how important
I was not.
I stopped running and finally got it:
That the moon and the sun don't cross the sky by my design.

So, thank you, Death.
You have made me a bed with the horizon.

RABBI BEN KAMIN (C78) is the founder of Reconciliation: The Synagogue Without Walls and the author of several books about Dr. Martin Luther King Jr. and the Civil Rights Movement.

Kaddish at Tiananmen Square

Israel Zoberman

The *Kaddish* letters grow
Small in this overwhelming
Space of invisible evil.
I shield them in my pocket,
Close to my heart,
Away from the menacing
Look of the Chinese soldier,
To protect memory.

ISRAEL ZOBERMAN, D. Min. (C74) is founding rabbi of Congregation Beth Chaverim in Virginia Beach, Virginia.

Shavuot Song

Kendrah Raye Whyte

Sing to the harvest, sing to the trees,
Welcome the fruit that comes from above,
Rejoice with the flowers,
Sing the darkness away,
Seek the rainbow, before the rain,
Seek the joy, before the song.

KENDRAH RAYE WHYTE lives in West Roxbury, Massachusetts, with her cat, Dena. She is an artist as well as a poet.

Jerusalem Word Play

Reeve Robert Brenner

Jerusalem, a pun on behold: peace
a play-on-words Yeru city
a yerusha received shalem
wholly city
Yeru—they will yet see peace
Yeru—a future peace
Shalayim—in multiplication
see now a piece of peace
two halves one peace
hello good-bye twice shalom
never knowing whether you're coming
or going, Yerushalayim
a city that plays with shalom
praises shalom
prays for shalom
whole and holy word
whole and holy city
Jerusalem
harm not her harmonies
—make whole her peace.

RABBI DR. REEVE ROBERT BRENNER (NY64) serves Bet Chesed Congregation in Bethesda, Maryland, and was the senior staff chaplain at the National Institutes of Health Clinical Center (retired). He has collected and edited with an introduction the poetry referencing Jerusalem published in English-language journals and magazines in the twentieth century: *Eternal Jerusalem: Poetry*.

Book Reviews

A Congregation, a Rabbi, and a Religious Movement
A Review Essay

Elliot B. Gertel

Reviewing

Sundays at Sinai: A Jewish Congregation in Chicago by Tobias Brinkmann (Chicago and London: The University of Chicago Press, 2012), 369 pp.

Max Lilienthal: The Making of an American Rabbinate by Bruce L. Ruben (Detroit: Wayne State University Press, 2011), 324 pp.

The Birth of Conservative Judaism: Solomon Schechter's Disciples and the Creation of an American Religious Movement by Michael R. Cohen (New York: Columbia University Press, 2012), 210 pp.

Three recent books—about a congregation, a rabbi, and a religious movement, respectively—provide fascinating glimpses into nineteenth and early twentieth century American Jewish life. They are also remarkably related in what they teach us, by commission and by omission, by design and by default, about the writing of histories and the value of narrative.

Chicago Sinai Congregation

Tobias Brinkmann's *Sundays at Sinai* is a comprehensive history of Chicago Sinai Congregation, which has taken pride since 1861 in being America's most radical Reform synagogue. Brinkmann focuses primarily on the nineteenth and early twentieth centuries in his highly readable and thoroughly researched volume, with special attention to Sinai's Sunday services, which have continued from 1874 to the present. He makes good use of newspaper accounts throughout the congregation's history. Indeed, Brinkmann suggests, and wisely so, that in the nineteenth century, too much "dialogue" between Sinai's board and rabbis was conducted openly in both the Jewish and general press. He vividly brings us into the temple's board room more than once, introducing us to the major players.

Brinkmann, an expert in nineteenth century Jewish immigration to America, posits that Sinai's strong and specific ideological beginnings were a result of Old World regional ties that led to "chain immigration." He attributes this insight to Hyman Meites (p. 11), the author of a groundbreaking *History of the Jews of Chicago*.[1] One hopes that Brinkmann will one day explore whether this is true of the more moderate Reform congregations, and of the few German/West European congregations that remained Orthodox or Conservative, such as B'nai Jeshurun and Ansche Chesed (in different incarnations) in New York, Chizuk Amuno in Baltimore, and Adas Israel in Washington, D.C.

Brinkmann declares that he wants to get beyond the "big men" approach to synagogue history and to explore "grassroots, gender and everyday life" (p. 6). Yet much of his book is a tribute to Rabbi Emil G. Hirsch (1851–1923) and his ability to influence other "big men." Brinkmann does note that Hirsch could be petulant, stubborn, and egotistical, and sometimes pauses to attribute megalomaniac intentions to Hirsch (pp. 230, 232), even suggesting that Hirsch considered himself an Ubermensch in the Nietzschean sense (pp. 137–38). Hirsch is treated like an ancient Greek hero, whose hubris leads to conflict and also to a downfall. Yet Brinkmann hardly makes the case that Hirsch was in danger due to his "criticism of the [First World] war and his pro-German stance" (p. 296).

Brinkmann presents Hirsch as one of the most brilliant and highly educated of nineteenth-century rabbis. He makes a case that Hirsch was a scholar in ancient Near Eastern languages who was worthy of his position at the University of Chicago, which he had helped to found, but none of the citations from Hirsch in this book would distinguish him as theologian or social commentator.

Sinai's radical founders were in contention with the energetic organizer of moderate Reform, Rabbi Isaac Mayer Wise (1819–1900) of Cincinnati, who supported Sinai's parent congregation, KAM, which had not been radical enough for Sinai's founders. Brinkmann delineates that dispute well. But he (or his editors) could have found a better, more respectful (and translatable) word to characterize Wise's manifold activities than to refer to him as a "Macher" (p. 34) True, Wise could be snide, and it was inappropriate of him, at the painful beginning of the Civil War in 1861, to refer to the Sinai folk as "secessionists." But Brinkmann certainly did not have to extend that metaphor by saying that five days after Sinai was established the Confederates attacked Fort Sumter (p. 53).

With regard to the Civil War and other matters, Brinkmann does justice to Bernhard Felsenthal, a gifted autodidact in Judaic studies and the pulpit rabbinate, who wrote the tract that led to the founding of Sinai Congregation, became its first rabbi, and spoke out early for the abolition of slavery. Founding Sinai members Alderman Edward Salomon and Michael Greenebaum, who bravely saved runaway slaves, are rightly praised, as is Felsenthal's involvement in protesting limitation of the military chaplaincy to Christians, along with anti-Semitic enactments by General Grant.

Brinkmann raises some good questions when he inquires as to whether radical Reform was the "driving force" behind the effective protests of Chicago Jews against slavery in the South and, in Chicago, anti-Jewish discrimination in insurance and other matters. These issues merit further exploration. Yet in his admittedly cursory treatment of Hirsch's successors, Brinkmann hardly makes his case that "the relatively powerful position of a socially conservative and cautious rabbi contributed to the loss of . . . [Sinai's] erstwhile influence" (p. 298). After all, Sinai did remain the largest and best-attended congregation on Chicago's South Side during the turbulent Sixties. To what extent was it preserved by "cautiousness"?

Brinkmann attributes Emil Hirsch's efforts, after a decade in Chicago, to develop Sinai into an "institutional synagogue"—that is, a congregation where members would socialize together and share in Jewish activities—to the influence of Orthodox synagogues. He depicts well the Zionist movement and the "Jews as race" discussions in the late nineteenth century, and utilizes iconic Chicago memoirs by Philip Bregstone and Bernard Horwich to depict Hirsch's increasing interaction with, and sympathy for, the Orthodox Jewish community on Chicago's West Side.[2] He highlights

Hirsch's helpful influence when Sinai members Hart and Schaff-
ner faced a grueling strike by workers, many of them West Side
Jews, and makes the case that these factory owners "were no cold-
blooded capitalists" (p. 256).

With regard to synagogue life in Chicago, Brinkmann offers use-
ful guideposts by providing the number of member units at KAM,
Sinai, and other congregations in various eras. It would have been
more helpful to readers and scholars had he indicated the sources
for such statistics. Does Brinkmann realize that it is households
that are counted and not "people" (p. 275)? He deftly traces trends
in the American Reform synagogue like mixed seating and changing prayer books. He also recounts well the bizarre removal of the
Holy Ark and *sifrei Torah* at Sinai and in Cleveland's Tifereth Israel
Temple by radical Reform rabbis who insisted that the "sacredness
attached to the Torah scroll had lost its religious meaning" (p. 172).

Brinkmann says that the founders of Sinai Congregation took its
name from David Einhorn's radical Reform journal by that name
(p. 53). One wishes that he had quoted any literature on the naming and offered clear evidence, as well, for his assumption that
the lay founders of Sinai's parent congregation, KAM (Kehillath
Anshe Maarav, Congregation of the Men of the West) misspelled
its Hebrew name (p. 37), as opposed to echoing a regional dialect
and/or showing an unfamiliarity with transliteration into English.
Also, Brinkmann never does tell us when "Chicago Sinai Congregation" became the congregation's official name.

Our author traces well the origins of Jewish women's organizations, both in the community and within Sinai Congregation. He
offers insight into the conflict within and among some of these organizations between traditionalists and reformers. He speculates
that these organizations may owe their origin to the "silent opposition of Sinai's male leaders to giving women more formal influence with the congregation beyond the right to full membership"
(p. 234). Yet he offers no documentation of widespread discussion
of this issue within the congregation, though he does observe that
the married women represented a vanguard of traditionalism in
their opposition to Sunday services (pp. 96–97). Impressive documentation is offered, however, in isolating various trends and
polemics in the growing interfaith movement, particularly with
respect to Jewish-Christian relations and to the 1893 World Parliament of Religions. In presenting the background of the Sinai Social

Center, Brinkmann offers a helpful overview of the YMHA/JCC movement.

There is no doubt that Brinkmann writes a compelling, remarkably engaging, well-detailed narrative. But the narrative raises questions about the layers of research. What research and what sociological and immigration theories originated with Brinkmann, and what represents an expansion of trends and concepts already uncovered and propounded by others?

Shockingly, there is not even an index reference in Brinkmann's book to Rabbi Morris A. Gutstein, whose history of Chicago Jewry, particularly of the synagogues, *A Priceless Heritage* (New York: Bloch, 1953), is itself a priceless compendium of research, arranged with care and skill. Brinkmann cites Gutstein once in a footnote (p. 310) and only for some documents in an appendix. Yet Gutstein recounted, pithily and with much detail, all the milestone events and internecine struggles that led to the split in KAM Congregation and resulted in the founding of Chicago Sinai Congregation. He also told of the background of Sinai's rabbis and, in great detail, of the conflict that arose between Rabbi Kaufmann Kohler and the temple board over the visit of Ethical Culture founder Felix Adler.

Gutstein even mentioned the trip to Germany by a Mr. Schoenman (Brinkmann spells it "Schonemann") in search of a candidate for Sinai's pulpit. Gutstein attributes this anecdote to Hyman Meites's pathfinding history of Chicago Jewry.[3] Brinkmann cites neither Meites nor Gutstein regarding this anecdote, but credits it to a lecture in German by Felsenthal (p. 317, n. 46), which the other two sources do not mention. What is the responsibility of the professional historian toward a community's iconic narrators?

Brinkmann devotes entire chapters to themes covered by Gutstein and Meites, and to other subjects such as dispute between Sinai and Isaac Mayer Wise spilling into B'nai B'rith meetings. But he does not indicate the extent to which these topics were treated in earlier works and what he has added to the narrative. True, he consulted primary sources that his predecessors could not find or to which they did not have access. But why the silence as to the specific contributions of an intermediate source like Gutstein?

Does Brinkmann offer a clue to this silence in his Preface remark about congregational histories having a "narrow focus" in contrast with professional ones (p. 5)? Brinkmann's narrative is a good one, but it is not better than many local synagogue histories.[4]

Do history departments in universities exist solely to create a class of professional historians, or is their success the cultivation of the grass roots amateur historians who actually preserve local history? Rabbi Gutstein devoted much effort to producing his milestone work, while tending to congregational and communal duties. Does Brinkmann really believe that the more a rabbi writes scholarly (and historical?) articles, the less he will take positions on social issues, as he suggests regarding Kohler (p. 104)? Brinkmann does credit Bernhard Felsenthal for the "pencil-written notes of a talk he gave to the Chicago Historical Society in 1863 on Chicago Jewish history," which "are the oldest extant history of the Chicago Jewish community (and of Sinai) and one of the few such documents that was not consumed by the 1871 fire" (p. 67).

Meites's landmark history is an "amateur" effort—Meites (1879–1944) was a Jewish newspaper publisher turned superintendent of the Chicago Water Department—but it did encourage Brinkmann in his exploration of immigration theory. I mean it as a compliment to say that Brinkmann himself writes like an amateur in the literal sense of the term: one who loves his subject and has made it his own. Brinkmann's English is most felicitous for one who had another first language, German. One wishes, however, that the editors at the University of Chicago Press had fine-tuned the wording.[5] There are also some errors that might be corrected in a second edition.[6]

Rabbi Max Lilienthal

While a worthy and impressive and enthusiastic effort, Tobias Brinkmann's *Sundays at Sinai* raises questions as to how to incorporate into the most recent narrative the local histories and related studies that came before and how to depict rabbinic and other leaders without glorifying, romanticizing, or even deprecating them. Bruce L. Ruben's study *Max Lilienthal: The Making of an American Rabbinate* goes a long way toward resolving those questions. It is beautifully and engagingly written, and well-edited.

Like Brinkmann's book, it is thoroughly researched and exudes enthusiasm not only for its specific subject, but for the history of American Judaism. No relevant detail or article about Lilienthal has failed to be woven, seamlessly and felicitously, into Ruben's exquisite narrative. This book is a model study in every way.

Max Lilienthal (1815–1882), rabbi, educator, poet, with impeccable German academic credentials, was, at the time of his death, the longest-serving rabbi in America. As a young rabbi he was hired by the Russian government to try to "Westernize" the Jews, facing coercion and censorship under the czarist regime and resistance from the Jewish communities, especially from Lubavitcher Chasidim. His memoirs reveal his own prejudice against the Russian Jew and thus raise questions that still persist about the extent of that prejudice and whether it led him, at first, to overzealous cooperation, to the point of collusion, with the Russian authorities. Ruben gives him the benefit of the doubt, especially in light of Lilienthal's later dedication as a rabbi, Jewish school principal, and community activist in New York and in Cincinnati.

Ruben deftly summaries Lilienthal's memoirs and many of his scholarly and popular articles, written in German and in English. He provides helpful detail about the histories of the Jewish communities and congregations Lilienthal served, about Lilienthal's own personal evolution and "reinvention" from Orthodox to Reform (pp. 95, 111), and about the resistance that he faced from the Orthodox both in Europe and in America. Ruben also pays all due deference to intervening sources, especially Moshe Davis's landmark work, *The Emergence of Conservative Judaism* (New York: The Burning Bush Press, 1963), which credited many of Lilienthal's contributions.

We learn that Lilienthal was one of the first American rabbis to have to deal with a ritual committee (p. 73) and with kosher butchers (p. 75), as well as with fights over new synagogue tunes (p. 79). He wrote the first Hebrew prayer for the American Government and was a major pioneer in the Jewish day school and Sunday school movements in the United States. Ruben vividly relates Lilienthal's efforts to develop Confirmation ceremonies in Europe and in America; modern pedagogy for children, including physical education; and a Jewish catechism.

Ruben does everything possible to weave helpful background studies into the text, covering the development of Jewish preaching styles in Lilienthal's youth; the effects of current synagogue music on his rabbinate; the outlook of his early, Orthodox teachers; even the costs of tuitions and salaries in the mid-nineteenth century. He also provides necessary background on German and Russian approaches to "emancipation," on the Haskalah (East

European Jewish Enlightenment movement), and on the Society of the Friends of Light (Lichtfreunde), formed to support the Jewish intelligentsia revolutionaries who had begun to emigrate from Germany in the late 1840s. We learn of Lilienthal's involvement in early campaigns for Sabbath observance, in major interfaith work, in the founding of the University of Cincinnati, in Church-State and anti-missionary polemics, even of his insights into Lincoln's relationship with the Jewish community. One might question, however, Ruben's remark that in the end Lilienthal "fully embraced materialism" (p. 232).

Ruben notes the effect of politics and economics on the kind of work that Lilienthal was trying to do and provides vivid portraits of Jewish life in Russian communities; of the development of the rabbinate in America; and of the role of the laity and of the rabbi in shaping American Jewish life. Ruben astutely traces this alongside the background of the Protestant and Catholic clergy, as does Brinkmann. We are treated to a touching portrait of Lilienthal's wife Peppie and of his family network. Ruben relates how Lilienthal learned community politics the hard way, how certain remarks or support in one area (such as the Lichtfreunde) could undermine his efforts in other areas (a union of synagogues). Lilienthal was certainly very patient, for the religious reforms he advocated came slowly, even in Cincinnati, where he was well-loved and well-established.

Ruben's study provides an excellent perspective, perhaps the best available, on the friendship and partnership between Isaac Mayer Wise and Lilienthal. The latter defended Wise against the prejudices of the self-styled elite Reform in Germany and in America. He played a key, diplomatic role in organizing the Cincinnati community so that Wise could have a base upon which to build a national following. Leadership roles took their toll on Lilienthal, while Wise thrived on the controversy. Ruben offers fine insight into Wise's psychology and into the personalities and ideological conflicts within the Reform Movement and among the different approaches to Judaism, well-documented with primary and secondary sources.

Ruben, who is a cantor and a teacher of cantors, pays special attention to Lilienthal's desire to improve synagogue music and to enhance the service with choir and organ. For this Lilienthal faced much adversity, especially from cantors who, according to Ruben's research, led in the reactionary opposition, at least in New York. Yet Ruben does not mention cantors and music directors in Cincinnati. One also misses any attempt to convey a sense of everyday life at Lilienthal's congregation—in the office, in events described in bulletins. Were there bar mitzvah ceremonies? Did they stop at a certain point? Also, Ruben might have taken a page from Brinkmann and recorded periodic membership statistics. One wishes, however, that Brinkmann had devoted more attention to music at Chicago Sinai Congregation.

Both Ruben and Brinkmann deal with the German Enlightenment concept of *Bildung* (cultivation of morality and reason) in one's individual life and in society, realizing worthy goals and helping others to do the same. They demonstrate that this concept was important, respectively, to the founders of Sinai Congregation and to Lilienthal. Ruben conveys its nuances better and weaves the literature about it into the narrative more tellingly. To their credit, both writers carry it through from beginning to end of their studies. (Someone should consider the influence of *Bildung* on German Modern Orthodox Judaism.) Ruben deals thoroughly, as well, with the concept of *Judische Wissenschaft*, the critical-historical study of Jewish tradition, which was important to Lilienthal, and which would be fundamental to the founders of Conservative Judaism. He notes that Lilienthal credited some of his own early research with the proper dating of the *Zohar* (p. 243, n. 101), while providing insight into Lilienthal's prejudice against Kabbalah.

Lilienthal's involvements anticipated, in many ways, the efforts of Mordecai Kaplan (1881–1983) to redefine Jewish life, religion, and education while seeking a rationale in American Jewish life for concern about the Jewish People worldwide. Brinkmann cleverly utilizes Kaplan's seventieth birthday celebrations in 1951 to illustrate Sinai's radical self-marginalization. Ruben sticks to his time-frame and does not mention Kaplan, but does provide in his final chapter a marvelous summary of Lilienthal's life against a panoramic overview of American Judaism in the years leading up to the establishment of the institutions upon which Conservative Judaism was built. He wisely asks whether a Conservative seminary would have been founded had the diplomatic Lilienthal lived another decade. It fell to Kaplan, who would play a key role in the Conservative

Movement, to solidify what Ruben describes as the shifting and evolving middle ground in American Judaism (p. 234).

Conservative Judaism

In *The Birth of Conservative Judaism*, Michael R. Cohen sets out to refute theories that a "historical school" of Judaism, with its origins in Zechariah Frankel's Breslau seminary, together with a coalition of like-minded rabbis and congregations, were already a "movement" when Solomon Schechter (1847–1915) was called to head the Jewish Theological Seminary of America in 1902. Cohen prefers a Conservative Movement that took its cue from Schechter and his disciples, from a Schechter molded after J. Gordon Melton's charismatic founders of "new religions" like Hare Krishna, the Spiritual Frontiers Movement, the Christian Gnostics, and the Amana Society.

But why pattern Schechter after such figures? Why not the paradigm of the Chabad Chasidic world from which Schechter emerged? After all, he was named after the first Lubavitcher rebbe, Shnuer Zalman of Liadi (1745–1812), who understood that a movement must have its own liturgical innovations, institutions, and approaches to Jewish law. And Schechter did write the first major essays in the English language defending Chasidic and Kabbalistic fellowship.[7] But even if one rules out such tendencies in Schechter's leadership style, there is certainly enough to link him to the Cambridge paradigm of college professor/president as mentor. Furthermore, Schechter *did* regard himself as a spiritual disciple of Frankel.[8]

Cohen equates Schechter's concept of "Catholic Israel" with the placing of authority to adapt Jewish law in a "unified Jewry" (p. 3), but the "Catholic Israel" concept, though vague, was an attempt to mediate authority between past generations and the problems facing those committed to the application of Jewish law in our time.[9] Certainly, Schechter's view of "Catholic Israel" was far closer to Frankel's notion of Jewish law as the "specifically Jewish" manifestation of "active religiousness" on the part of the most "committed representatives of Jewish consciousness," to cite Louis Ginzberg's paraphrase of Frankel,[10] than to "new religions" spirituality, which denies classical religious authority. Indeed, Schechter mocked the New Age spirituality of his time.[11]

Dogmatic indeed is Cohen's either/or regarding the origins of a Conservative Movement—either the disciples of Schechter or an "historical school." He is not quite sure where to place the laity in all of this, whether working for the rabbis or against them—another either/or. Here, Charles S. Liebman's notion of a tension between "elite religion" and "folk religion,"[12] sometimes working in tandem, sometimes working at odds, would have been helpful. Bruce L. Ruben points to this dynamic in the efforts of Max Lilienthal and Isaac Mayer Wise to involve and even defer to the laity in establishing the Union of American Hebrew Congregations and the Hebrew Union College (pp. 205-215), as does Tobias Brinkmann in his account of Emil Hirsch's consistent enlistment of lay leaders.

Cohen credits Schechter's concept of "Catholic Israel," seen by some of his disciples and opponents as an inhibiting factor, with allowing for the "institutionalization of diversity . . . that allowed the emerging movement to successfully outlive Schechter and move into its postcharismatic stage" (p. 8). He does show that the association of Seminary graduates was a coalition rather than a movement. But how does that disprove a sense of an "historical school" movement at various stages?

The books by Brinkmann and Ruben demonstrate the importance of histories of congregations and of the dynamics between rabbis and congregations to understanding religious movements. That requires narrative. Yet Cohen makes every effort to minimize narrative. The result is a book closer in style to the Synoptic Gospels than to the solidly crafted historical accounts by our two other authors. Cohen tells us about the birth of the Orthodox Union—in response to Schechter's coming? (p. 22)—in various chapters, like the accounts of Jesus' birth in different gospels. He collects testimonies and then incorporates them into independent essays without sequence or chronology.[13]

Even in his depiction of the disciples, Cohen withholds narrative. He provides a detailed portrait of some disciples but not of others. Consistently and annoyingly, he cites some Seminary graduates by name and refers to others, and even to some of the same rabbis, without naming them, or by naming them in a footnote. One gets the impression that he does this to free his essays of biographical baggage, but it is precisely the depiction of congregations and rabbis that fleshes out the theory. It is a pity, by the way, that Cohen does not mention the names of many of the congregations or say something about their cultures.[14] The failure to name synagogues in a particular city can lead to misconceptions as to which one is being referenced.

Cohen certainly does copious research and has a good feel for the issues and challenges in the early days of the fledgling Conservative rabbinate. He depicts well the fragile world of those early disciples. He can be impressively resourceful, as when he checks to see which rabbis attended or didn't attend Conservative or Orthodox functions (p. 79). But the structural problems with the book, and his failure to state his theory concisely and clearly at the outset, hamstring his efforts. The responsibility for this rests squarely with the editors at Columbia University Press, who even allowed unexplained numbers in parentheses (pages in the closest footnoted sources?) to proliferate in the text.

Cohen offers some intriguing references to the role of women in Conservative Judaism. Was that role more far-reaching than that of women in the early Reform Movement? If so, was this because of the rise of Conservative Judaism in a later epoch? Here, again, Cohen's research is impressive. He makes a good case that the Women's League pioneered in publications propounding the perspectives of Conservative Judaism, and in the use of the term "liberated," to describe the political and religious status of women, and actually conferred authority upon the rabbis (pp. 92–93,124–26), demanding that they remedy the *agunah* situation.

Wisely, Cohen notes the effect on Schechter's disciples of Reform Judaism and of Zionism. That Cohen himself refers to Hebrew Union College as "more progressive" than the Seminary shows what challenges Schechter and his disciples had cut out for them. One wishes that Cohen had looked more probingly at the very term "conservative." Why did Schechter use it? Was he reacting to the use of "liberal" by the Reform Movement, or was his pluralism a natural outgrowth of classical conservative thinking, both politically and socially, as advocated by Edmund Burke's conservatism?[15] Cohen does note that the liberals, like Kaplan, were "less inclusive" (p. 70).

Cohen deals with differences on Zionism within both the Conservative and Reform camps, but he misses at least one good opportunity to show just how controversial the topic was. In bringing the important memoir of Rabbi Jacob Kohn (1881–1968) to light, he ignores a key passage in which Temple Ansche Chesed's president made the "repugnant" suggestion that "all allusion in sermon and liturgy to Zionism and the hope of Israel's restoration [be dropped] because in his imagination this idea was repellant to the wealthier Jew long settled in America."[16]

Cohen is on to something when he quotes some of the disciples to the effect that the Conservative rabbis needed to move beyond being a counter-Reform Movement. But if they were seen as Orthodox from the left, then they were also seen as Reformers by the right, particularly within their own congregations. Did Cohen find pronouncements on how Schechter and his disciples dealt with such profiling? Surely, Schechter had thoughts about what parts of the traditional prayer book had to be preserved—and what did not.[17] Did any of the early Seminary graduates or their teachers record observations about how to learn from the abuse suffered by the early Reformers, like Lilienthal, at the hands of more orthodox lay people, and from the similar abuse suffered by the orthodox synagogue members at the hands of their rabbis and neighbors?

Perhaps these are the key and abiding questions raised by all three authors in a time when even a spirit of religious pluralism, both within and among religious movements, seems so elusive.

Notes

1. Hyman Meites, *History of the Jews of Chicago* (Chicago: Jewish Historical Society of Illinois, 1924). One could credit James G. Heller with noting that Isaac Mayer Wise regarded German background in a region exposed to Reform teachers as indicative of openness to Reform Judaism. See James G. Heller, *Isaac M. Wise, His Life, Work and Thought* (New York: The Union of American Hebrew Congregations, 1965), 238, 258.

2. See Philip P. Bregstone, *Chicago and Its Jews: A Cultural History* (Chicago: privately published, 1933) and Bernard Horwich, *My First Eighty Years* (Chicago: Argus Books, 1939). Appropriately, in discussing the founding of Sinai Congregation and of Jewish women's organizations, Brinkmann refers to the autobiography of Hannah Greenebaum Solomon, *Fabric of My Life* (New York: Bloch Publishing Company, 1946).

3. See Morris A. Gutstein, *A Priceless Heritage: The Epic Growth of Nineteenth Century Chicago Jewry* (New York: Bloch Publishing Company, 1953), 113, 455 n. 69. Gutstein even deals at length in a chapter on "Synagogue Life" with such matters as service times, decorum, preaching, and Torah reading.

4. Among the finest recent congregational histories are Peter Eisen-stadt, *Affirming the Covenant, A History of Temple B'rith Kodesh, Rochester, New York, 1848–1998* (Rochester: Temple B'rith Kodesh, 1999); Gerry Cristol, *A Light in the Prairie, Temple Emanu-El of Dallas 1872–1997* (Fort Worth: Texas Christian University, 1998); Fred Rosenbaum, *Visions of Reform: Congregation Emanu-El and the Jews of San Francisco 1849–1999* (Berkeley, CA: Judah L. Magnes Museum, 2000); Jan Bernhardt Schein, *On Three Pillars, The History of Chizuk Amuno Congregation* (Baltimore: Chizuk Amuno Congregation, 2000); and Wilfred Schuchat, *The Gate of Heaven, The Story of Congregation Shaar Hashomayim of Montreal 1846–1996* (Montreal: Congregation Shaar Hashomayim with McGill-Queen's University Press, 2000).

   For other histories of congregations, see Elliot B. Gertel, "From Beth Tefila to Beth Midrash: Learning from Synagogue Histories," *American Jewish History* 74, no. 3 (March 1985): 312–22. For my reviews of two fine local histories, *Rodfei Zedek, The First Hundred Years* (1976) by Carole Krucoff, and *B'nai Amoona for All Generations* (1982) by Rosalind Mael Bronson, see, respectively, the Fall 1978 and Winter 1983–1984 issues of *Conservative Judaism*.

5. Better words could have been employed in some places. Are the founding German Jewish families in Chicago best characterized as "social climbers" (pp. 16, 163) or as "upwardly mobile"? Was Hirsch "vulnerable" to personal attacks (p. 131) or "sensitive" to them? Brinkmann writes: "Sinai expected to recruit new members from a constituency considered susceptible to their brand of Reform" (p. 281). Does he mean "susceptible" or "amenable"?

   Sometimes, the author's meaning is just not clear, as in the sentence: "As one of very few rabbis in America, Hirsch had emancipated himself almost completely from the board of his congregation" (p. 196).

6. Rabbi Jacob J. Weinstein is called "Jacob I." in the Acknowledgments. Louis Mann's previous pulpit, Mishkan Israel, was in New Haven, Connecticut, when Mann came to Sinai, not yet in the Hamden suburb mentioned on p. 272. Also, while not wrong in noting that Bernhard Felsenthal was the first clergyman in Chicago to have received a life contract (p. 67), Brinkmann might add that the first rabbi to have been hired on such terms, according to James G. Heller, was Isaac Mayer Wise. See Heller, *Isaac M. Wise*, 237, 239.

7. See Solomon Schechter, "The Chassidim," in *Studies in Judaism* (London: Adam and Charles Black, 1896) and "Safed in the Sixteenth Century—A City of Legists and Mystics," in *Studies in Judaism, Second Series* (Philadelphia: The Jewish Publication Society of America, 1908).

8. See Solomon Schechter, *Seminary Addresses and Other Papers* (Cincinnati: Ark Publishing Company, 1915), 74, 173-193, where

Schechter argues against the misappropriation of studies by Frankel and others.

9. It is telling that Schechter employs the term "general use" as a synonym for "Catholic Israel." See Schechter, *Studies in Judaism* (1896), xxiii. To Schechter, Catholic Israel referred to the Jewish People committed to Jewish law and observance as sanctioners of practice. "Unity" in and of itself was not a core value of Schechter's conception of "Catholic Israel." In fact, Schechter opposed various synod proposals for American Jewry out of fear that, in the name of "unity," they would impose a "remedy . . . worse than the disease" by calling for the abolition of aspects of "the practice of the Law." See Norman Bentwich, *Solomon Schechter: A Biography* (Philadelphia: The Jewish Publication Society of America, 1938), 298–99.

   The formulation "Catholic Israel" is ambiguous, as I noted in an article, "Jewish Theological Seminary of America (JTSA)," in *Jewish American Voluntary Organizations*, ed. Michael N. Dobkowski (New York and Westport, CT: Greenwood Press, 1986), 281–93. Unfortunately, a typographical error entered the final printed version of my article so that the word "unwillingness" became "willingness" in a pertinent sentence that should have read: "The ambiguity of Schechter's concept of 'Catholic Israel' lies not only in the vague nineteenth century rhetoric (e.g., 'ideal aspirations and religious needs of the age') but in his unwillingness to identify that body or to articulate a theory of revelation" (p. 283).

10. See Louis Ginzberg, *Students, Scholars and Saints* (Philadelphia: The Jewish Publication Society of America, 1928), 205, 209. These sentiments are echoed by Schechter in the previous footnote. Clearly, Ginzberg is paraphrasing Frankel's writings and not projecting Schechter upon them. See the passage by Frankel anthologized by Mordecai Waxman in *Tradition and Change: The Development of Conservative Judaism*, 1958), 43–50.

11. See, for example, Schechter, *Seminary Addresses*, 134.

12. See Charles S. Liebman, *The Ambivalent American Jew: Politics, Religion and Family in American Jewish Life* (Philadelphia: The Jewish Publication Society of America, 1973), 45-49.

13. I would characterize Cohen's "gospels" as follows: Schechter as Charismatic, The United Synagogue as Communion, The Rabbinical Assembly as Last Supper for Schechter's Disciples before Lay Leadership, and the Later Generations of Conservative Rabbis as Resurrection of the "Catholic Israel" Concept.

14. In discussing Rabbi Herman Rubenovitz, Cohen does discuss the culture of Congregation Mishkan Tefila in Boston, as understood by Rubenovitz in Herman H. Rubenovitz and Mignon L. Rubenovitz, *The Waking Heart* (Cambridge, MA: Nathaniel Dame and

Company, 1967). Yet Cohen missed an opportunity in not considering the career of Rabbi Louis Egelson at Congregation Adas Israel in Washington, D.C., against the background of Rabbi Stanley Rabinowitz's telling study, *The Assembly: A Century in the Life of The Adas Israel Hebrew Congregation of Washington, D.C.* (Hoboken, NJ: Ktav Publishing Company, 1993).

15. See Elliot B. Gertel, "Is Conservative Judaism—Conservative?" *Judaism* 28 (Spring 1979): 202–15. In discussing the "historical school" and offering a "theological programme" for it, Schechter described "its attitude towards religion" as "an enlightened Scepticism combined with a staunch conservatism which is not even wholly devoid of a certain mystical touch." Schechter, *Studies in Judaism* (1896), xx.

See also, Schechter's letter to Cyrus Adler (September 10, 1901): "You know my conservative tendencies both in life and thought, but I am thoroughly convinced that if the Seminary should become a real blessing, it must not be de-graded into a battle-ground of the various parties. It must be above them all and give directions to both orthodox and reform." Cited in Bernard Mandelbaum, ed., *The Wisdom of Solomon Schechter* (New York: The Burning Bush Press, 1963), 120. This booklet, compiled by Mandelbaum as "A United Synagogue Jubilee Publication (1913–1963)," remains the best sampling of Schechter's thought and maxims.

16. Jacob Kohn, unpublished *Memoir* (in Ratner Archives, Jewish Theological Seminary), "New York After WWI," 12.

17. "We could, with little difficulty," Schechter wrote to Judge Mayer Sulzberger, "compile a Prayer Book, entirely placed on Talmudic and Gaonic authority, which would prove acceptable to the communities and form an antidote to . . . the Hebrew Union Prayer Book, as you indicate in your letter. The only question is whether the Orthodox Rabbis (. . . who justify their existence only by their opposition to the Seminary) could be won over to give their approval to such a Prayer Book" (December 1, 1908). Cited in Bernard Mandelbaum, *Wisdom of Solomon Schechter*, 129.

RABBI ELLIOT B. GERTEL (JTS81) has served pulpits in New Haven and Chicago. He is the editor of *Jewish Belief and Practice in Nineteenth Century America* (2006).

The JPS Bible Commentary—Ruth
Commentary by Tamara Cohn Eskenazi and Tikva Frymer-Kensky
(Philadelphia: Jewish Publication Society, 2011), 178 pp.

This JPS Commentary on Ruth follows a similar pattern to their previously published volumes on Jonah, Esther, and Ecclesiastes. Here, renowned scholars each in her own right, Tamara Cohn

Eskenazi, professor of Bible at HUC-JIR/LA, was joined by the late Tikva Frymer-Kensky, professor of Hebrew Bible and the History of Judaism in the University of Chicago's Divinity School. The result is a formidably researched, and at the same time, an eminently readable study of the Book of Ruth. The book earned the 2011 National Jewish Book Award.

As in the previous volumes, a major introductory chapter precedes the text itself; the text, translation, and commentary cover a bit more than half of the volume. Similar in format to *The Torah: A Modern Commentary* (both the original and revised editions) and *The Torah: A Women's Commentary* (the co-editor of which is Eskenazi) there is a running commentary at the bottom of the page, which allows the authors to reflect on the plain meaning of the text, as well as often offering background context on the environment of the ancient Near East. The commentators sometimes use this running explication to offer midrashic insights or to point out connections to material that will appear later in the story or in other parts of the Bible. The names of characters and places, as well as institutions, or specific verbs utilized in the text are analyzed. Unlike the Torah commentaries, because the focus here is on only one small four-chapter book, there are comments on each and every verse in this *m'gillah*.

While this commentary on Ruth was a joint effort of these two well-respected scholars, sadly Frymer-Kensky died while working on the project. Fortunately, she left extensive notes addressing the first two chapters, as well as some notes for the introduction. Eskenazi's voice is reflected in chapters 3 and 4, as well as the principal voice of the introduction.

The near ninety pages of introduction provide the reader with a wealth of information. For example, although many scholars and commentators in the past suggested that the Boaz-Ruth marriage was a levirate union, that does not appear to be the case, and such a view "is nowadays challenged by a number of scholars" (p. xxxv). Although there is no way to prove or disprove this point, today several "scholars entertain the possibility that the author was a woman. They note the unusual extent to which the book is attentive to women's lives and perspectives (comparable only to Song of Songs in this respect)" (p. xvi). Another view put forth is that this book may have been written by "a circle of women" (p. xvii), which contrasts with the more common androcentric approach to the Bible.

The introduction itself divides into seventeen sections: Authorship and Date, Genre/Style, Ruth's Place in the Canon, Ruth's Relationship to Other Biblical Books, Ruth and Shavuot, Background Issues and Themes, Levirate Marriage, The Marriage of Boaz and Ruth, Intermarriage, Conversion, The Status of the Moabites, *Hesed*, The Theology of the Book of Ruth; Redemption in the Bible, Pre-Modern Rabbinic Interpretations, Later Jewish Interpretations, and Contemporary Readings. In this last category are subsections that include Feminist Interpretations and Modern Jewish Interpretations.

The JPS Bible Commentary—Ruth is a product of the contemporary world. Over the past forty years there have been a number of major commentaries written by Edward F. Campbell (1975), Robert L. Hubbard, Jr. (1988), Jack M. Sasson (1989), Frederick W. Bush (1996), Kirsten Nielsen (1997), and Tod Linafelt (1999). To a greater or lesser degree, these earlier commentaries cover similar ground as found in this study. That stated, the focus in this volume on intermarriage and conversion, as well as feminist interpretations makes it unique. As the most recent commentary written, it also allowed the authors the opportunity to reflect on scholarship produced over the past number of decades. For example, they write that in recent years the Book of Ruth has become "recognized as a spiritual source for contemporary women and men as a sophisticated contribution to understanding the dynamics of class, gender, and ethnicity, both in the past and the present" (p. lxv). They also take note of a study by Danna M. Fewell and David N. Gunn, which is quite critical of Naomi's role (p. lxvi).

The authors appear to have enjoyed writing this book, which is often both witty and wise. At times the language itself is playful, including statements that feature alliteration, or other plays on words. They describe the book of Ruth as a "story [that] is simple but never simplistic" (p. xvi), a work that is filled with "*hesed* and *hutzpah*," telling the story of "a journey from famine to fullness, from futility to fertility" (p. xv). Chapter 2 is titled "Finding Favor and Food in the Field" (p. 27); chapter 4 is titled "Redemption and Restoration" (p. 69).

Each chapter begins with a paragraph overview followed by a three-single-sentence outline with appropriate verse numbers. These divisions help define for the reader the direction of the chapter itself. In addition, as one reads through the commentary, each of these chapter divisions features additional introductory explanations for the section it addresses.

The text of the English translation comes from the latest JPS *TANAKH* volume. Those readers who have become used to a gender-sensitive avoidance of a masculine word for God will be somewhat dismayed to see that the word "LORD" still appears in this commentary.

The JPS Bible Commentary—Ruth is a natural for synagogue libraries, and the libraries of colleagues and laypeople as well. It provides a great amount of interesting material that could be used for classes on biblical books, programs for *Tikkun Leil Shavuot,* or discussions about conversion or intermarriage in the contemporary world.

DAVID J. ZUCKER, Ph.D. (C70) recently retired as rabbi/chaplain at Shalom Cares, a senior continuum of care center, as well as Shalom Hospice in Aurora, Colorado. His latest books will be published this year: *The Bible's PROPHETS: An Introduction for Christians and Jews,* as well as *The Bible's WRITINGS: An Introduction for Christians and Jews* (Wipf and Stock, 2013). He publishes in a variety of areas. See his website, www.DavidJZucker.org.

Call for Papers: *Maayanot*

The CCAR Journal: The Reform Jewish Quarterly is committed to serving its readers' professional, intellectual, and spiritual needs. In pursuit of that objective, the *Journal* created a new section known as *Maayanot* (Primary Sources), which made its debut in the Spring 2012 issue.

We continue to welcome proposals for *Maayanot* —translations of significant Jewish texts, accompanied by an introduction as well as annotations and/or commentary. *Maayanot* aims to present fresh approaches to materials from any period of Jewish life, including but not confined to the biblical or Rabbinic periods. When appropriate, it is possible to include the original document in the published presentation.

Please submit proposals, inquiries, and questions to *Maayanot* editor, Daniel Polish, dpolish@ optonline.net.

Along with submissions for *Maayanot,* the *Journal* encourages the submission of scholarly articles in fields of Jewish Studies, as well as other articles that fit within our Statement of Purpose.

The *CCAR Journal: The Reform Jewish Quarterly*
Published quarterly by the Central Conference of American Rabbis.

Volume LX, No. 4. Issue Number: Two hundred thirty-eight.
Fall 2013.

STATEMENT OF PURPOSE

The *CCAR Journal: The Reform Jewish Quarterly* seeks to explore ideas and issues of Judaism and Jewish life, primarily—but not exclusively—from a Reform Jewish perspective. To fulfill this objective, the Journal is designed to:

1. provide a forum to reflect the thinking of informed and concerned individuals—especially Reform rabbis—on issues of consequence to the Jewish people and the Reform Movement;

2. increase awareness of developments taking place in fields of Jewish scholarship and the practical rabbinate, and to make additional contributions to these areas of study;

3. encourage creative and innovative approaches to Jewish thought and practice, based upon a thorough understanding of the traditional sources.

The views expressed in the Journal do not necessarily reflect the position of the Editorial Board or the Central Conference of American Rabbis.

The *CCAR Journal: The Reform Jewish Quarterly* (ISSN 1058-8760) is published quarterly by the Central Conference of American Rabbis, 355 Lexington Avenue, 18th Floor, New York, NY, 10017. Application to mail at periodical postage rates is pending at New York, NY and at additional mailing offices.

Subscriptions should be sent to CCAR Executive Offices, 355 Lexington Avenue, 18th Floor, New York, NY, 10017. Subscription rate as set by the Conference is $100 for a one-year subscription, $150 for a two-year subscription. Overseas subscribers should add $36 per year for postage. POSTMASTER: Please send address changes to CCAR Journal: The Reform Jewish Quarterly, c/o Central Conference of American Rabbis, 355 Lexington Avenue, 18th Floor, New York, NY, 10017.

Typesetting and publishing services provided by Publishing Synthesis, Ltd., 39 Crosby Street, New York, NY, 10013.

The *CCAR Journal: The Reform Jewish Quarterly* is indexed in the *Index to Jewish Periodicals*. Articles appearing in it are listed in the *Index of Articles on Jewish Studies* (of *Kirjath Sepher*).

ISBN: 978-0-88123-200-4

GUIDELINES FOR SUBMITTING MATERIAL

1.   The *CCAR Journal* welcomes submissions that fulfill its Statement of Purpose whatever the author's background or identification. Inquiries regarding publishing in the CCAR Journal and submissions for possible publication (including poetry) should be sent to the editor-elect, Rabbi Paul Golomb, Rabbi@Vassartemple.org.

2.   Other than commissioned articles, submissions to the *CCAR Journal* are sent out to a member of the editorial board for anonymous peer review. Thus submitted articles and poems should be sent to the editor with the author's name omitted. Please use MS Word format for the attachment. The message itself should contain the author's name, phone number, and e-mail address, as well as the submission's title and a 1–2 sentence bio.

3.   Books for review and inquiries regarding submitting a review should be sent directly to the book review editor, Rabbi Laurence Edwards, at *LLE49@comcast.net*.

4.   Inquiries concerning, or submissions for, *Maayanot* (Primary Sources) should be directed to the *Maayanot* editor, Rabbi Daniel Polish, at *dpolish@optonline.net*.

5.   Based on Reform Judaism's commitment to egalitarianism, we request that articles be written in gender-inclusive language.

6.   The *Journal* publishes reference notes at the end of articles, but submissions are easier to review when notes come at the bottom of each page. If possible, keep this in mind when submitting an article. Notes should conform to the following style:

a. Norman Lamm, *The Shema: Spirituality and Law in Judaism* (Philadelphia: Jewish Publication Society, 1998), 101–6. **[book]**

b. Lawrence A. Hoffman, "The Liturgical Message," in *Gates of Understanding*, ed. Lawrence A.Hoffman (New York: CCAR Press, 1977), 147–48, 162–63. **[chapter in a book]**

c. Richard Levy, "The God Puzzle," *Reform Judaism* 28 (Spring 2000): 18–22. **[article in a periodical]**

d. Lamm, *Shema*, 102. **[short form for subsequent reference]**

e. Levy, "God Puzzle," 20. **[short form for subsequent reference]**

f. Ibid., 21. **[short form for subsequent reference]**

7.   If Hebrew script is used, please include an English translation. If transliteration is used, follow the guidelines abbreviated below and included more fully in the **Master Style Sheet**, available on the CCAR website at *www.ccarnet.org*:

"ch" for *chet* and *chaf* "ei" for *tzeirei*

"f" for *fei* "a" for *patach* and *kamatz*

"k" for *kaf* and *kuf* "o" for *cholam* and *kamatz katan*

"tz" for *tzadi* "u" for *shuruk* and *kibbutz*

"i" for *chirik* "ai" for *patach* with *yod*

"e" for *segol*

Final "h" for final *hei*; none for final *ayin* (with exceptions based on common usage): atah, Sh'ma, <u>but</u> Moshe.

Apostrophe for *sh'va nah*: b'nei, b'rit, Sh'ma; no apostrophe for *sh'va nach*.

Hyphen for two vowels together where necessary for correct pronunciation: ne-eman, samei-ach, <u>but</u> maariv, Shavuot.

No hyphen for prefixes unless necessary for correct pronunciation: babayit, HaShem, Yom HaAtzma-ut.

Do not double consonants (with exceptions based on dictionary spelling or common usage): t'filah, chayim, <u>but</u> tikkun, Sukkot.